D1175423

BILLS AND ACTS

LEGISLATIVE PROCEDURE IN EIGHTEENTH-CENTURY ENGLAND

Bills and Acts

LEGISLATIVE PROCEDURE IN EIGHTEENTH-CENTURY ENGLAND

SHEILA LAMBERT

CAMBRIDGE

AT THE UNIVERSITY PRESS

1971

Published by the Syndics of the Cambridge University Press
Bentley House, 200 Euston Road, London N.W.1
American Branch: 32 East 57th Street, New York, N.Y.10022

© Cambridge University Press 1971

ISBN: 0 521 08119 X

Printed in Great Britain
at the Aberdeen University Press

CONTENTS

PREFACE

All students of this subject must acknowledge their debt to the work of the late Dr O. C. Williams. His intimate knowledge of the House of Commons and its ways produced three books which are an inexhaustible mine of information.

I am grateful to the benchers of the Honourable Society of Lincoln's Inn, and to their Librarian, Mr C. W. Ringrose, for permission to consult the volume of Robert Harper MSS.

Dr P. D. G. Thomas was good enough to allow me to see the typescript of his forthcoming book, *The House of Commons in the eighteenth century*.

I am indebted to Mr Maurice Bond, Clerk of the Records of the House of Lords, for much valuable advice and criticism, most kindly and generously given.

S.L.

Cambridge
August 1970

ABBREVIATIONS

Numbers in square brackets in the text refer to the list of Robert Harper's bills in Appendix I. A description of this material, and of the British Museum references used in footnotes, is given in the introduction to the appendix.

Abbreviations used for parliamentary references are explained in the note on parliamentary sources, Appendix II.

Clerical Organization   O. C. Williams, *The Clerical Organization of the House of Commons, 1661–1850* (Oxford, 1954).

Clifford   Frederick Clifford, *A History of Private Bill Legislation* (2 vols. 1885).

Courthope   *The Minute Book of James Courthope*, ed. O. C. Williams, in *Camden Miscellany*, xx (Royal Historical Society, 1953).

Holdsworth   Sir W. S. Holdsworth, *A History of English Law* (16 vols. 1903–66).

Liverpool Tractate   *The Liverpool Tractate*, ed. Catherine Strateman [Mrs C. S. Sims] (New York, 1937).

Parliamentary Practice   Thomas Erskine May, *A Treatise upon the Law, Privileges, Proceedings and Usage of Parliament*. 1st ed., 1844, and 12th ed., 1917, are cited.

Precedents   J. Hatsell, *Precedents of Proceedings in the House of Commons, under Separate Titles; with Observations*. The first three volumes appeared in 1776, 1781, 1785, and were reprinted, with the fourth, in 1796. New ed. 4 vols. 1818.

Private Bill Procedure   O. C. Williams, *The Historical Development of Private Bill Procedure and Standing Orders in the House of Commons* (2 vols. H.M.S.O., 1948).

Thomas   P. D. G. Thomas, *The House of Commons in the eighteenth century* (Oxford, 1971).

INTRODUCTION

Being engaged in preparing a list of printed House of Commons sessional papers for the eighteenth century, I found myself relying upon a collection of such papers in the State Paper Room of the British Museum. Many of the printed bills bore manuscript annotations and notes of amendments, and at first I assumed they had belonged to a member of parliament and wondered whether it might be possible to identify him. I noticed that many papers also bore contemporary ink reference numbers and sometimes the initials 'R.H.'; then I found one or two whose docket was endorsed 'To Mr Harper' and others marked 'as drawn by R.H.'. Finding no member of that name, I set off in search of a lawyer named 'R. Harper'. This book is the result of the search. It centres round the work of one attorney, hitherto completely unknown and without any official status. Its purpose is to illustrate the procedures by which legislation was prepared and enacted in the eighteenth century.

The legislative output of the century was so great that historians in political and economic fields who have little concern with legislation as such can scarcely escape touching upon the subject at some time. My purpose is to go behind the formal rules of procedure to show, by illustration, what actually took place in a number of cases and thus to suggest how any particular bill may have been initiated and put through to the statute book.

The British Museum's collection of private bills is probably, thanks to Robert Harper, the most complete now in existence. The manuscript annotations of this material have previously been incomprehensible because their origin was unknown; I hope that the identification of Harper's authorship will encourage its use. In particular I hope that those interested in family history, the inclosure movement, or those aspects of local history that are touched upon in the collection may find here some suggestions for new material, as well as for the better use of well known sources.

1

ROBERT HARPER AND
PARLIAMENTARY AGENCY

On Friday the 30th ult. died, Robert Harper, Esq., of Lincoln's Inn, Counsellor at law, who is deservedly supposed to have been one of the most able conveyancers in England for more than half this present century. He was deeply versed in the laws of his own country, and well acquainted with the language and history of the modern and ancient nations. His knowledge was great; but his humanity and good temper were above all the modes of expression. He was born at Farnley in this parish; educated at the Free-School in this town; and was the elder brother of Samuel Harper Esq., Alderman of this borough.[1]

The eldest son of Samuel Harper of Farnley, Yorks, gentleman, Robert Harper was born just before the turn of the century and was admitted to Lincoln's Inn on 14 March 1717. On 5 February 1735 he was called to the bar and on 30 May 1746 to the Bench of Lincoln's Inn. Robert's brother Samuel was born about 1700. He did not attend university but despite the lack of any indentifiable legal training he assisted his brother in his London practice. In later life he returned to Leeds. From 1758 the local paper records property of his in the town to be let.[2] On 26 October 1762 he was chosen common councilman, and two weeks later alderman; the following year he was elected mayor – a rapid rise. His tenure of office seems to have been uneventful,[3] and when he died on 13 February 1775 his obituary records merely that he had served the office and was in the 75th year of his age.[4] He was buried at Farnley. Nothing is known of his descendants, if any.

Robert Harper had two sons, Robert born 16 February 1729 and Samuel born 28 December 1732.[5] Robert junior entered

---

[1] *Leeds Intelligencer*, 10 November 1772, printed *Publications of the Thoresby Society*, xxxviii, 82.
[2] *Publications of the Thoresby Society*, xxviii, 107, 126, 167, 168, 220; xxxiii, 156, 169; xxxviii, 149. [3] *Ibid.*, xli, 294, 397–8. [4] *Ibid.*, xxix, 403.
[5] *The Records of the Honorable Society of Lincoln's Inn* (London, 1896), ii, 453.

Lincoln's Inn in 1745 and was called to the bar in 1754. In 1763 he married Ann Rhodes of Ripon and went to live in Yorkshire; by 1772 he was a widower with only one child, a daughter, Sarah;[1] he died in 1793.[2] Samuel was the only member of the family not to follow a career in the law. After attending school in Fulham he was admitted to Trinity College, Cambridge, in 1750, graduated in 1754, M.A. 1757, and being ordained in 1756 became curate of Gamston, Notts, and in 1775 Vicar of Rothwell, Leeds[3] (very close to Farnley). But it seems likely that he was non-resident, for his career was made in the British Museum. The claim of his obituary in 1803 that he had been 'upwards of 47 years librarian to the British Museum and 37 years chaplain to the Foundling hospital'[4] is exaggerated so far as the Museum is concerned but it seems probable that he was employed there in some capacity for the whole of his career after coming down from Trinity. In 1763 he was described as 'of the Parish of St. George's Bloomsbury'[5] and his sons went to school in London between 1768 and 1772.

On 27 July 1765, Dr Thomas Percy enquired of Dr Thomas Birch: 'please to inform me by return of the post whether Mr Empson's place in the British Museum is yet filled up, and if not, whether Mr. Harper hath obtained a promise from any of the three electors, and whether any other candidate hath offered or is likely to succeed.'[6] The place was that of one of the three under-librarians or 'keepers of departments' and the implication is that Harper was already working in the Museum. Dr Matthew Maty, publisher of the *Journal Brittanique* and editor of Chesterfield's works, was under-librarian of the Museum from its first institution in 1753 and principal librarian from 1772 to his death in 1776.[7] In 1765 Maty became secretary of the Royal Society and in 1766 Samuel Harper became a

---

[1] 12 Geo. III pr. c. 86.   [2] *Musgrave's Obituary.*
[3] J. & J. A. Venn, *Alumni Cantabrigiensis* (London, 1922).
[4] *Gentleman's Magazine* (1803), p. 697.
[5] 12 Geo. III pr. c. 86.
[6] John Nichols, *Illustrations of the Literary History of the Eighteenth Century* (London, 1817–58), vii, 577–8.
[7] John Nichols, *Literary Anecdotes of the Eighteenth Century* (London, 1812–15), iii, 257.

Fellow of the Society.[1] Maty's son, Dr Paul Henry Maty was assistant librarian from 1778 to 1784 and of the catalogue of printed books, in two volumes folio, of 1787, it is said that 'about two-thirds were compiled by Dr Maty and Mr Harper and the remainder by Mr Ayscough'.[2] Harper also assisted in 1786 with the publication of the facsimile edition of the Alexandrine MS of the New Testament by Dr Woide.[3] When Maty died in 1788 'His remains were attended by Mr Penneck, Mr Harper, Mr Planta, Mr Woide and Mr Southgate, his Associates in the Museum.'[4] Shortly before his own death, Harper's considerable private library was sold; his late colleague Joseph Planta, then principal librarian, obtained a copy of the fifty-seven page catalogue,[5] went to the sale and purchased several items on behalf of the Museum.

The Reverend Samuel Harper had two sons, again called, predictably, Samuel and Robert, who attended Westminster School.[6] Samuel, born about 1761, was admitted to Lincoln's Inn in 1778 and became a Law Stationer; his *Practical Hints for abstracting title deeds* went through three editions between 1817 and 1829. Robert John, born in 1764, was admitted to Lincoln's Inn in 1781 and became keeper of the records and Deputy Clerk of the Council of the Duchy of Lancaster, in which capacity he 'kindly assisted' Richard Gough with his *History and Antiquities of Pleshy*.[7] In 1816 Robert John sought, and was given, permission to restore at his own expense the tombstone of his grandfather, Robert, in Lincoln's Inn Chapel.[8]

To return to the latter: almost nothing is known of Robert Harper's life outside of the Inn where his children were baptised and he himself was buried. His chambers in the Inn, from December 1734, were on the ground floor of staircase 25 in Gatehouse Court.[9] From the time of his call to the bench in

[1] The identification is queried by Venn, but *The Signatures in the First Journal-Book and the Charter Book of the Royal Society* (1912), leaves no doubt about it.
[2] Nichols, *Lit. Anec.*, ix, 55.   [3] *Ibid.*, p. 10.
[4] *Ibid.*, iii, 260.   [5] BM 821. g. 16(1).
[6] *The Record of Old Westminsters*, ed. G. F. Russell Barker (London, 1928).
[7] Nichols, *Lit. Anec.*, vi, 302. There is a considerable amount of Harper's correspondence on Duchy business in the Liverpool papers (BM Add. MSS 38,446–51).
[8] *The Records of the Honorable Society of Lincoln's Inn. The Black Books* (1899), iv, 142.
[9] The Red Book, p. 328.

1746 the Red Books show that Harper was diligent in his attendance at meetings of the Council, and from 1752 he served in turn the principal offices of the Inn, being Master of the Walks in 1752, Keeper of the Black Book in 1753, Dean of Chapel in 1755, Treasurer in 1760 and Master of the Library in 1761.[1] The following year he represented Lincoln's Inn on the committee which settled a joint admissions policy for the four Inns of Court and received the thanks of his fellows for his services.[2]

The volume of manuscripts at Lincoln's Inn which bears Harper's name consists for the most part of the indexes to his working papers, but it also indicates that Harper, like many of his generation, had some antiquarian interests. He possessed a seventeenth-century manuscript copy of Hooker's translation of the 'Modus tenendi parliamentum' and also of Hooker's own tract 'The Order and Usage how to keep a Parliament in England'.[3] A client gave him a copy of 'Wise William Pierrepont's reasons against a public register'[4] of about 1671, which was afterwards printed from manuscript in the *Harleian Miscellany*.[5] Like Speaker Onslow, he subscribed for the 1732 edition of Whitelocke's *Memorials*. The nature of these items emphasises the parliamentary bias of Harper's interests.

Harper's practice must have been lucrative, but we have no information about his estate except that he owned some land in the City which he settled on his eldest son and which was worth £1,000 by 1772.[6] It is sad to have to record that in the year of his death, when his son's marriage settlement needed revision, 'Robert Harper the Elder Esquire in the Bill named is so very far advanced in years and under so great an Imbecillity of mind as to be incapable of signing the petition or of

[1] *The Black Books*, iii, 349, 353, 355, 357, 368, 369.
[2] *Ibid.*, 374–5. There is a tradition at Lincoln's Inn that Harper 'ghosted' *An Examination of the Scheme of Church Power, laid down in the Codex Juris Eccleseastici Anglicani* (1735), ascribed to Sir Michael Foster. I can find no justification at all for this belief.
[3] These manuscripts are rather rare. They occur together with a list of the parliament as in Yelverton MS vol. cxxii, now BM Add. MS 48,110, and in the printed edition of *The order and usage of the keeping of a Parliament*, published in 1575. The manuscripts may be copies of the printed book.
[4] BM 357. c. 12(83). Copy attested by Samuel Shering, the Duke of Kingston's attorney.   [5] 1745 ed., iii, 305–11.   [6] 12 Geo. III pr. c. 86.

testifying his consent'.[1] Perhaps this is the reason he died intestate. Letters of administration were granted the following year to his son, the Reverend Samuel of the British Museum. Even his tombstone cannot now be traced in spite of his grandson's attempt at restoration. But Robert Harper left his own memorial, till now unrecognised, and it is to his indexes that we must turn for the clue to his career.

The Reverend Samuel inherited his father's library and this was sold, with his own, in 1802. As a result the British Museum acquired an item described as 'Private Acts of Parliament of George I, II and III. 62 vols. bound; and a great number unbound'. This was part of the working library of Robert Harper's law office; but unfortunately the Museum did not obtain the manuscript indexes to it; these are in the volume of Harper MSS at Lincoln's Inn.[2] At the Museum, Harper's papers appear at first to have been catalogued in their original order, but later, in the absence of the indexes, their provenance was ignored, the volumes split up and their contents reclassified and dispersed. With the aid of the indexes I have been able to reconstruct the greater part of the collection and have ascertained that almost the whole of the Museum's set of so-called 'Private Acts'[3] up to 1767 belonged to it. If it were not for Harper's collection, the Museum's holdings of eighteenth-century parliamentary papers would be thin indeed.

At the Museum there is only one, subsidiary, index, headed 'Orders, Petitions and proceedings in extraordinary and special cases'.[4] Only three pages in length, the references in this index go up to volume 36 (1759) and cover a wide variety of papers including 'cases' and 'reasons' in connection with public acts. For instance a sequence taken at random reads:

	Vol.	No.
Mr Potters Bill for numbring the people	30	40
Case of Clerk Assistant in the House of Lords	30	42
Bill for a Method to bar Entails in Maryland	31	31
Mary Visscher's petition for a Denization	32	pa. 65
Security on the Duties of Ellenfoot Harbour	33	43

[1] HLRO. Judges report on *ibid.*
[2] Presented to the Inn by Mr Hubert Stuart Moore, F.S.A., in 1915.
[3] State Paper Room, BS Ref. 2.   [4] Misbound following 357. b. 1(104).

5

The most interesting item mentioned is Harper's own memorandum on passing private bills which originally formed part of his 'great precedent book' and which is discussed in chapter five.

The indexes at Lincoln's Inn are in two main sections. The first is an index to precedent books, covering twenty-seven volumes, three being called simply 'precedent books' 1, 2, and 3, the others being referred to by the letters C (seven volumes), M (seven volumes) and S (ten volumes), which one may guess mean Conveyances, Mortgages and Settlements respectively. These volumes are all lost except for part of volume 1 'the great precedent book' which has been split up and a few pages dispersed in different volumes at the Museum. From these survivals it can be seen that the volumes were entry books containing summaries of the documents in each case, written by various clerks at different times in hasty, cramped handwriting with many abbreviations – definitely volumes for use, not ornament. The index to them is elaborate, though roughly written, with many cross-references. A typical entry reads:

Annuity

Proviso to apportion it for a broken half year	1pb,691
Secured by a Mortgage & defeasance thereof	M7,350
Secured for 2 lives out of Exchequer Annuities	2pb,587

This index to the precedent books seems to have been made contemporaneously; the form of the second section of the index, on the other hand, shows that it was not compiled until the collection was almost complete. This is the index to Acts of Parliament, the main part of which, running to over 100 pages, covers forty-four volumes, most of which have been traced at the British Museum.[1] The contents of the first four volumes cover various dates in the first quarter of the century and begin to be in annual sequence from volume 5, 1 George II, suggesting that the earlier papers were put in order at that date. From 1728 the papers were kept in regular sessional order, a volume for each year usually beginning with the printed private bills of the session, followed by public bills and other parliamentary

[1] The indexes and the papers themselves are discussed in more detail in Appendix I.

papers, and concluding with a manuscript section containing copies of the various supporting papers required for the passing of the private bills which Harper himself had drawn.

In addition to this main index of Acts, there are in Lincoln's Inn six subsidiary indexes (or rather lists in date or volume order) whose entries are duplicated in the main index and which must have been drawn out separately for convenience of reference. Three cover Estate Acts, Change of Name Acts and Divorce Acts. Another covers Inclosure Acts and this contains references to additional volumes A2, B and C which do not appear in any other index and which I have not been able to trace ('C' is evidently not the same as the 'C' for Conveyances volumes of precedents). The fifth subsidiary index also covers Inclosure Acts but from the point of view of form, not content, for instance: 'Articles recited pretty long'; 'Articles recited very short referring to ye Act'; 'Allotments made copyhold'. Another five page index, headed 'Kingston' itemises all the papers relating to the Duke of Kingston's property.

The compilation of such lengthy indexes near the end of a working life throughout which he had apparently managed without them suggests that Harper was preparing to hand over his practice to a successor, or perhaps it was simply due to a slightly senile pride in his achievement. One cannot suppose that any successor would need the final list at Lincoln's Inn, which was evidently made by running straight through forty-three of the forty-four volumes of 'Acts' in the numerical order in which Harper then had them in his possession. This list is headed 'Acts drawn by RH'[1] and extends to the amazing total of 613 items covering the years 3 George I to 6 George III. Beginning with one or two bills in each of the years 1717, 1718, 1720–2, the number then gradually increases until sixteen to twenty bills each session are common in the 1740s with no less than twenty-six in 1747; later there is some decline, but still ten in the last year, 1766. The evidence of this list is confirmed by the papers at the Museum: Harper put his

---

[1] Harper may be forgiven the misnomer. He was not accustomed to his bills failing to pass. 93% of the numbered items in his list did become acts and of the remainder some were never introduced and others succeeded at a second attempt.

initials 'RH' in the top left-hand corner of the copy of each bill he drew personally, and the manuscript material in the volumes, which could have been known only to the lawyer concerned, refers only to bills so marked. Nor is the list complete. It was made up to the end of 1766 but in 1767 Harper drew seven more bills. There is also evidence, from the presence of manuscript petitions amongst the papers that Harper was responsible for at least two dozen more bills over the whole period which he overlooked when compiling his list.

Robert Harper was a conveyancer, which explains the lapse of eighteen years between his admission to the Inn and his call to the bar. Conveyancing was a separate branch of legal practice, its practitioners having more in common with barristers than with attorneys, but since they were allowed to be members of their Inn, could work from their chambers, and had no occasion to plead in court, there was no reason why they should be called to the bar and they usually did not take this step; they remained 'practitioners under the bar'.[1] In 1729 attorneys were required by act[2] to register if they were to continue in practice and Robert Harper was duly enrolled on 27 November 1730 before Mr Justice Denton at Serjeant's Inn as an attorney in the Court of Common Pleas.[3] Perhaps he thought this a necessary precaution and did not intend to practise, or perhaps he thought the Inn would not proceed severely against an old established member who was really a conveyancer and only incidentally an attorney. It was not yet an absolute rule that practice as an attorney must cease for at least two years if one was to be called to the bar.[4] Any way, Harper changed his course and in 1735 was called. We can only guess at his motives: perhaps the Leeds Free School boy had become the type of good college man who, having established himself in his profession, looked forward to service in the offices of his Inn and ultimately the Mastership as his greatest remaining ambition and the reward of his labours. Membership of the bar, though unusual for a conveyancer, did

---

[1] Holdsworth, vi, 448.   [2] 2 Geo. II c. 23.
[3] *Additional Lists of Attornies and Solicitors* (1731), p. 68.
[4] Holdsworth, xii, 23. The rule was laid down by the committee of which Harper was a member, in 1762. Above, p. 4.

not preclude his continuance in that practice, the chief difference being that he would usually be called upon to settle,
rather than actually draw the clauses of, acts or other documents. Harper's call in fact seems to have made no difference
at all to the nature of his activities.

In 1760 the Society of Gentlemen Practisers in the Courts of
Law and Equity (the forerunner of the Law Society) was
concerned to defend its rights against the invasions of members
of the Scriveners Company. When the case came on before
the Recorder of London on 11 December Harper gave evidence
on behalf of the Society and being asked how long he had been
in the profession replied 'Why, Sir, I may reckon it above forty
years.' Counsel then asked 'You have more particularly had
Conveyancing business brought before you. Pray how long
have you followed that branch?' to which Harper replied 'Why
I believe I may say ever since any body would trust me'.[1]
Even so, and although it stands first in his list of 'Acts drawn'
it is hard to believe that Harper was solely entrusted with his
first private bill, and that the very valuable marriage settlement
of the Marquis of Granby, at the age of 17. It seems more likely
that he had entered chambers where he was able to assist with
drawing the bill. There are some hints that these may have
been the chambers of Peniston Lamb, uncle of Sir Matthew
Lamb, M.P., who named his son, later the first Lord Melbourne,
for his great-uncle, having inherited from him a fortune
reputed to be £100,000.[2] In his will, which is very brief and
businesslike, Peniston Lamb left almost his whole estate to his
nephew. Apart from some small bequests and annuities to
female relatives, the only monetary legacy is one of £20 to
Samuel Harper, who was one of the witnesses of the will.
Lamb left mourning rings to seven of 'my friends' including
'Mr Robert Harper'.[3] Peniston Lamb was a conveyancer, who
entered Lincoln's Inn in 1708, perhaps only for the sake of
residence there, since he was already well established in his

---

[1] *The Records of the Society of Gentlemen Practisers in the Courts of Law and Equity*,
ed. E. A. Freshfield (London, 1897), p. 274.
[2] G.E.C., *The Complete Peerage*, sub Melbourne.
[3] P.C.C. Ducie 33. The will is dated 27 Jan. 1734/5. Lamb died on the 29th and was
buried at Lincoln's Inn on 3 Feb. (*Records*, ii, 649).

profession and was never called. He was a witness to the preliminary agreement for the Marquis of Granby's marriage settlement and a trustee under the act. Another of his clients was the Duke of Kingston, as shown by a letter he wrote in 1707 to the Duke's man of business concerning 'what Deeds we have in our custody' relating to Samuel Pierrepont's estate;[1] Harper notes items relating to the late Samuel Pierrepont's estate in his list of Kingston papers, which also shows that he had copies of many deeds and other instruments relating to the Kingston estates. The only letter of Robert Harper's so far discovered is in the same collection, addressed to Samuel Shering at Thoresby, concerning the surrender of a mortgage.[2]

If the Duke of Kingston was perhaps his most important client, Harper also drew all the Cowper family bills [Nos. 80, 106, 162, 186, 374]; he probably drew the 1735 petition of William Cowper and other creditors of the Hanaper for arrears of salary;[3] and he had copies of the papers in the case of the clerk of the parliament's claim to appoint his own clerk assistant;[4] so he may have been the family's man of business. Harper was quite often named as a trustee under acts [Nos. 13, 30, 52, 100, 110, 255, 286, 306, 311, 363, 425, 493, 518]; sometimes his brother Samuel was co-trustee [Nos. 286, 518]; and sometimes Samuel acted alone [Nos. 204, 309, 498]. Trustees were necessary if a strictly settled estate was to be relieved: the property was vested in trustees, freed from the restrictions of the settlement, for the use of the parties entitled to the property. Usually the property was to be sold by the trustees as quickly as possible, thus terminating the trust, when the cash or other property bought from the proceeds was again vested in the person concerned under the terms of the settlement. But occasionally the trust was a permanent one, to administer estates on behalf of a lunatic, for instance. It may be guessed that when Harper acted as a permanent trustee

[1] BM Egerton MS 3516 f. 76.

[2] BM Egerton MS 3516 f. 100. Another hint is that in 1731 Peniston Lamb and Samuel Harper jointly certified a copy of an act from the Parliament Office, BM 3 Geo. I pr. c. 7.

[3] BM 357. c. 2(91).   [4] BM 357. d. 10(42)–(44).

he was the family lawyer, and that this activity was a function of his ordinary practice as an attorney rather than of his parliamentary business. But on many occasions he was evidently concerned only as a parliamentary expert and cooperated with the family's man of business. There are two copies of the Duchess of Bolton's bill in 1725 [No. 14], one 'As it was first drawn by RH' and the other 'As alter'd by the Dutchesses' Counsel'. In 1728 the Duchess of Portland's bill [No. 26] 'was first drawn by Mr. Walter to answer the prayer of the petition. But that being thought not proper to answer the main design of the parties I drew it as it now stands.' Lord Irwin's bill in 1756 [No. 479] was altered by Mr Booth and in 1765 a clause in Dobinson's bill [No. 598] was 'drawn by Dr Blackstone and inserted at the Committee ... instead of the Clause ... prepared by me'.

It was in 1732 that Robert Harper first drew more than ten bills in one session and he never again dropped below that number until 1763 when, as the deterioration of his handwriting and the small number of his bills show, he was ill. He recovered, but remained in practice for only four more years. During the thirty-one years of his prime, 1732 to 1762, altogether 1,238 private acts received the royal assent and of these 458 or 37% were drawn by Harper. About a quarter of all private acts were for change of name or naturalisation; with these Harper had little to do – presumably they were too simple to require his attention. His speciality was private estate acts of which he drew 350, or 56% of the total in this group. Up to 1754 he drew the same percentage of all the inclosure acts, but when the inclosure movement really began to get under way, Harper continued to draw only the same number – between two and six each session – so his overall percentage for inclosure acts drops to 31%; however, his activity in this field in the early years of the movement must have had considerable influence on the development of the form of these bills.

Since one must grant that many private estate bills were drawn by the parties' own solicitors, the figures indicate that Harper's practice was so extensive as to leave almost no room for any one else to operate in the field. Certainly no attorney

Robert Harper and parliamentary agency

could have rivalled him as a parliamentary draftsman. The details of Harper's work will be further discussed under the appropriate headings. We need here remark only that he was sometimes involved in the opposition to local and inclosure bills. He clearly kept an eye on bills other than his own in the interests of his practice. He noted on Warden's name bill, for instance, that the clause enabling him to bear the arms as well as take the name of Sergison had, unusually, been struck out of the bill.[1] He many times noted the time and place of meeting of a parliamentary committee, even for bills he had not drawn, many others appear in his indexes, and in one case he noted that 'this bill was desired to be amended in ye Recitalls by the Chairman of the Committee of the Lords and was so amended by me',[2] which looks as though he was acting as agent for a bill drawn by the party's solicitor. Harper's papers are by no means complete and there may well have been more than the five occasions on which we know he had power of attorney empowering him to sign consents 'at the Committees of both houses of Parliament ... and also to consent to any alterations that shall be made ... by the Committees' [Nos. 38, 84, 109, 130, 289]. On the last such occasion, Harper is joined with his brother Samuel, who is actually described as an 'agent' presenting a petition out of time, in the index to Robert's precedent book.[3]

In view of all this evidence of Harper's parliamentary connections, it comes as no surprise to find that he was left a mourning ring in the will of Samuel Richardson, printer to the House, his name occurring immediately after that of Jeremiah Dyson and before those of the other Commons clerks.[4] We may assume that, as a later House printer was to

---

[1] BM 6 Geo. II pr. c. 18. [2] BM 4 Geo. II pr. c. 28.
[3] See Appendix I following [No. 515]. Samuel also had power of attorney for [No. 159].
[4] Harper is the only recipient of a ring who has not been identified by the literary scholars. Samuel Harper, who also received a ring, has been tentatively identified as the Reverend Samuel of the British Museum, but he was only twenty-four when the will was made and had no known parliamentary connections, so the reference is almost certainly to his uncle, who was closely connected with Robert Harper's practice. For details of the will see *Notes & Queries*, 12th ser., xi, 342–4, 383–7; and vol. ccix (1964), 300–4.

remark, 'although the connection and interest were not of the most exalted kind, yet it ensured regard and consideration being such (and that not of an unsolicitous kind) which is bestowed on the conduit-pipe that conveys the necessary supply from the fountain'.[1] From 1705 both Houses required printed copies of private bills to be delivered to them. An attorney responsible for as many as twenty such bills each session, who had the selection of the printer, was a far more valuable client even than the House itself, which never at this time ordered anything like that number of public bills to be printed; yet the work of printing public bills was eagerly sought after by printers.[2]

Dr O. C. Williams[3] demonstrated that the statement made by Clifford[4] and exaggerated by Holdsworth[5] suggesting that the clerks of the House had the exclusive privilege of soliciting bills in parliament is incorrect. His evidence was a group of solicitors' accounts for a variety of different private bills, dating from 1661 to 1734. In 1948, Dr Williams enquired whether in the mid-eighteenth century there were already 'professional men in London who made a regular business of parliamentary agency'.[6] By 1954 he was satisfied that there were not, but that the work was performed 'not as a specialty, but by solicitors and attorneys in the ordinary course of their practice' and 'although some solicitors may have had more practice in Parliament than others, there is no reason to suppose that such firms only carried on what came to be called parliamentary agency. There was not enough business.'[7]

There is however more evidence to show not only that this work was done by private solicitors but that they were officially recognised, by the House itself, to have a special position. On 9 April 1742,

A complaint being made to the House, that Mr. Gilbert Douglas, a Solicitor for several Bills depending in this House, was, upon Monday last, arrested as he was attending this House;

[1] P. and G. Ford, *Luke Graves Hansard, His Diary* (Oxford, 1962), pp. 72–3.
[2] S. Lambert, 'Printing for the House of Commons in the Eighteenth Century', *The Library*, 5th ser., xxiii (1968), 34. [3] *Clerical Organization*, pp. 185–9.
[4] Clifford, ii, 878. [5] Holdsworth, xi, 334. [6] *Private Bill Procedure*, i, 28.
[7] *Clerical Organization*, p. 186 and n. 3.

And the Journal of the House of the 2d Day of May 1678 (in relation to the Allowance of the Privilege of this House, to Mr. John Gardner, Solicitor in the Case concerning Lindsey Level, who was arrested as he was coming to attend on the House), being read;
And a Witness being called in, and examined, in order to prove, that the said Mr. Gilbert Douglas was so arrested;
And the House being informed, by several of their Members, that he did that Day attend on the House as Solicitor for several Bills then depending;
Ordered, That the Privilege of this House be allowed to the said Mr. Gilbert Douglas; and that he be discharged from his Arrest.[1]

The presence of a private solicitor is evidently as essential as that of the members to the work of the House, and the members therefore extend their own privilege to him, to enable him to perform his functions, as they had done in a similar case more than sixty years earlier.

The Lords recognition of a private solicitor has a somewhat harsher tone, but his responsibility is clearly as great: on 23 January 1706 'The solicitor on Goulston's Bill was called in and owns he follows Mr. Goulston's Bill, and he was reprimanded for not providing a sufficient breviate. He says the brief was drawn by the Clerk of the House of Commons and was reprimanded and ordered to make a perfect brief.'[2] Williams remarked that the clerk of the House might be regarded as 'the universal parliamentary agent'[3] but even so the Lords would not allow a private solicitor to hide behind Jodrell's negligence: the solicitor 'following' the bill was responsible for it to the House. The presence of an 'agent' is quite often mentioned in the Lords committee books, but the name of the person concerned is seldom given.[4]

[1] *CJ* xxiv, 170. Douglas was admitted a solicitor in Chancery in 1730 (*Additional Lists of Attornies and Solicitors* (1731), p. 184). In 1734 he acted as parliamentary solicitor to the Georgia Trustees (H.M.C. *Egmont Diary*, ii, 25, 32, 37, 44). He seems to have been unfortunate: the Commons had to rescue him from his creditors twice in 1756 (*CJ* xxvii, 447, 537), and again in 1758 (*CJ* xxviii, 251). Christopher Picard was similarly relieved, on Douglas' precedent, in 1753 (*CJ* xxvi, 797).   [2] H.M.C. *House of Lords MSS*, vi, 429.
[3] *Clerical Organization*, p. 188.
[4] Agents were ordered to prepare additional evidence [Nos. 23, 38]; and to give their clients notice of proceedings [Nos. 14, 384]. In the case of Jervoise [No. 45] Harper was present at the Lords committee and proved an attested copy of a

Robert Harper and parliamentary agency

Robert Harper practised as a conveyancer, not exclusively for parliamentary work although he certainly specialised in this branch. He was primarily a draftsman and it is not suggested that he acted as agent in the House for all the bills he drew.[1] In any event the work of an agent in the eighteenth century could not have been exactly the same as that of the nineteenth-century firms which developed to cope with the ever-increasing complexity of the standing orders. We will see that in the eighteenth century the task of putting a bill through parliament might be handled in a variety of different ways. Clifford defined an agent as one who had an 'exact knowledge of precedents ... and of the ... rules embodied in the Standing Orders and practice of the two Houses', in order to 'prepare Standing Order proofs, to draft most of the Bills which go before Committees, to frame notices, petitions, memorials as to non-compliance with Standing Orders, and all other documents required in promoting or opposing Bills at their various stages'.[2] In so far as these criteria apply in the pre-standing order period, Robert Harper had this knowledge, carefully set out in his precedent books, and performed all these functions.

We will see that agency by the Commons clerks developed a good deal earlier than Dr Williams supposed, but in 1812 John Dorington, acknowledged to be the leading agent after George White, promoted only 17 bills[3] and in 1832 only the largest firm of agents promoted more than 26 bills;[4] by which time of course the total number of bills was very much greater than it had been in Harper's lifetime. The promotion of at least ten bills in every year from 1732 to 1762, rising to twenty-six in 1747, makes good Harper's claim to be one of the first parliamentary agents and one with a practice as extensive as many of his successors until well into the nineteenth century.

---

document (Com. Bk. 8 Apr. 1730), but his function is not mentioned. Williams deduced that there were no agents in the seventeenth century because none is mentioned in Courthope's minute book (*Clerical Organization*, p. 186) but this is not conclusive since *Courthope* does not record the members present and sometimes does not mention even the chairman.

[1] See below, p. 49 for two occasions on which Commons clerks acted as agents for bills drawn by Harper.

[2] Clifford, ii, 879.   [3] *Clerical Organization*, p. 183.   [4] *Ibid.*, p. 262.

2

TREATISES AND HANDBOOKS

Even in the pre-standing order period the rules and conventions of both Houses were complicated enough. In 1765 for the first time the statute book contained more than 200 items. As the need for private legislation increased, parliamentary procedure began to be of concern to more than the members of the Houses. There was need for guidance to the public as to the ways in which parliamentary activity might affect, not only their daily lives as citizens, but their private and business concerns.

The pioneering treatises on procedure, such as those of Lambarde, Hooker, Hakewill and Elsyng, came to an end when Henry Scobell used his position as clerk of both Houses to publish books based on materials that he found among the official records.[1] It is broadly true that no new book on procedure then appeared until Hatsell began to publish his *Precedents* in 1776. One excludes from this discussion books on the jurisdiction of parliament, notably those of William Petyt[2] and Sir Matthew Hale;[3] and books on election cases.[4]

[1] *Memorials of the Method and Manner of Proceedings in Parliament in Passing Bills* (1656). *Remembrances of some Methods, Orders and Proceedings. Heretofore used and observed in the House of Lords. Extracted out of the Journals of that House. By H.S.E.C.P.* (1657). There is a mystery as to how the *Remembrances* came to be published when they did, and by the Commonwealth equivalent of the King's Printer. There was no House of Lords at the time, as Scobell emphasises by converting the phrases of the Lords orders into the past tense. Nonetheless the format of the volume is that of a pocket book for easy reference, measuring scarcely $3 \times 5\frac{1}{2}$ inches.

[2] *Miscellanea Parliamentaria* (1680); *The Ancient Right of the Commons Asserted* (1680); and *Jus Parliamentorum* (1739).

[3] Hale's work is fully discussed and his manuscripts described by Francis Hargrave in his excellent introduction to Hale's major work on jurisdiction, *The jurisdiction of the Lords House, or Parliament, considered according to ancient records* (1796). See also *A Collection of Tracts relative to the Law of England, from Manuscripts, now first edited by Francis Hargrave, Esquire, Barrister at Law* (1787).

[4] For instance, William Bohun, *A Collection of debates ... touching the right of electing members ...* (1702). Thomas Carew, *An Historical Account of the Rights of Elections ...* (1755). In the later eighteenth century reports of proceedings on controverted elections became a branch of law reporting. In 1775 J. Topham and Richard Blyke edited Glanville's reports of 1624 from a manuscript belonging to Nicholas Hardinge.

The books that appeared before the Restoration were addressed primarily to members and were concerned with the regulation of business within the Houses. The conventions governing debate and order had been settled in their broad outline by the later seventeenth century. Between 1685 and 1717 the particular orders were made which regulated the conduct of private business for the greater part of the eighteenth century and these included regulations for matters to be dealt with outside the Houses as a preliminary to business within. The books published after 1660 are of three sorts. There continues to be a historical or antiquarian interest. Members' handbooks become an established thing when George Petyt's publishers think it worth while to bring out a new edition to coincide with the opening of three successive parliaments. What is new is the publication of the standing orders themselves, for the use of the public outside the House, and the appearance of the first handbook for the promoters of private bills.

The continuing interest in parliamentary history need not be laboured. Hooker's translation of the medieval Modus appeared in *Somers Tracts* in 1751 and his *Usage* in Mountmorres' *History of Ireland* in 1742. Lambarde's tract was printed in the *Harleian Miscellany* in 1744. The definitive edition of Elsyng's *Manner of Holding Parliament* was published by the clerk of the Commons in 1768.

All the principal early tracts went through new editions in the late seventeenth century and in 1690 there appeared George Petyt's *Lex Parliamentaria: Or a Treatise of the Law and Custom of the Parliaments of England. By G. P. Esq.*[1] This work combined the essential parts of Hakewill's and Scobell's writings into a practical handbook. The information contained in the volume, apart from the attributions,[2] is usually correct. That

[1] The book is usually ascribed to George Petyt, but I cannot trace any person of this name in any of the usual biographical sources. None of the printed editions give anything but the initials 'G.P.' as does the advertisement of the first edition. The earliest attribution of the name seems to be in the Bodleian catalogue of 1738. I am indebted to Mr P. Melville of the Cambridge University Library for this reference.

[2] Mrs Sims has written that 'Comparison of the quotations with their sources indicates that the compiler was very careful indeed' and 'his critical faculties and his bibliographical knowledge were obviously great' (*Liverpool Tractate*,

it was found of use as a handbook is indicated by the production of new editions for the opening of the parliaments of 1734, 1740 and 1748, and it had influence even in the New World.[1] It is cited as an authority in a small private precedent book made by a peer active *c.* 1704–7, who also adapted its title for his own collection: 'Lex Parliamentaria in Domo Superiori.'[2]

The Lords standing orders were officially collected and enrolled in 1621.[3] We have no earlier manuscript versions, but the wording of many of the earliest orders is most informal;[4] it does seem most likely that the committee, including Selden, who were then being 'guided through' the work of establishing the privileges of the House by Henry Elsyng senior[5] incorporated in the first roll a collection of precedents already well established and subsisting in written form in the clerk's office.[6] One may remark also that the title of the roll, 'Remembrances ... leaving the solemnity belonging to his Majesty's Coming, to be marshalled by those Lords, to whom it more properly appertains' has an echo in Elsyng's 'The Moderne Forme of the Parliaments of England':[7] 'The manner of his Majestys comeing for the Order and State thereof, I leave to the Heraulds, and will onely shew what is done in the House that day.'

The roll was deficient, for everyday use, in that it was inevitably kept in chronological order. Scobell, in his published version[8] remedied this by sorting the orders into chapters in logical sequence and adding (very rightly) a summary of

---

pp. lix–lx). But, alas, Petyt used the 1671 edition of Hakewill's book, *The Manner how Statutes are enacted in Parliament by passing of Bills*, which followed that of 1659 in confusing Hakewill's and Starkey's tracts, so that many of the citations which Petyt ascribes to Hakewill, for instance pp. 30–1 and pp. 125–6 are by Starkey. What is worse is that the 1671 edition of Hakewill's book was sold bound up with Scobell's *Memorials* and Petyt cites this sometimes as 'Scobell' and sometimes as 'Memorials in Hakewill'; see for instance pp. 163–75 where he uses the latter title for Scobell's long section on divisions.

[1] *Proceedings in Parliament, 1610*, ed. E. R. Foster (Yale, 1968), i, xv n.
[2] Cambridge University Library MS Dd. xiv. 19.
[3] Printed *in extenso* H.M.C., *House of Lords MSS*, x, 1–27.
[4] See particularly the anecdote of Lord Chief Justice Popham, who would not be seated, though infirm, *ibid.*, p. 4.
[5] M. F. Bond, 'The Formation of the Archives of Parliament, 1497–1691', *Jour. Soc. Archivists*, i (1957), 151–8.
[6] The earliest MS copy I have seen is in the Braye MSS, but it does not predate the roll.   [7] Ed. C. S. Sims, *Amer. Hist. Rev.*, liii (1947–8), 292.   [8] Above, p. 16.

Selden's *Baronage*. It is therefore not surprising that his successors in the office used his work as a basis for their own precedent books.[1] But Scobell's book seems not to have been favoured by peers, who preferred to use manuscript copies of the official roll[2] until the need for these was superseded by the appearance of a printed edition.[3] This was published in 1744 and was directed not only to peers but to 'all Others concerned in the Laws of Great Britain and Ireland'; a second edition appeared in 1748.[4] Like Scobell's *Remembrances*, these publications present the orders in logical, rather than chronological, order. The House of Lords also posted those orders that had to be complied with by promoters of private bills in the lobby of their House; these, handsomely printed on broad sheets,[5] might be copied by lawyers' clerks attending the House.

The Lords orders contained some specific rules concerning procedure on bills, but the great majority of them are not really orders, but precedents concerning privilege and the

---

[1] BM Add. MS 36,102 and Hargrave MS 167 are interleaved copies of Scobell's printed book, with later MS additions, both belonging to 'John Walker, Deputy to John Browne, Cler. Parl.'. The House of Lords Record Office recently acquired a greatly enlarged MS copy of the 'Remembrances', compiled *c.* 1710 by John Relf, a clerk in the Parliament Office.

[2] Innumerable copies of these exist in manuscript collections. Probably every active peer possessed one. BM Add. MS 3571 was specially transcribed by James Merest, clerk assistant, as a gift to Sir Hans Sloane. Lansdowne MS 500, which, since it contains orders up to 1749, appears to post-date the printed editions, does not in fact do so: it originally contained the orders only up to number 121 (1732); the later orders are added in a different hand.

[3] *Remembrances: or, a Compleat Collection of the Standing Orders of the House of Lords in England. Extracted from and compared with the Journals of the said House. Very useful for all, but more particularly the Nobility, Gentry and all Others concerned in the Laws of Great Britain and Ireland.* Published by the Editor of the Parliamentary Debates in England, as a proper Supplement to the same. Printed in the Year 1744.

I have not been able to identify the publisher. The edition of the debates referred to is presumably *A Collection of the Parliamentary Debates in England from the year 1688 to the present time.* 24 vols., no place (1739–49). Another edition in 13 volumes has 'Dublin printed, London reprinted' (1739–41).

[4] The title is the same as that of 1744 from *A Compleat Collection* ..., the imprint being simply 'London, 1748'. The BM copy belonged to Francis Hargrave and is bound up with his copy of the Commons Standing Orders (see below p. 25). This edition was advertised in the *London Magazine*, September 1748. No publisher's name is given. The price was 3s.

[5] There is a fine copy of the orders as printed by the Queen's Printer, 1708, in the Cambridge University Library. Some of the printed copies, 1661–1727 have been cut up and pasted inside the cover of the manuscript copy of the 'Remembrances', BM Lansdowne 500 (see above n. 2).

customary forms of the House. They are, as their title says, 'Remembrances for order and decency'. Just as 'Remembrances' is the keyword for the Lords orders, so 'Observations' is the keyword for the Commons,[1] and similarly, the 'Observations' are a collection of precedents, rather than of rules laid down by the House, but their history is much more obscure than those of the Lords. The seventeenth-century collection 'Observations, rules and orders, collected out of divers Journals of the House of Commons' appears to date from the early seventeenth century and is frequently associated with a copy of the 'form of apology' of July 1604; this document gradually became permanently associated with the manuscript 'Observations' and was finally absorbed into its table of contents. The 'Observations' seem to have been a collection of very hasty notes drawn from the Journal and the quality of the text has not been improved in transmission. Precedent books of course were common; most of the clerks and many members must have kept them; but this one does seem to have a special connection with the House. In its original form,[2] the latest precedent is the order of 16 June 1607 for a committee to supervise the Commons Journal. Later some additional precedents of the reign of Charles I were added. John Browne, clerk of the parliament,[3] and speaker Bromley,[4] owned copies of this version. A Commons

---

[1] The word occurs in the title of the later editions of Scobell's *Memorials* as 'gathered by observation out of the Journal books'. A copy of Lambarde's treatise, usually called 'Some certain notes of the Order ... of the lower house ...' in the Braye MSS is there titled 'Observations of the house of commons ...'. At the end of the eighteenth century, Hatsell's *Precedents* are still divided into 'Precedents' and 'Observations' thereon.

[2] All the manuscripts I have seen are copies. The earliest appears to be BM Lansdowne MS 480 which contains 'Observations', ff. 3–55 and the form of apology, ff. 56–74 in the same hand, but as two separate entities with several blank folios between. The book has a note on the title page 'This book was given to mee in June 1688 by my honoured friend William Sacheverell Esq.'. The volume belonged to Lord Somers, passed to Sir Joseph Jekyll and was bought by Edward Umfreville at Whiston's sale in 1739. BM Harleian MS 6283 is earlier than Harleian 7201 and both appear to have come from the Harley family papers. Hargrave's MS 195, ff. 1–51 has on the fly-leaf 'Herberts book transcribed out of a manuscript belonging to Sir Hugh Grahme May ye 8th 1678.'   [3] HLRO Braye MS 6.

[4] BM Add. MS 36,854, ff. 1–178. This contains the text of the 'Observations' to James I, with some of James II added in another hand. The volume also contains a manuscript copy of Scobell's *Memorials*.

clerk in the later seventeenth century combined the 'Observations' and Scobell's *Memorials* to form the basis of his own precedent book.[1] As late as 1820, John Bull, clerk of the Journals, used the 'Observations' in the same way and his section on prayers in fact contains no additional matter.[2]

The 'Observations' were printed in 1707, with an attribution to Lord Chief Justice Hale,[3] and again printed separately in 1717.[4] Hale, though much younger, was a friend of Selden and executor of his will, and also renowned as a collector of manuscripts, so one would hope that the history of this book might throw some light on that of the 'Observations'. But Francis Hargrave was quite clear that the attribution was spurious; no such manuscripts even existed in Hale's collection, much less were they written by him. In the notes on his printed copy, now in the British Museum,[5] Hargrave declared that the first

[1] HLRO Ambrose Kelly's book.   [2] HLRO John Bull's book.

[3] *Original Institution, Jurisdiction and Power of Parliaments. In Two parts: The First comprehending the Nature and Method of all Parliamentary Transactions; The Second consisting of Observations, Rules and Orders, Collected out of divers Journals of the House of Commons. Being a manuscript of the late Judge Hales* (London, 1707).

Mrs Sims identified BM Add. MSS 33,249; 36,858 and Harleian 1243 as the manuscripts of part 1. To these may be added Cambridge University Library MS Dd. xii. 66. BM Add. MS 36,858 belonged to speaker Bromley. These MSS are all copies, fair written, with a title page drawn out like that of a printed book. Mrs Sims' identification of the manuscripts of part 2 is incorrect and her comment also far from the facts (*Liverpool Tractate*, p. ix, n. 111). The 'Observations' are not 'a compilation based on various tractates and especially on Hakewill and Scobell'; the section on the speaker, which she cites particularly, bears no resemblance at all to Hakewill's account. Add. MS 36,854 is not the version used for the printed part 2, though it is similar to it. Add. MS 8878, also cited by Mrs Sims, is not a manuscript of the 'Observations' at all. It is someone's private precedent book and a very excellent one. It appears to have been compiled about 1678–9; the only identification we have is a note on the fly-leaf that it was bought for the Museum 'at the Fairfax sale' in 1831, but I have not been able to trace the item in the sale catalogue, which included many of Thomas Fairfax's manuscripts.

[4] *Observations, Rules and Orders, collected out of divers Journals of the House of Commons, entred in the reigns of Edward VI, Q. Mary, Q. Elizabeth, K. James I, K. Charles I and K. Charles II* (London. Printed for Bernard Lintot ... 1717). This edition follows the order of the original manuscripts but adds precedents from James I up to 1679 under each head. At the end, following the Apology, is an extra section giving some additional precedents for the time of James I and Charles I. We have no information at all about this book or the MS on which it was based. Lintot was at this time one of the printers of the Commons *Votes*, but these printers always did much private as well as official work.

[5] Pressmark 1130. f. 2. The *D.N.B.* accepts Hargrave's argument but states that the MS to which he refers is lost. It is not: it is Hargrave MS 195 (see above p. 20 n. 2).

part of the volume is 'a grossly piratical compilation' from well-known books, notably those of Coke, and as for part 2, to attribute it to Hale is 'an imputation on him'.

So the history of the 'Observations' remains obscure. They are almost certainly a good deal older than Hale's time and could not have been his. The text of the printed version is so poor that it can hardly have been of much practical use. The only interest of the book is that it was thought worth while to publish it at all, under cover of a famous name. The same is true of *Arcana Parliamentaria*[1] where the name of Sir Thomas Smith is prominently displayed to cover a feeble compilation from Smith, Starkey and Coke, but again, a Commons clerk thought it worth while to transcribe this into a volume in the Journal Office, with some much more respectable companions.[2]

That there was sufficient public interest to make such publications worth while is also illustrated by the history of the printing of the *Commons Journals*. When Jodrell became clerk in 1683 he found the papers of the House in confusion.[3] He endeavoured to remedy this situation by obtaining a house at Westminster in which they might be kept[4] and in 1688 appointed a clerk to supervise the records.[5] Jodrell gave particular attention to the Journals, making an inventory of them[6] and taking immediate action when he discovered that booksellers of Westminster had 'by some indirect means got some books which they pretend to be a copy of the Journals and design

---

[1] *Arcana Parliamentaria: or Precedents concerning Elections, Proceedings, Privileges and Punishments in Parliament. Faithfully collected out of the Common and Statute Law of this Realm with Particular Quotations of the Authors in Each Case. By R.C. of the Middle Temple Esq. To which is added, The Authority, Form and Manner of Holding Parliaments. By the learned Sir Thos. Smith, Doctor of Laws* (London, 1685).

[2] HLRO. The volume contains transcripts of Scobell's *Memorials* (1670 ed.), Doddridge's *Opinions of Sundry Antiquaries* (1685 ed.) and Elsyng's *Bills* (1685 ed.).

[3] If Jodrell had been clerk assistant from 1678 as suggested by Williams, some responsibility for the muddle rests with him (*Clerical Organization*, pp. 30, 36).

[4] *Ibid.*, pp. 38–9. The negotiation fell through despite the fact that Jodrell was one 'whom the King is disposed to gratify' (*Calendar of State Papers, Domestic*, 1685, p. 109). He received other favours from the Crown (*Clerical Organization*, pp. 43, 58).

[5] Williams suggested this may have been Zachary Hamlyn (*Clerical Organization*, p. 40 n. 1) but he was a child of ten at the time (see below p. 39).

[6] Report of committee on printing the Journals, *CJ* xxiv, 164.

to print the same'.[1] This was not a new practice, and one cannot avoid the suspicion that the booksellers' chief fault may have been their failure to 'square' the reversioner of the clerkship. In William Goldesborough junior's time the sale of manuscript copies at high prices had encouraged booksellers to print the Journals for the sessions of 1678 and 1679.[2] This commercial activity can scarcely have gone on without the connivance of the clerk, and Jodrell did not put a stop to the making of manuscript copies for sale. Humfrey Wanley noted in his diary '18 December 1724. One Mr. Payne came, saying that he hath a complete sett of the Journals of the House of Peers; that is, from the beginning of K. Henry VIII's reign to the dissolution of the last Parliament; all fairly and regularly written in one Hundred Volumes in Folio, which he offers to my Lord for Six Hundred Guineas.'[3] Payne was evidently in a big way of business and counted even the King among his customers: 'Thomas Payne Esq., for transcribing Journals of the House of Lords, House of Commons and Parliament Rolls £1,637. 17. 0.'[4]

Jodrell presumably simplified this commercial copying when he began to make a fair copy of the Journal at the end of each session, and he was put in charge of the transcription of the

---

[1] Jodrell's petition of 16 November 1683 printed *Clerical Organization*, pp. 36–7.

[2] I am most grateful to Mr D. C. L. Holland, Librarian of the House of Commons, for drawing my attention to these volumes. They are *A coppy of the journal-book of the house of commons for the sessions of parliament begun at Westminster, October 21, 1678 ...* (London, 1680), and *A True Copy of the journal-book of the last parliament begun at Westminster the sixth day of March 1678/9 ...* (London, 1680). It was the Journal for 1679 which Pepys borrowed and which he returned to Jodrell when the writs went out for the 1685 parliament. The first thirteen folios, presumably containing the entries for the first session, 6–13 March 1679, were already missing, though they had existed and were printed in the 1680 volume, which Hardinge considered to be authentic. Pepys' reference to the volume 'coming into my hand in the manner it did' does not suggest he received it from the clerk, although Jodrell knew he had it. (Pepys' letters are printed in *Clerical Organization*, pp. 37–8.) On 13 May 1684 Sunderland had ordered Jodrell to allow L'Estrange to borrow the Journals and other papers concerning the popish plot, and in November and December Dr Samuel Parker, the king's chaplain, was to have access to some unspecified papers (*Calendar of State Papers, Domestic*, 1684, pp. 15, 118, 195, 236).

[3] *Diary of Humfrey Wanley*, ed. C. E. and R. C. Wright (London, 1966), ii, 324.

[4] *CJ* xx, 532. Some of Payne's accounts for this transcribing are bound into a manuscript volume of Commons standing orders, BM Lansdowne MS 481.

earlier Journals by a committee of 1698.[1] But although this work was completed it was not well done. Hardinge considered all manuscript copies of the Journals 'very erroneous'.[2] Hardinge set about this side of the clerk's business in a much more scholarly and workmanlike manner, as befitted a scholar of Eton and Fellow of King's. He first made a complete catalogue of the Commons papers[3] and then had the Journal abstracted under the main heads of elections,[4] conferences with the Lords,[5] and proceedings on the election of a speaker.[6] He may also have been responsible for making a new index-calendar of the Commons, and possibly even of the Lords Journals.[7] Nor did he rely solely upon the papers available in the office but aimed to make the record complete by raiding the Petyt collection for materials that had gone astray there.[8]

All this activity suggests that Hardinge may have had it in mind, from the time of his first appointment, to publish the Journals as a commercial enterprise. It has not been noticed that this was the proposition he put to the House. He wished to print 1,000 copies, 600 for members and the remainder for sale; or, if the House did not wish to embark upon any public

---

[1] *Clerical Organization*, pp. 40, 191.
[2] Report of committee on printing Journals, *CJ* xxiv, 264.
[3] BM Lansdowne MS 553. 1 vol. 1547–1733.
[4] BM Lansdowne MSS 545–9. 5 vols. 1603–1730. Lansdowne 544 is a summary volume which serves as an index to the five.
[5] BM Lansdowne MSS 550–2. 3 vols. 1660–1732.
[6] BM Lansdowne MS 507. 1 vol. 1553–1734.
[7] Calendars are of course as old as any sort of record-keeping by the clerks, and these cannot be ascribed with any certainty to Hardinge's tenure of office. The surviving volume for the House of Commons, now in HLRO, covers 1546–1642, and by analogy with the other compilations I judge this was the first of a three volume set. The Lords took their records in hand, and ordered their calendar to be 'perfected' in 1717 (HLRO Memorandum No. 13, p. 8 where the surviving volumes are listed). There are three Lords volumes in Lansdowne 554–6, the last of which may be a copy from the set in Add. MSS 5120–2 which belonged to Sir Thomas Tyrwhitt, clerk of the Commons 1762–8.
[8] 'Upon a motion of Mr. Annesley that the clerk of the House of Commons may have liberty of inspecting the books given to this Society by Mr Petyt and now in the Library, and take copies of such parts thereof as may be of use or service towards completing the journals of the House of Commons, the Library keeper to lay before the Table tomorrow such directions as are made for the use of the books so given by Mr Petyt or such order to be then made as shall be expedient' 19 May 1732. (F. A. Inderwick, *A Calendar of the Inner Temple Records* (5 vols. 1896–1937), iv, 258.)

expenditure, he offered to undertake the whole publication commercially, by subscription. In that case he intended to have a complete monopoly: 'It is not doubted but that the House will effectually restrain the printing or selling of any Edition of the Journals or any abridgement thereof, or any Collections therefrom which shall not be warranted by their own order.'[1] Hardinge was able to persuade the committee to agree to his first proposal but the House would not countenance this commercial enterprise on the part of the clerk and the order finally made was that copies should be printed for the use of members only, not for sale.[2] Hardinge was awarded £1,000 compensation for the loss of copying fees[3] and was paid in full for the expense of printing; whereupon he attempted to bilk the unfortunate printer.[4]

In view of this interest in the Journal it is not surprising that there was sufficient public interest to encourage the printing of the Commons standing orders in the middle of the century. What is extraordinary is that the publication was permitted to appear without any warrant whatsoever from the House, as was also the case with the Lords orders.[5] The standing orders alone would not have made a book: the publisher took also the sessional orders and a selection of precedents from the Journal to make a compilation of a similar sort to the Lords Remembrances.[6] The only comparable manuscript, which presents

---

[1] *CJ* xxiv, 266.

[2] *Clerical Organization*, pp. 200–1. The vote of the House did not settle the matter. As was usual with money votes, Hardinge had to go through the whole investigation again before the Treasury Board, who treated the printing as his own scheme. (*Cal[endar of] T[reasury] B[ooks &] P[apers]*, 1742–5, pp. 53, 54, 57, 62, 66.)

[3] Which may be a hint as to how much Jodrell had been making out of Thomas Payne.

[4] *Clerical Organization*, pp. 64–5. William M. Sale, *Samuel Richardson: Master Printer* (Cornell, 1950), pp. 77–83.

[5] *Orders, Standing Orders and Resolutions of the Honourable House of Commons, Relating to their Forms of Proceedings, Privileges &c. Collected out of the Journals and Digested under their several heads*. Printed for A. Steward in Flower de Luce Court, Fleet Street. (Price Three Shillings) 148 pp. no date. Advertised in *London Magazine*, September 1747. Steward's name does not occur in Plomer's *Dictionary of Printers*. The first edition is thus of 1747 not 1745 as stated by Clifford, ii, 753. Nor, of course, was it published by a committee clerk. F. H. Spencer made this extraordinary suggestion by misapplying one of Clifford's footnotes: *Municipal Origins* (1911), p. 64, n. 2.   [6] Above pp. 19–20.

the orders in chronological sequence, with elaborate index tables,[1] may have been a product of Hardinge's reorganization,[2] but it seems more likely that even this was a commercial enterprise, since the volume contains Thomas Payne's accounts for copying the Journals.[3] The publications seem to have had a polemical intention and the preface is worth quoting in full:

If it is reasonable to wonder, that this Manual was never published before, it will be so much the less necessary to apologise for publishing it now: and surely, if it appears, that not only all who have seats in Parliament, or who are in a capacity to sit, or who have Business to transact there, but the whole People in general are interested in the Rules and Orders of their Representatives, it will not be disputed that they ought to be acquainted with them; and the Persons will rather deserve their thanks than Censure, who put it in their power to be so.

Now barely to read them, is to be convinced of this, for they will be found to reach almost all Orders of Men, either mediately or immediately, from the Judge to the Bailiff's Follower, and from the Petitioner at the Bar to the Footman on the Stairs and the Vagrant in the Street; and it is fit for those without Doors to reflect, with a due mixture of Reverence and Attention that the Word Privilege is become as sacred as the word Law; and that Ignorance in case of an offence may be held as insufficient a Plea in transgressing against the one as the other.

Then for those within: it can scarce be said that they are qualified for the Trust reposed in them, till they are acquainted, in some degree, with the methods in which it is to be discharged: And this is a known Truth, that Men of very slender Parts, by rendering themselves thorough Masters of the Forms of the House, have made themselves considerable, have fancied themselves to be more so; and by the mere Dint of calling to order and quoting Journals and Precedents have sometimes defeated Arguments they could not answer.

In the first edition, the latest precedent is of 16 June 1746. The second edition[4] appeared nine years later and was greatly

---

[1] BM Lansdowne MS 481. 'The rules, orders, declarations and resolutions of the House of Commons, to the 15th May 1730.'   [2] Above, p. 24.   [3] Above, p. 23.
[4] *Orders, Essential Fundamental and Standing Orders, Reports, Declarations, Memorandums, Rules, Agreements and Resolutions of the House of Commons relating to their Forms of Proceedings, Privileges &c. Collected out of the Journals. And the matter relative to the same subject chronologically connected, whereby the Judgement of the House at sundry times is at once seen. To which are added, Proceedings of the House against the Honourable*

enlarged, containing all the proceedings of the House against Alexander Murray, 1750–1, and also a complete and correct copy of the 1732 table of fees. It contained the same preface, and was dedicated without permission, perhaps ironically, to the Earl of Egmont.

The preface to the *Orders* states succinctly enough, and perhaps exaggerates, the influence parliament had come to have upon the lives of ordinary citizens, but there is still a lapse of eleven years before the appearance of the first handbook on private bill procedure.[1] It was quite shortly followed by the first magazine article on the procedure of the House. Coinciding with the beginning of newspaper reporting of the debates,[2] the article begins with the remark: 'As the end of instituting of parliaments is universally understood it is a little extraordinary that the *forms* are not better known.'[3]

Handbooks on private bill procedure did not become common until the early nineteenth century, and the first one is a not very adequate example of its kind, but its importance is that its intention was strictly practical: to advise solicitors on the procedure for passing a private bill. With the *Method of Proceedings* we come to some of the procedural developments which cannot be traced from official collections of precedents or from standing orders. The author was almost certainly a lawyer; he had read, and approved of, Daines Barrington's *Observations on the Statutes*. The book describes briefly the procedure to be followed to obtain a private act, from the first petition to the royal assent; it is, in legal parlance, a collection

---

Mr. Murray. The Second edition. Corrected and brought down to this time. London: Printed for James Lymans; and Sold by the Booksellers of London and Westminster. 1756. 290 pp. James Lymans appears in Plomer's *Dictionary* in respect of this publication only.

[1] *The Method of Proceedings, in order to obtain a Private Act of Parliament.* London: Printed by His Majesty's Law-Printers, for W. Owen, between the two Temple-Gates, Fleet Street. 1767. 24 pp. Owen was a well-known publisher, notably of periodicals, but although Strahan's ledgers contain accounts for some of Owen's private work, these do not contain any accounts for the law printing patent, and so yield no information about this book.

[2] P. D. G. Thomas, 'The beginning of parliamentary reporting in the newspapers, 1768–1784', *English Hist. Rev.*, lxxiv (1959), 623–36.

[3] *The London Magazine* (1770), pp. 621–4, 656–8. The article is a competent, if rather formal, summary of some of the main procedural points, probably based on George Petyt's *Lex Parliamentaria*.

of forms, giving the appropriate form of words for a petition, order of reference, certificate of swearing a witness, brief for the judges, judges' report, and brief of the bill for the lord chancellor. The example used, which is imaginary, is for a bill to vest an estate in trustees to be sold for the benefit of infant heirs under a will.

Hatsell's *Precedents* began to appear in 1776 and held the field until the publication of May's *Parliamentary Practice* in 1844. The first volume has a very oldfashioned air: concerned entirely with privilege and containing no precedents later than 1628, one feels it might well have been written by Henry Elsynge senior. But from the appearance of the second volume in 1781, the work piles precedent on precedent, cataloguing the increasing complexity of procedural change through the war and the Union with Ireland, increasing in bulk with each edition to the massive, and unusable, four volumes of 1818. In the preface to the third volume (1785) Hatsell promised a chapter on bills for the next volume, but this promise was never performed, so the work is of little assistance for the consideration even of the formal alterations in legislative procedure, which were themselves but a small part of the changes that took place in the eighteenth century.

3

THE CLERKS: FEES AND AGENCY

'Theise private bills benefitt yow, Mr. Speaker', said Sir
Henry Poole in 1621.[1] Indeed they did, to the tune of £200 in
1597,[2] and £500 a year by the 1730s;[3] and not only the speaker,
but every official in both Houses from the chancellor down to
the doorkeepers.[4]

This being so, the first thing to be decided by the promoters
of a bill was whether to proceed with it as a public or a private
measure. In many cases they had no choice. As Sir John Neale
remarked, the problem of distinguishing between public and
private bills in the sixteenth century was solved by the officials
'in a very simple way. Could they extract fees from someone?
If so, it was a private bill.'[5] But on the border line, if the promoters had the cash, they were well advised to proceed by the
private method,[6] otherwise they might well find their bill

[1] *Commons Debates, 1621*, ed. W. Notestein, F. H. Relf, H. Simpson, 7 vols. (New
Haven, 1935), iii, 279.
[2] Sir J. E. Neale, *The Elizabethan House of Commons* (London, 1949), pp. 336–7.
[3] *Clerical Organization*, p. 308.
[4] Sir John Neale (*op. cit.*, p. 341) suggested that the Serjeant's fee of £1 for every
private bill was not fixed before the seventeenth century, but Hooker in his
'Order and usage how to keepe a parlement in England' stated distinctly that
the fee was already 20s in 1575. (Holinshed, *Chronicles*, 2nd ed. 3 vols. 1587,
ii, 126.) This discrepancy may arise because Neale quoted from Hooker's
original manuscript at Exeter. In his printed edition, Hooker corrected the
error he had made in his manuscript in referring to the members for London
and York as 'burgesses' instead of 'citizens'. Neale also introduced from this
manuscript a 'little board' for the clerk to write on (p. 364). This reading,
calculated to delight those who like their House of Commons to be romantic,
is adopted by Williams (*Clerical Organization*, p. 11, n. 2, p. 12) but it is a mistake
for the much more mundane 'table board'. All the early pictures of the House
show a very substantial piece of furniture. The 1575 edition of Hooker's treatise
is said by Mrs E. R. Foster to be 'much fuller and more useful' than the version
printed in the *Chronicles* (*Bulletin Inst. Hist. Res.*, xliii (1970), 38 n), but apart from
spelling and punctuation there is no material difference at all between the two.
Since the 1575 edition is a very rare book, it seems preferable to refer to the
Chronicles.   [5] Neale, *Elizabethan House of Commons*, p. 336.
[6] In 1585 Recorder Fleetwood said 'I did advise him to make [it] a private bill
but he would not, and therefore he shall see what will come of it' (*ibid.*, p. 383).

jammed in the clerical machinery with the session drawing rapidly to an end. It was in 1607 that the speaker ruled a bill to amend the highways of 'only three shires' to be a private bill,[1] a dictum upon which Hatsell was still relying heavily in 1781.[2]

Professor Neale's chapters on the officers and on procedure[3] give a vivid picture of the importance of fees in the promotion of business in the sixteenth-century House of Commons and, in particular, his examples show how Elizabethan speakers exerted themselves to defend the financial rights of themselves and the officials of the House. The Elizabethan speakers could exert great influence because they usually had the power to decide in what order bills were to be put forward.[4] The speaker's power in this respect is clearly stated by Hooker[5] and Hakewill,[6] although the latter strongly suggests that public bills ought normally to be preferred to private and that the latter 'should be offered to be read and passed in such order as they were preferred'.[7] Even the medieval 'Modus tenendi Parliamentum' maintained that 'he who layeth first his bill in shall be first heard'.[8] At the time that Hakewill was writing it was within the sphere of public bills that the speaker's discretion was of real importance. In the early Stuart parliaments, speaker Phelips would manipulate the rules of the House to postpone a bill displeasing to the government,[9] even in desperation going to the length of adjourning the House before any members arrived in the morning if he could think of no better expedient.[10] But the political implications of the speaker's

[1] Neale, *Elizabethan House of Commons*, p. 336.   [2] *Precedents* (1781 ed.), ii, 191.

[3] Neale, *Elizabethan House of Commons*, pp. 332–48, 364–418.

[4] *Ibid.*, pp. 338, 391–3.

[5] 'Of the bils brought in he hath choise, which and when they shall be read: unlesse order by the whole house be taken in that behalfe.' (Holinshed, *Chronicles*, ii, 125.)

[6] 'The Clerk being usually directed by the Speaker (but sometimes by the House) what Bill to read ...' *The Manner how Statutes are enacted in Parliament by passing of Bills* (1671 ed.), p. 137. The great extent of the speaker's discretion is further emphasised in Hakewill's separate chapter on the office of speaker, published by Mrs Strateman Sims, *Amer. Hist. Rev.*, xlv (1939–40), 90–5.

[7] *The Manner how Statutes are enacted ...*, p. 134.

[8] Hooker's translation, published in *Somers Tracts* (2nd ed. 1809), ii, 179.

[9] *The Parliamentary Diary of Robert Bowyer, 1606-7*, ed. D. H. Willson (Oxford, 1931), pp. 54–5 and *passim*.   [10] *Ibid.*, p. 297.

powers do not concern us here.[1] Members accepted the necessity to pay fees on private bills provided that measures in which
they were concerned made progress; but they were perfectly
willing for the manipulation of the order of business to occur
in the case of bills for naturalisation of foreigners, in whom no-
one took any interest, and from whom the officers of the House
made a considerable proportion of their fee income.

Like the speakership, the clerkship of the House had always
been a political appointment. The clerk assistantship, like the
chairmanship of committee of the whole House, was in origin
an attempt by the House to resist undue political influence from
the senior posts, but by the eighteenth century this had been
virtually forgotten.[2] The clerkship never became a complete
sinecure, but by 1797 Hatsell executed the office by deputy and
advised that deputy to leave the work to his assistants.[3] The
clerkship changed hands for £6,000 in 1748 and was worth
far more than that per annum by the end of the century; yet
both Nicholas Hardinge and Jeremiah Dyson were willing to
resign the office for seats in parliament and junior government
posts. The clerk assistantship was recognised to be much the
more active post, since it involved attendance on committees
of the whole House. It was said to be worth £3,000 in 1760
and no one thought it odd that a London solicitor should offer
to buy the place.[4] Of course, none of the officers was required
to attend the House except during the session, which did not
take up much more than half the year.

The first eighteenth-century clerk, Paul Jodrell, stood very
high in the favour of the crown.[5] His assistant, subsequently
his successor, was his own nominee. Jodrell was a product of
an older parliamentary tradition, when annual parliaments were
not yet the rule. By profession a solicitor, he was solicitor to the
Court of Chancery, agent to the Earl of Meath, and active
in private practice.[6] He referred to the clerkship of the House
as 'my parliamentary business' and at first intended his son to

[1] They are discussed at length by Dr Thomas.
[2] *Clerical Organization*, pp. 50–2. See also S. Lambert, 'The Clerks and Records of
the House of Commons, 1600–40', *Bulletin Inst. Hist. Res.*, xliii (1970), 215–31.
[3] *Clerical Organization*, p. 150.   [4] *Ibid.*, p. 81.
[5] *Ibid.*, pp. 38–9, 43–5, 58.   [6] *Ibid.*, pp. 26 n. 1, 35–6.

succeed him in it, but Paul Jodrell junior confined himself to the private side of the practice. He became a successful practitioner at the parliamentary bar, and later a member; he was intended for the solicitor generalship under the Leicester House plan of 1750.[1]

The clerk's parliamentary business was always very lucrative, probably, in the early eighteenth century, a good deal more so than has been supposed, because of the effect on his income of fees upon naturalisation bills. Aliens living in Britain needed to be naturalised by private act in order to hold or inherit real property or engage in certain important types of trade. The usual procedure was that a bill would be introduced for the naturalisation of one, or a group, of persons, which would be read twice and committed. Any other person wishing to be naturalised could then petition to be added and upon paying his fees would have his name added in committee. Naturalisation bills might be introduced in either House and names added by either House.[2] Of course it could always be arranged that a more important person, or anyone willing to pay, could have a bill to him-, or more usually her-, self: foreign born brides of the nobility, for instance.

A comical feud arose between the speaker and his deputy in 1657, from which it appears that members were not above using his reliance on the multiple-bill fees to punish a speaker displeasing to them. In January of that year Bulstrode White-locke took over temporarily from the speaker, Sir Thomas Widdrington, who was ill. The House promptly appointed a day for the reading of private bills, from which the acting speaker would benefit, whereupon

Sir Thomas Widdrington being informed of the great favour of the Parliament to me their Speaker during his Absence, and the

---

[1] A. N. Newman, 'Leicester House Politics, 1750–60', *Camden Miscellany*, xxiii (Royal Historical Society, 1969), 116.

[2] Details of the names may be found in William A. Shaw, *Letters of Denization and Acts of Naturalization for Aliens in England and Ireland* (Huguenot Society Publications vols. 18, 27, 35 (1911–32)). In 1699 the Commons objected to the addition of nearly eighty names to one of their bills, because so great a number could not be properly considered and also because many of them were soldiers, at a time when many English troops were out of employment, but in the end they gave way (*ibid.*, i, 178).

Interest I had gained in the House, and that several private Bills were ready to pass, and particularly for naturalizing of many Strangers, and every one of them was to pay £5 to the Speaker for his Fee, which I would receive in case Sir Thomas Widdrington did not take his Place again before the passing of those Bills; he being desirous of the Money, though to the hazard of his Life, came again to the House and took his Place, though very weak and feeble.[1]

Three or four bills only were involved in this transaction, but the important one was for the naturalisation of no less than ninety-seven individuals,[2] which involved fees, to the Speaker alone, of £485 – a sum well worth squabbling over.

In 1685 a plea was made to Jodrell to allow a naturalisation bill to pass since the parties 'have already paid their fees three times and lost them by the bills being delayed by the late Clerk ... for getting more in the bills than was first for his own advantage'.[3] The allegation thus made against William Goldesborough junior was that he had put off the meeting of the committee in order to collect more names, and fees for no additional work, but carelessly left the business too late and was overtaken by the prorogation.

There is therefore a great mystery surrounding the clerks' claim for loss of fees during the short period in Anne's reign when a general naturalisation act was in force which made private acts unnecessary.[4] The claim[5] purports to show the actual number of fees received on this account over a ten year period, as a basis for the compensation they held to be due to them, but the details of the claim are inexplicably written down to much below the correct figure. As the table shows,[6] the total number of persons naturalised by act in the ten years was 1,578; yet the clerks claimed for only 333. The numbers claimed in each year do not correspond to any figures at all in the table: neither those for one (of several) acts, nor the number of names originally offered in the acts, nor the number added, or introduced in the Commons (as opposed to the Lords).

Yet there seems to be no doubt that the clerks were charging, as they were perfectly entitled to do by the table of fees, a single

[1] *Memorials of the English Affairs* (New ed. 1732), p. 655. [2] *CJ* vii, 487.
[3] *Calendar of State Papers, Domestic*, 1685, No. 1098. [4] See below, p. 77.
[5] Printed in full, *Clerical Organization*, pp. 286–94. [6] Below, p. 35.

fee from 'every private person taking benefit of any private act'. Indeed, if they were not, the claim would be completely incomprehensible since the small number of acts involved could not possibly produce even 333 fees by any other method. Some of the individual bills were of the nature of estate bills,[1] as well as containing naturalisation provisions, and it appears that the clerks were leaving these out of account and concentrating only on the multiple bills, since they made no claim for 1703 on the ground that 'this year the Bill lost',[2] but this makes very little difference to the overall figures.

In 1702 on the third reading of Benovad's bill the House was informed 'that several of the persons who had passed the Committee refused to pay their fees, although of good Ability so to do' and four names were consequently ordered to be struck out of the bill.[3] The last phrase might give rise to the extraordinary supposition that the clerks benevolently refrained from exacting fees from those who were not of 'good ability' to pay; but there is no other reason to believe this. Perhaps the clerks hoped to arouse the generosity of members, as occurred the same year in the Lords on St Leger de Balcolon's bill. The Lords committee being informed that John Constantine and three others had not paid their fees 'Earl Feversham undertook for the fees of the first of these',[4] so his name was retained. It would be a matter of indifference to the officers who paid the fees, so long as someone did so.

---

[1] Robert Harper did not draw many naturalisation bills. Their form was standard unless they contained other provisions. One such was Mary Noguier's act [No. 432]. Her husband had been naturalised and settled in Harper's part of the world, Armley, near Leeds. He left a complicated will, effectively disinheriting his son, and though his widow, Mary, had full power to dispose of the estate it was doubted if she could do so effectively even if she were now naturalised, since she had not been so at the time of her husband's death. So the bill set out the whole story and arranged the estate as well as her naturalisation at the same time. There is a letter from the son, Anthony, concerning his sister's marriage settlement, in the volume of Harper MSS at Lincoln's Inn – the sole surviving relic of what must have been a huge correspondence with clients.

[2] Hack's bill, which failed in the Commons for lack of time. It would have contained at least fifty-four names and the parties had presumably paid their fees in the House of Lords. (H.M.C. *House of Lords MSS*, v, 184–6.)

[3] *CJ* xiii, 903, 904. In fact, according to the committee report, these four and six others had already been struck out by the committee.

[4] H.M.C. *House of Lords MSS*, iv, 473 n.

The Clerk's petition is printed in full, *Clerical Organization*, 286–94. The numbers of persons naturalised are taken from Shaw, *Acts of Naturalization*, and are approximate. The names can be obtained only from the original acts at the House of Lords, and Shaw's explanations of names added and subtracted during the passage of each bill are very difficult to follow. I have not attempted to work out the details for the first two years. There is also a possibility that the clerks' claim was calculated on a different year-basis from that of the Statute book. The discrepancy between the two sets of figures is so enormous that the details hardly matter.

| | Number of fees claimed by clerks | Statutes of the Realm | Number of names | | | |
| | | | inserted | | omitted | total |
			HL	HC		
1699	130	10 Wm. III				
		23 acts				381
1700	38	10 & 11 Wm. III				
		6 acts				220
1701	15	12 & 13 Wm. III				
		2 acts				2
		c. 30	3	1		4
		c. 31	2	6		8
		c. 35	22	6		28
		c. 36	8	3		11
1702	41	1 Anne				
		1 act				1
		c. 78	21			21
		c. 76	73	13	1	85
		c. 77	140	18	10	148
1703	—	1 Anne st. 2				
		c. 32	2	1		3
1704	23	2 & 3 Anne				
		2 acts				2
		c. 28	—	17		17
		c. 29	38	24		62
		c. 50	25	13		38
		c. 51	20		1	19
1705	9	3 & 4 Anne				
		3 acts				3
		c. 45	3	—		3
		c. 52	5	2		7
1706	35	4 & 5 Anne				
		4 acts				4
		c. 16	12	24		36
		c. 67	3	1		4
		c. 68	93	94	1	186
1707	23	6 Anne				
		3 acts				3
		c. 47	37	64		101
		c. 48	11	32		43
1708	19	6 Anne				
		2 acts				2
		c. 13	31	68		99
		c. 29	—	2		2
		c. 30	16	19		35
	333					1,578

I can offer no explanation of the discrepancy between the fees apparently receivable on naturalisation bills and the amounts stated in the claim of 1709, unless perhaps the clerks were thinking of their land tax assessments.[1] There seems no doubt that the full fees were normally charged to each individual named in a multiple bill, and if so the average number of fees a year lost by the general naturalisation was some 175, not 37 as claimed. In the case of the clerk, this means a figure of over £900 a year, instead of the £200 he claimed. The speaker benefited to about the same amount and the lower officers proportionately. Dr Williams overlooked the effect of these multiple bills on the income of the clerks. His table of fee-attracting bills must be revised upwards[2] and will affect his conclusion that the clerk's income from fees was only moderate before 1750.[3] If naturalisation fees had not been charged in this way, the speaker's return of his income for 1728–31[4] would point to a very much larger number of bills, other than those for naturalisation, for which multiple fees were charged than is suggested by any other evidence. In 1730, for instance, the speaker received 105 separate fees for forty-three bills, which would mean that a number of bills must have paid two-double or even higher fees. But if the sixteen naturalisation fees are first deducted one is left with the much more reasonable figure of eighty-nine fees for forty bills of other types.

This argument does not affect Dr Williams' conclusion for the latter part of the century when multiple naturalisation became much less usual and the great increase in other types

[1] Compare the committee report of 1759, *CJ* xxviii, 528–30.
[2] It is not really useful to average the number of naturalisation bills, since the number of names included varies so much. Exact figures for three of the years cited by Williams may be taken as examples.

	Cler. Org., p. 318 list of fee-attracting bills	Number of naturalisation bills	Number of persons naturalised	% increase of fees
1730	43	3	16	30
1736	58	5	19	24
1740	30	4	18	46

[3] *Clerical Organization*, p. 110.   [4] *Ibid.*, pp. 308–9.

of legislation makes what little is left in the way of naturalisation fees a much smaller proportion of the whole. As he stated,[1] the accounts make it clear that the average charge for all local and private bills was between 2 and 2½ fees; one should remember also that the real figure must have been even lower than this since Williams took no account of bills that failed, some of which had certainly paid their fees.

The figure usually cited by modern authors for the cost of a naturalisation bill is £100,[2] but the evidence for this is that of Henry Walmisley, Lords clerk and parliamentary agent, in the last year of procedure by private act, before the procedure was rendered obsolete by the general naturalisation act of 1844.[3] Walmisley told the 1843 committee that he charged his clients a flat rate of £100, but he did not specify how much of this represented his own fee.[4] This committee had quite forgotten about the multiple bill procedure; they discussed the possibility of having an annual naturalisation bill in which a great number of names might be included to reduce the cost; Lord Brougham thought such a system might be set up.[5]

The general naturalisation controversy provides an amusing example of the way in which parliamentary fees were commonly misquoted in argument even by contemporaries who were perfectly expert in the facts. In the 1748 debate on the naturalisation of foreign protestants, the summary of the arguments given in the *Parliamentary History* indicates that the opponents of the measure poured scorn on the idea that the 'small expence' of a private bill was any deterrent, being 'not above £20 or £30' each if several persons were named in one bill.[6] In 1753, by contrast, Nicholas Hardinge, late clerk of the House, supporting the second reading of the Jewish bill, went out of his way to stress the 'great expense' of a private act so that 'the bill would in practice open the door only to the rich'.[7]

In fact the Commons committee of 1732 stated distinctly that the average cost of a naturalisation act for a single individual was £63: £3 more than the cost of an ordinary single

[1] *Clerical Organization*, pp. 318–19.   [2] E.g. Holdsworth, ix, 90.   [3] 7 & 8 Vic. c. 66.
[4] HC (307) 1843, qu. 293.   [5] *Ibid.*, qu. 111.   [6] *Parl. Hist.*, xiv, 147.
[7] *Ibid.*, cc. 1375, 1396. Dr Perry, (cited below, p. 78 n. 9) p. 79 and n. 16 conflates the two arguments and speaks of the 'great expense' of '*at least* £20 or £30' (my italics).

fee bill because of the additional cost of proving the sacrament and taking the oaths.[1] Even this figure seems high if the table of fees is strictly interpreted, but assuming that it is correct, an individual paid £43 13s 4d for the basic fees of the two houses and the cost of the oaths, leaving about £20 to cover incidental charges, committee fees and ingrossment. This additional cost would be shared amongst the persons taking advantage of a joint bill, so their total outlay would depend upon the number of persons named – though one cannot avoid the suspicion that not one would be allowed to escape without at least adding an individual tip to the doorkeepers, so that the financial saving on fees would not be very great. Probably people were attracted to joint bills by the relative simplicity of the procedure and the saving in solicitor's fees. Procedure in the House was kept to a minimum; the bills did not have to be printed; petitions for additional names are not formally entered in the Journal; the seven days notice required for select committees was ignored for naturalisation bills. The clerks evidently had this aspect of procedure firmly in their own hands and probably found it very lucrative even apart from the fees. Harper's manuscripts contain a complete account of 'Mr Ayscoughe One of the Clerks of the house of Lords his bill for the Act to naturalize Lady Howe'.[2] The total cost was £86 16s 4d, that is about £65, the recognised cost of a naturalisation bill, plus £21 as Ayscoughe's fee as agent.[3] The amount

[1] *Clerical Organization*, p. 307.   [2] BM 357. b. 1(27).

[3] No person of this name held an identifiable post at the House of Lords, but in that House at this time all the subsidiary officials were the personal servants of the clerk and their names are not recorded in official lists (HLRO Memorandum no. 22). The Lords committee book (15 March 1726) records that 'Mr. Aiskew was also called in and heard' before the committee on fees. This may be the same person (the name is spelt indifferently also as Askew, Ayscoghe, etc.) or it may possibly be the almost equally mysterious Michael Aiskew, clerk assistant of the Commons, who was called to give expert evidence. However, if that had been the case, one would expect Aiskew to get formal leave of the Commons before attending a Lords committee and there is no trace of such permission in the *Journal*.

Apart from Ayscoughe, we know of no Lords clerk acting as agent until the rise of the exceedingly numerous Walmisley family in the nineteenth century. But there is no reason to suppose that Lords clerks did not carry on some agency work, although it is unlikely that they would ever have had anything approaching the amount possible to their Commons equivalents. A clerk was not likely to act as agent except for a bill originating in his own House, which limited Lords

of trouble involved cannot have been great, yet no less a person than Paul Jodrell junior attended as counsel at the Commons committee. Only the lady's social status can have justified feeing counsel at all in such an affair.

This digression has indicated that the clerks' fees on private bills in the early part of the century were probably a good deal higher than has been supposed. Even so, Jodrell's £5 fee on each bill was only part of his income. He acted as agent for private bills,[1] and received a gratuity of 100 guineas in addition to his fees on the London Orphans Bill of 1694 and got away with it while speaker Trevor was expelled for accepting a gift on the same occasion.[2] He took the bulk of the ingrossing fees on all bills public and private[3] and was paid by the Treasury to see the finance bills through the House.[4]

When it became clear that parliaments were to be annual, he increased his establishment, at first by the old-fashioned method of employing a private clerk to assist him.[5] We do not know who was the first holder of this post or at what date or by what influence Zachary Hamlyn came up from Devon and succeeded to it. What is certain is that there is no need to pity Hamlyn because he was not one of those 'fortunate men who obtained salaried positions' and never 'saw his name printed as clerk of the papers in the Court and City Register'.[6] He does not appear to have had any formal legal education but his work brought him a very considerable fortune, so that by 1729 he was

---

clerks from the first. During Harper's lifetime, he handled the majority of private bills that began in the Lords, but someone must have taken over that practice when he died.

[1] *Clerical Organization*, pp. 22, 230, 316–17.   [2] *Ibid.*, p. 45 n. 4.
[3] *Ibid.*, pp. 295–7.   [4] *Ibid.*, pp. 43–4.   [5] *Ibid.*, pp. 39–40.
[6] *Clerical Organization*, pp. 71, 52. Zachary Hamlyn, son of William Hamlyn and Gertrude Cary, was born at Woolfardisworthy, Devon on 14 July 1678. (I am most grateful to Dr Joyce Youings, of Exeter University, for obtaining this information for me from the bishop's transcript of the parish register in the possession of the Devon & Cornwall Record Society.) He did not marry, and at his own request was buried simply at Woolfardisworthy on 2 July 1759, leaving his estate to the descendants of his sister Thomasin. His will is PCC Arran 237. Thomasin, b. 1670, married Richard Hammett and their grandson James was chief beneficiary under the will, in accordance with which he changed his name to Hamlyn (33 Geo. II pr. c. 15). James became M.P. for Carmarthenshire 1793–1802 and was created baronet in 1795. He had been admitted to Lincoln's Inn in 1750 but was never called.

able to buy the Clovelly estate of his mother's family[1] and later also bought extensive property in Carmarthenshire.[2] He had chambers at Lincoln's Inn[3] and was left a mourning ring in Samuel Richardson's will.[4] The account for Harper's first bill [No. 1] includes a payment of ten guineas for Hamlyn's advice.[6] He collected the committee fees on another occasion [No. 8]. In 1722 he advised the promoters of the Don navigation,[5] and in 1726 the promoters of the Weaver bill paid him a sum that almost certainly includes a private fee; by this time he had a clerk of his own who was worth a tip.[7] In 1727, although George Legh handled the Weaver bill with great competence and specified precisely in his account all the small fees of both Houses, yet he paid Hamlyn his additional 'demand' of sixteen guineas.[8] In 1748 the town clerk of Exeter instructed Hamlyn to attend the city's members to discuss a bill to suppress players, which the clerk optimistically hoped would not involve much expense, but 'if you'd give me a hint what you think it may cost I'd be obliged to you and take care to send you the Mony as soon as demanded'.[9] Undoubtedly Hamlyn was a parliamentary agent and very well placed to be one as unofficial clerk of the Journals, Jodrell's servant, and with one of Jodrell's sons in the committee office and another at the parliamentary bar.

Jodrell's other innovation was the appointment of the four clerks without doors. They were all, when appointed, young gentlemen of good families and no doubt they bought their places.[10] From 1696 they received allowances of 25 guineas each,[11] raised to fixed salaries of £50 from 1701, for assistance

[1] Charles Worthy, *Devonshire Wills* (London, 1896), p. 403.
[2] Mentioned in his will, above p. 39 n. 6.
[3] He was admitted to Lincoln's Inn 14 Jan. 1732 and to the Middle Temple 21 June 1736, but presumably only for social reasons. His chambers cannot have been within the precincts of the Inn proper, since there is no reference to them in the Red Book and he was able to leave them in his will to his nieces Mary and Anne Hammett.
[4] *Notes & Queries*, 209 (1964), p. 303. The bequest was later cancelled because Hamlyn predeceased Richardson.   [5] Below, p. 124.
[6] T. S. Willan, *The Early history of the Don Navigation* (Manchester, 1965), p. 111.
[7] Below, p. 158.   [8] Below, p. 165.   [9] H.M.C. *Exeter MSS*, p. 172.
[10] *Clerical Organization*, pp. 55–6, 68–71.
[11] *Ibid.*, p. 55. I am not quite convinced that Jodrell instituted these appointments since in 1673 the clerk had received £100 for distribution amongst the under-

with public business.[1] There is no need to describe the Treasury formula for the payment[2] as 'a fiction', for there is no evidence that these men were originally appointed to act only as committee clerks, or that they were ever confined to this function only. George Cole assisted at the Table of the House in 1694, as Robert Yeates was to do in 1761.[3] There is positive evidence of actual personal service as committee clerks for only a few of them and definite evidence that committees were often attended by persons who were not of their number. John Burman attended several committees before he held any office in the House, but there is no record of his attending any committee in the twenty years after he officially became a committee clerk.[4] It is probably incorrect to regard the committee clerks as a homogeneous group. We know only of James Courthope that he did serve both as a committee clerk and as a parliamentary agent; he was also a clerk in the Lottery Transfer Office.[5] George Cole, another of the original group of four committee clerks, was probably also an agent.[6]

The committee clerks received fees from the parties for all the private bill committees they attended, and this includes, of course, committees on many bills that became public acts. They were not required to serve for many of the truly public acts since these were taken, not in select committee, but in committee of the whole House, where the clerk assistant officiated. Special select committees of enquiry were usually

---

clerks under a very similar rubric (*ibid.*, p. 297). An excellent seventeenth-century precedent book preserved in the Journal Office was kept by one Ambrose Kelly who describes himself as 'Clerk to the Committees of the House of Commons', and is described in the *Journal* on 23 Jan. 1690, as 'one of the Clerks of the Office, attending this House', *CJ* x, 340.

[1] *Clerical Organization*, p. 54.

[2] *Ibid.*, p. 53: 'writing copying and ingrossing several bills, writings and other papers for His Majesty's Service.'

[3] *Ibid.*, pp. 53, 165.

[4] *Ibid.*, pp. 133, 330–5. To Dr Williams' list of Treasury payments to clerks attending committees should be added a payment for the 1732 committee on fees; the clerk is not named (*Cal. T.B.P.*, 1731–4, p. 231).

[5] *Clerical Organization*, pp. 54–7 and *Courthope*, p. viii.

[6] *Clerical Organization*, p. 186 n. 3. Williams did not identify George Cole with Mr Cole the 'solicitor in parliament' who was agent for a bill in 1719, but I see no reason not to do so.

separately remunerated, so the amount of work involved each session for the salary of £50 would not be very great.[1] The clerks petitioned in 1701 claiming that their private business (meaning, of course, only their official fees for private committees) had not brought them in £30 apiece,[2] but after this we hear no more complaints except in the petition of 1709 when they pleaded that their losses (alone) from estate bills beginning in the Lords because of the new standing orders of that House, would be £50 a year.[3] After this private business continually increased and the Commons standing order of 1717 that petitions for local bills should also be committed doubled the fee-potential of each of these bills for the committee clerks.[4]

At the very first vacancy among the committee clerks, Jodrell appointed his own son Edward, to their number, so the remuneration was presumably worth having.[5] To make sure of it, Jodrell altered the order of seniority to make Edward senior of the four since in that capacity he received an additional, and certain, fee of 10s on every bill as collector of the fees of the House.[6] However it does not seem likely that he did

[1] I here take issue with Dr Williams, *Clerical Organization*, p. 130, based on *Courthope*, pp. xi–xiii. The proportion of private and local bills over public bills going to select committees increased very markedly during the eighteenth century, so that his calculations based on 1698–9 do not hold good for very long. His proportion of eighteen private to twenty-two public committees for 1698 is arrived at by including in the latter category twelve select committees of enquiry, which in the eighteenth century were usually separately remunerated; see the long list, *Clerical Organization*, pp. 330–5. And some of the bills classified as public probably paid fees. The Assize of Bread bill for instance (*Courthope*, xii) failed on this occasion, but passed in 1709 as 8 Anne c. 19 and certainly paid fees when it was renewed in 1719 (5 Geo. I c. 25), for the account is printed in *Clerical Organization*, pp. 316–17.

[2] *Clerical Organization*, p. 130. Williams confirmed this figure by a calculation which gives an average of about 30s for each bill but all the actual figures of committee fees we have are a good deal higher than this. E.g. £4 6s 8d in one case and £7 5s in another (*ibid.*, pp. 316–17).

[3] *Ibid.*, p. 290. Williams' gloss on this statement, p. 57, is not correct. Only one (the senior) of the committee clerks claimed on account of the general naturalisation act, for committee fees and for his 10s as collector of the fees on each bill.

[4] Dr Williams does not notice this point, in calculating that if a committee clerk's income was £90 in 1709 it would not be 'much above £100' in 1730 (*ibid.*, p. 130).

[5] Edward was also a pluralist, but the nature of his other appointment at Westminster is unknown (*Clerical Organization*, p. 57n).

[6] Edward Jodrell was receiver of the fees in 1732, before the death of Hicks Burrough who was ostensibly senior clerk (*Clerical Organization*, p. 310, compare p. 281).

any work for the money. Not one of the accounts for private bills that have been found makes any reference to him. In his time, as in that of his predecessor John Hookes, the fees were actually collected by Zachary Hamlyn.[1]

Nicholas Hardinge became clerk of the House in 1732 and soon made many changes.[2] One of his first acts as clerk was to get himself a salary of £200 a year – probably all that the traffic would bear without raising the salaries of his juniors – in addition to the ancient fee of £10 a year which had been the clerk's only official stipend up to that time.[3] Hardinge was a fellow of King's College, Cambridge,[4] a brilliant scholar, and also attorney-general to the Duke of Cumberland.[5]

We have already noticed Hardinge's activity in reorganising the House papers and arranging for the printing of the Journal.[6] At the same time, in 1733, the House printing was taken away from William Bowyer and given to Samuel Richardson, in whose will Hardinge of course received a ring.[7] He obtained an allowance of £100 a year for John Grover, which was charged on Richardson's printing account.[8] Grover had been in line for appointment as a committee clerk at the next vacancy, but when this occurred, on the death of Hicks

---

[1] *Clerical Organization*, pp. 42 n. 1, 52,307.

[2] Dr Williams rightly emphasised the political nature of the appointment (*Clerical Organization*, pp. 62–3), but there is no direct evidence of the reason for it. Hardinge did know speaker Onslow earlier: BM Lansdowne MS 566 is a copy of a treatise on the King's power of pardoning which Onslow gave to Hardinge before 1 December 1731. [3] *Clerical Organization*, p. 108.

[4] He gave a fourteenth-century bible to the College on the occasion of his election and held his fellowship until 1737 when he wished to marry the daughter of Lord Chief Justice Pratt.

[5] Dr Thomas considers that Hardinge was 'a failure as a Parliamentarian', but his only reference is to a remark of Horace Walpole's describing the debates of 1751 on the Regency Bill, in which he says that Hardinge was 'not well received' by the House, simply because he had been clerk (*Memoirs of the Reign of George II*, i, 134). Jeremiah Dyson was very unpopular for the same reason, as Dr Thomas shows at length. In the passage mentioned, Walpole describes Hardinge as 'a sensible, knowing man', and praises him for having said on this occasion that even the Duke of Cumberland might be removed from the Regency Council: this 'was the more honest, as he was actually the Duke's Attorney'.

[6] Above, pp. 24–5.

[7] *Notes & Queries*, 209 (1964), p. 301. This bequest, like Hamlyn's and another to John Read, clerk assistant, was cancelled because they all predeceased Richardson.

[8] I have shown elsewhere that this payment was not connected with the payment of copy money to the clerk. S. Lambert, 'Printing for the House of Commons in the Eighteenth Century', *Library*, 5th ser., xxiii (1968), 43–4.

Burrough, Grover succeeded him as ingrossing clerk[1] but not as committee clerk.[2] The post of fourth committee clerk went to John Naylor, aged twenty-five, whom Hardinge brought in from Cambridge. He is only known to have attended one committee, but although so junior in the office was permitted to deputise for the clerk assistant at the Table, during Aiskew's frequent illnesses.[3] Evidently this post was his ambition, but it was not until 1740 that Aiskew was persuaded to resign his 'place of £500 a year'.[4]

By the time the clerk assistantship fell vacant, Naylor seems to have fallen from favour. He obtained this post (no doubt he had paid for it and the contract had to be performed) but not the clerkship of elections which should have gone with it. This went to John Grover (he being once again passed over for a clerkship without doors) so that Newdigate Poyntz, aged twenty-five, could come in as fourth committee clerk. Since Naylor's successor, John Read, also from Cambridge and only twenty-three, took back the clerkship of elections as soon as it was released by Grover's death, one feels that Naylor's resignation in 1744 was probably not voluntary. He took orders and was then hanging about London looking for preferment which he was not expected to, and did not, receive quickly.[5]

The clerkship of elections was not nearly so important a post at this time as it was to become after 1770. Dr Williams has shown that very few election cases were actually considered by

[1] Jodrell may have invented the post of ingrossing clerk for Hicks Burrough when he promoted his son Edward over Burrough's head, providing for the latter from a small proportion of his own ingrossing fees. Burrough is described as ingrossing clerk in the 1727 River Weaver accounts; this is six years before the previously earliest known reference. (*Clerical Organization*, p. 56.)

[2] In spite of this Grover served as clerk to two committees for which he was paid by the Treasury. The second of these, that on the navy debt in 1734, is not noted by Williams, *Clerical Organization*, p. 331; see *Cal. T.B.P.*, 1735–8, pp. 5–6.

[3] *Clerical Organization*, pp. 68–9.

[4] *Clerical Organization*, pp. 67–8, 99. Almost nothing is known of Aiskew. See note above, p. 38. He may well have been the Michael Askew who was Steward to the Duke of Beaufort and died in 1746 (*Gentl. Mag.*, p. 164). This Askew signed the Lords committee book, 14 March 1730, as trustee for some of the Duke's affairs.

[5] *Clerical Organization*, pp. 68–9. Most of the biographical information on the clerks in these pages is given by Dr Williams, but my interpretation of it differs from his at several points.

the committee,[1] and cases of privilege were quite rare. Grover would have had no difficulty in combining the post with the clerkship of ingrossments any more than Burrough would have had in combining the latter with a committee clerkship. Grover did have the skill to write the ingrossing hand, but it seems doubtful if a man drawing a Treasury allowance equal to the clerk assistant's salary actually did much work of the sort except on the rare occasion when he was called in to ingross at the Table. Certainly, from very soon after Grover's death, ingrossing was being done by a man who was not to achieve the post of ingrossing clerk for twenty years.[2]

In 1748 the clerkship of the House of Commons changed hands, and in 1750 Robert Yeates was appointed to the newly invented post of second clerk of ingrossments by his patron and friend Jeremiah Dyson, to hold that office only until there was a vacancy for a committee clerk. Yeates was almost certainly already a parliamentary agent. From December 1749 'Mr Yates' received a retainer of ten guineas a year to watch the parliamentary interests of the Protestant Dissenting Deputies.[3] Yeates was almost immediately appointed to assist with Treasury drafting and became effectively the first Parliamentary Counsel to the Treasury.[4] Even after his appointment as a Treasury clerk and while actually officiating at the Table during the illness of the clerk and clerk assistant, he found time to act as agent for the Weaver bill,[5] but he later claimed that the demands of his Treasury work had compelled him to give up his private practice.

After his appointment to the Treasury, and while remaining a Commons clerk, he had election literature printed for two or three government seats at the general elections of 1761 and 1768.[6] The bill was not paid, and when it was finally settled by

---

[1] Williams maintained that Grover's position (1740–9) was 'by no means a sine-cure' but that Hardinge Stracey (1757–70) 'can not have incurred much labour' as clerk of elections, whereas his table shows that each had exactly the same number of committees to attend – six at two general elections. (*Clerical Organization*, 218–20).   [2] *Ibid.*, pp. 84, 230.

[3] B. L. Manning, *The Protestant Dissenting Deputies* (Cambridge, 1952), pp. 41–2.

[4] Below, pp. 67–8.   [5] Below, pp. 166–8.

[6] There is some evidence that he also acted as agent in the localities (*Clerical Organization*, p. 167 n. 2). BM Lansdowne MS 497 is a pocket-size index to the

Yeates' executor in 1769 there had been added to it sixteen dozen of rum and one of madeira, bought in 1762, and some books, including *Gil Blas* and Coke's *Institutes* bought in 1768.[1] Yeates must have been on close terms with Strahan since these items are quite out of the latter's usual way of business. Strahan evidently expected the government to take over the cost of the printing since after Yeates' death he first charged the outstanding amount to George White's account, until Yeates' executor, Rosier, settled it. Strahan's accounts do not include any printing of bills for Yeates (who probably employed Richardson for this work, since he received a mourning ring), but Yeates' friend and deputy John Rosier was giving Strahan two or three bills a year from at least 1762.

Yeates' versatility is striking. He officiated at the Table of the House, acted as clerk to select committees, and as parliamentary agent for private parties; he concerned himself with elections, did confidential work for Jenkinson; served as a Treasury clerk and as Treasury draftsman.[2] In September 1767 Yeates received a most unusual grant of a civil list annuity of £750 a year in recognition of his services to the government and in compensation for having given up his private agency.[3] He must have been a remarkable person, but something like

---

official Commons collection, 'the Rights of electors determined', titled 'Yates's Notes of Election Cases'; the latest precedent is of 1747.   [1] See below, p. 48 n. 1.
[2] *Clerical Organization*, pp. 166–8.
[3] The Letters Patent, no doubt reciting his petition, state that the grant is in consideration not only of 'the good and acceptable services performed by our Trusty and well beloved Robert Yeates Esquire in the punctual and faithful discharge of his duty as one of the principal clerks of our Treasury but also the very useful and important assistance given by him from time to time with great assiduity and ability in the carrying on of many other branches of the publick service for which he hath not received any allowance or compensation whatsoever and that by his anxious attention and persevering diligence in the execution of the Business as well official as extraordinary entrusted to his care his health hath been greatly impaired and it having been represented unto us that the said Robert Yeates in order that he might be able duly to attend to the said extraordinary publick business did several years ago voluntarily relinquish the Sollicitations of private bills and other affairs in our Houses of Parliament and that such Sollicitations were attended with emoluments not only superior to the profits of his said office in our Treasury but capable of being considerably increased'. (PRO C. 66. 3714 no. 4.) The grant was backdated to 5 July 1767 and was punctually paid (T. 53/50 p. 441) for the rest of Yeates' life (Civil list accounts, *CJ* xxxii, 596, 603).

this multiplicity of activities was perhaps not unusual amongst the clerks in the first half of the century. By the time of Yeates' death in 1769 the increase of business was beginning to require greater specialisation. His work was divided amongst three people: Danby Pickering succeeded him as Treasury draftsman, Thomas Pratt as Treasury clerk,[1] and George White as Commons committee clerk. In addition Rosier, who had been Yeates' unofficial assistant, was formally appointed as Treasury agent in the House, to assist Pickering, at the same time succeeding George White as clerk of the Journals.[2]

Dr Williams maintained that 'there is no evidence that any established firms of parliamentary agents ... existed before George White and John Dorington started about 1780 the two businesses which lived in the memory of the next generation'.[3] The first example of agency by a clerk which he was able to discover was a payment by the Board of Works to John Speed for 1767,[4] but Speed in fact held no official position at this time; he did not become a clerk until he succeeded Rosier as clerk of the Journals in 1774. I suggest that Speed, like Yeates and White, became a clerk because he was already an agent, not the other way round. The first account that Williams found, relating to the session of 1781, refers to the 'firm' of 'Messrs White';[5] these things do not grow up overnight. George White Junior appears in the *Journal* as agent for a Bill in 1776[6] when he was only an (unofficial) deputy committee clerk, twelve years before he was appointed clerk to the Committee of Privileges. There is no reason to doubt the statement that 'Mr. Dorington's father practised [as an agent] previous to 1780';[7] Dorington senior held no official position, but he married Robert Yeates' only relation – his cousin Roberta.

Williams quite rightly used Hansard's printing accounts as a guide to the size of the practices of nineteenth-century agents. If a three-figure debt to the printer is proof of substantial agency,[8] George White senior was thoroughly in

[1] PRO T. 29/40 p. 102.   [2] *Clerical Organization*, p. 169.
[3] *Ibid.*, p. 184.   [4] *Ibid.*, pp. 187–8.   [5] *Clerical Organization*, p. 183.
[6] *CJ* xxxv, 636.   [7] *Clerical Organization*, p. 184.   [8] *Ibid.*, p. 183 n. 1.

business by 1762 when William Strahan's ledger states his account at £246 17s 0d in respect of fourteen local and inclosure bills, including the very controversial Bridgewater canal bill in connection with which Strahan printed for White two cases as well as the bill. White could not suddenly have been responsible for fourteen bills in one session had he not been in business for some time; the explanation may be that Strahan obtained this work along with the Law printing patent which he took over at this time.[1] In the first ledger there are no

	No. of bills	White	No. of bills	Rosier
1762	14	£246 17s 0d	2	£26 15s 6d
1763	11	£149 6s 9d	3	£34 18s 3d
1764	12	£85 6s 3d	—	—
1765	15	£258 10s 9d	3	£24 7s 10d
1766	15	£508 10s 3d	2	£18 14s 8d
1767	7	£110 10s 3d	2	£28 14s 6d
1768	4	£84 10s 6d	2	£25 9s 0d
1769	7	£101 1s 3d	} 3	£52 3s 3d
1770	1	£37 15s 0d		
1771			6	£117 9s 6d
1772			3	£33 16s 6d
1773			7	£132 16s 6d
1774			—	—
1775			4	£53 11s 0d
1776			1	£22 1s 0d

accounts for the printing of bills except for Rosier and White. White was at this time clerk of the Journals; he was succeeded by Rosier and then by John Speed, all holding the post first held, unofficially, by Zachary Hamlyn. The accounts show that George White handled up to fifteen bills a year from 1762, but the number begins to decline from 1767 and there are no accounts for White after 1770 when he was promoted from the clerkship of the Journals to the sinecure committee clerkship.

[1] Strahan's MSS at the British Museum are in process of reclassification and refoliation so one cannot give precise references. Yeates' account, including the rum, is in a small cash book now Add. MS 48,803 (formerly 48,802 A). The other accounts are in the two main ledgers dated 1739–68 and 1768–85 now Add. MS 48,800 and 48,801 (formerly 48,803); these are indexed, so the items can quite readily be found. The second ledger, though said to extend to 1785, in fact contains no accounts for work done later than 1776; the entries of later date (with the exception of the very last entry in the volume) are all of belated payments.

After this date White was increasingly employed on government work, but the firm of 'Messrs White' was still very much in business as a parliamentary agency. At the end of the century Hansard did most, if not all, of their printing,[1] so perhaps the transfer of the account to the rival establishment began at this time. In any case it is not certain that the Strahan account at any time represents all the bills for which White and Rosier were responsible; later agents made a practice of dividing their patronage amongst several printers.

White's account is made up of a variety of local bills, with some inclosure and estate bills. Rosier's much smaller account includes the East India Stock bills of 1765 and 1766. The accounts become available only towards the end of Harper's career and coincide with his list in respect of two items: Rosier was responsible for the printing of John Woods bill of 1762 [No. 565] and White for that of the Yorkshire cloth bill of 1766 [No. 613], so presumably they were the agents in these cases and Harper only the draftsman. The second ledger, from 1768, also shows that there were some other firms of outside agents at work.[2]

The clerkship of the Journals and Papers should have had some duties attached to it. Jodrell and Hamlyn put the papers in good order; Hardinge found a good situation on his accession, which he further systematised; and the printing of the Journals from 1742 is a considerable achievement. Yet by 1800 the papers

---

[1] *Clerical Organization*, pp. 181–3.

[2] James Cecil Esq., paid for the printing of the Duke of Ancaster's Estate bill in 1776, but presumably he can be left out of the discussion. A Mr Kiernan, however, had nine bills between 1769 and 1771 and the range of subjects covered indicates that he was a professional agent. Edward Moore, presumably the gentleman who indexed the *Commons Journals*, but who was not a clerk, ran a little side-line with one bill in each of four sessions between 1770 and 1776. 'Mr Woodcock of Lincoln's Inn' with one estate bill in 1771, becomes 'Messrs Woodcock and Barnard' the next year; they had nine bills printed over the next five years, interspersed with the printing of particulars of estates and conditions of sale – evidently solicitors acting for clients. Finally there is a fully-fledged firm of agents specialising in Scottish bills. In 1768, Henry Davidson was in partnership with a Mr Ross, then alone until 1773 when 'Messrs. Davidson, Seton and Langlands' appear and they continue to conduct five or six Scottish local bills every session. Each of the partners also had an individual account, Davidson being solicitor to the Clyde Navigation, for whom he ordered a great deal of miscellaneous printing other than bills.

of earlier date than 1770 were in chaos: it would require 'several clerks for many months'[1] to put them in order. This lapse must be traced to the reign of George White, clerk of the Journals, 1756–70. It would appear that Rosier, Speed and the two Bensons, his successors, though all of them were parliamentary agents, at least employed a clerk to attend to the ostensible duties of their official position.

The clerkship of the committee of elections was a post which could easily be combined with a clerkship without doors and with parliamentary agency. Even after the reforms of 1770 made a great deal more work, this occurred almost exclusively in the first year of a new parliament when legislation was likely to be less in bulk; thereafter the clerk of elections had the great advantage of an office at the House and a staff free to turn their attention to private bills.

The committee clerks were certainly all sinecurists by 1772, in the sense that they drew their fees and performed the work by deputy paid out of the proceeds.[2] But since the office was held for life, it seems certain that, after the first few years, some must have continued to hold office when disqualified by age from active employment, and there is very little evidence of any of them actually functioning as committee clerks. But it was an appointment that carried prestige and provided, if not an actual office, at least a desk and access to the House records. The importance of such a foothold in the House to a parliamentary agent can scarcely be over-estimated. No outside agent could have done what Edward Barwell, committee clerk, was able to do for a client in 1774: he promised to give the client warning when a petition in which he was interested was to be presented to the House; he was able not only to do this, but to give his client a copy of it before it was presented, so that he might prepare his opposition.[3]

The ostensible offices held by the Commons clerks make misleadingly neat and tidy tables in the *Court and City Register*.

[1] Arthur Benson's evidence to the select committee on public records. (First Series, xv, pp. 66–7.)

[2] *Clerical Organization*, p. 141.

[3] *Parl. Hist.*, xvii, 1007–8. This is the case of John Horne (Tooke) and the Tottington inclosure, see below, p. 98.

Some used their sinecures for an easy, leisured life; some took office in the House as a stepping stone to politics; many were active in private parliamentary agency; and any of them might be employed from time to time on work for the Treasury or other government departments. This not because the Treasury 'set up and paid an agency of its own in the Clerk's department',[1] but because in this, as in other ways, the government worked through the ordinary legislative machinery, feeing an agent to watch their interests as private organisations did, paying a clerk to attend a committee as an individual was compelled to do, paying the full ingrossing fees on public bills as individuals did on private, and promoting all but the essential finance bills through the normal bill procedure with the aid of draftsmen and agents who might be Commons clerks or outside practitioners.

[1] *Clerical Organization*, p. 159.

4

PARLIAMENTARY BUSINESS

Mr Hatsill [*sic*] writes to me that above 360 private petitions have been presented for Bills, being above fifty more than in the last Session, and three times as many as the average twenty years ago. He attributes this to the superaccretion of wealth; and, at the same time, the bankruptcies in the *Gazette* are ten times as many as the old average.

Thus Lord Auckland to Lord Grenville on 11 February 1811.[1] The legislative output of that year resulted in 128 public and 295 local and private acts. Of the latter, one was for change of name, two for divorce, six concerned the settlement of private estates, 133 were for inclosure; the remainder, some 150, concerned local affairs. The majority of this last class were for turnpike roads, some were for canals or bridges, others for churches, and a number for purely local matters – the streets or poor rates of a given town.

In 1711, only seventy-four acts, public and private,[2] were passed. Some may be called matters of state: encompassing the death of a privy councillor; a quarantine act was necessary; three, including the mutiny act, related to the army. There were nine financial measures, six acts were concerned with trade and transport and one or two related to social matters – there was a game act and provision for the building of fifty new churches. There were three turnpike road acts. About half the total related to private estates.

The pattern of 1711 is typical of the beginning of the century. The government's chief business was finance and often several acts were necessary to complete the supply. Occasionally matters of state such as a royal marriage or the completion of a treaty required legislative enactment. A private act was

---

[1] H.M.C. *Fortescue MSS*, x, 121.

[2] My reason for not distinguishing between the public and private acts will be found in chapter 9.

necessary for naturalisation, change of name, or divorce; such an act was also desirable, and sometimes essential, for many dealings in property. The inclosure movement began in 1709 but did not get into its stride until 1754, reaching a peak after the end of the century. The turnpike road acts are the forerunners of an ever-increasing amount of local or sectional legislation.

Since the length of the parliamentary session was not increased and, however long individual sittings, the day still contained only twenty-four hours, it is obvious that the enormous increase in the quantity of legislation must have been accompanied by changes in procedure. We must now chart the outline of these changes, as they appear from formal sources, and as they grew, unavowedly and almost imperceptibly, in the practice of parliament.

When the Commons standing orders were first officially published in 1810,[1] they contained only seven public orders, of which only three were of earlier date than 1715 and the next in date were of 1772. For the greater part of the eighteenth century, the only public standing orders of importance were those that ruled that government bills concerning public money could be introduced only in the Commons and there only in committee of the whole House with the recommendation of a minister of the crown. Other public bills might be introduced in either House after leave was given to a motion for that purpose. The Lords had no particular standing orders relating to public bills. The orders of both Houses relating to private bills were somewhat more elaborate, dealing much more with things to be done outside parliament; they will be discussed in the next chapter.

From very early times attempts were made by temporary orders to try to limit the encroachment of private business upon the time of parliament. Stubbs suggested that the exclusion of lawyers from the parliament of 1404 and its summons to Coventry – away from the law courts – was an attempt to reduce the number of private petitions.[2] In 1581 the first of the 'things that lengthen the session' was named as 'the number

[1] HC (355) 1810, ii, *211.*   [2] *Constitutional History,* iii, 47.

of private bills of singular persons'.[1] In 1656, 'it is private business jostles all out'.[2]

In earlier times the attempt to stem the flood usually took the form of a prohibition on the receipt of bills for a given period. This was tried in the 1650s. For instance, on 26 May 1657 there was a motion to exclude private business for fourteen days, but Mr Bond moved 'to make trial for a week; for if you have not private business you will have no house'; the speaker agreed 'for when private business was excluded for two months you did less public than when you took in private. Haply you may not sit a month.'[3] At the beginning of the next session private business was again excluded for a month.[4] Later, the usual expedient was a rule that all private petitions must be presented by a certain date and none received after that time. This was the usual practice from the Restoration.[5] After 1811 it was provided by standing order that petitions for private bills must be presented in fourteen days from the first Friday of any session.[6]

Efforts were made from time to time to improve progress with private business. Under Elizabeth, for instance, there were attempts to get the London bills sorted out and grouped before the opening of the session.[7] In 1702 when there was a huge number of petitions concerning forfeited estates, special days were set aside to receive them and they were read in

[1] Neale, *Elizabethan House of Commons*, p. 383.
[2] Thomas Burton, *Diary*, ed. J. T. Rutt (4 vols., London, 1828), i, 190.
[3] *Ibid.*, ii, 133.   [4] *Ibid.*, ii, 376. *CJ* vii, 540.
[5] In the first fourteen years of the eighteenth century such an order was made in five sessions. Perhaps one can assume the trouble was not so pressing in the others.

Session began	Order made	No bills after
Oct. 1704	19 January	that day
Oct. 1705	21 January	24 January
Dec. 1706	19 March	that day
Oct. 1707	18 February	28 February
Nov. 1709	11 March	16 March

[6] In 1841 the period was extended to twenty-one days (*Private Bill Procedure*, ii, 211).   [7] Neale, *Elizabethan House of Commons*, pp. 383, 386–7.

batches and referred to the same select committee, which reported from time to time.[1] In 1706, after the order that no new bills were to be received, days were set aside to make progress with those already begun.[2] In the early eighteenth century, turnpike bills that had a geographical relationship with each other were sometimes referred to the same select committee and in 1714 an experiment was tried of appointing a sort of expiring laws committee for turnpike bills.[3] But these expedients did not help very much. Most private bills, especially the estate bills, were essentially individual matters and no grouping of them was possible.

Since not much could be done to prevent the large number of private bills coming into the House, all that could be hoped for was to arrange that some definite time was reserved for public business. In the sixteenth century, when the House met at 8 a.m., first readings of private bills were taken until 9 a.m. 'when usually the House groweth to be full';[4] and it was already at that time becoming customary to treat the first reading as a formal stage.[5] But although orders concerning the time of private business which appear superficially to be very similar continue to be made throughout the seventeenth and eighteenth centuries, their intention alters. In the early seventeenth century these orders were intended not so much to restrict private business as to allow members to know when public business would be taken. Attendance was often small and the political activities of the speaker made it desirable that he should not be allowed to get important measures through in a very thin house. After the Restoration the orders for time of private business are worded in the opposite form: instead of 'that no public business should pass but between 9 and 12' we have 'that no private business be taken after nine o'clock', sometimes supplemented by orders that private business 'must cease and be adjourned' at the time set.[6] Clearly the intention of these orders is simply to restrict the time for private business.

[1] *CJ* xiii, 739, 748, 750, 751, 757, 789. [2] *CJ* xv, 116, 118–19.
[3] *CJ* xvii, 491, 500, 572, 585, 603–4. [4] Hakewill (1671 ed.), p. 135.
[5] Neale, *Elizabethan House of Commons*, p. 371.
[6] Report of committee on attendance of members, 1744, *CJ* xxiv, 684–5.

From 1689 to 1770 the official time to which the House stood adjourned was 9 a.m., and thereafter 10 a.m.[1] How far this was a dead letter by 1819 is shown by Brougham's joke about Charles Wynn: 'many persons imagined he really came down to the House every morning at 10 o'clock.'[2] Although there is evidence that in the early eighteenth century the House did sometimes meet at the official hour of 9 a.m.,[3] it is by no means certain that it did so regularly. The time fixed for the end of private business was 10 a.m. from 1701 until in 1744 it was fixed at 1 p.m.,[4] which suggests that the House actually met at 11.30 a.m. or noon. There is no need to suppose that any great innovation was made when, in 1761, 2 p.m. was fixed for the beginning of public business[5] – this simply reflects the later time of meeting of the House, with the usual allowance of one, or at the most two hours for private business. Indeed Hatsell credits Onslow with establishing 2 p.m. as the time for public business, despite the order of 1744.[6] Hatsell in later years recollected following Onslow's state coach as it passed 'at 12 o'clock punctually' through Palace Yard.[7] But Hatsell and Onslow coincided only in 1761, a very quiet session because of the war, the new reign and the pending general election. From 1763 controversial business was sometimes specially ordered to be taken at noon.[8] By the end of the century public business began at

[1] Report of committee on attendance of members, 1744, *CJ* xxiv, 684–5.
[2] A. Aspinall, *Lord Brougham and the Whig Party* (Manchester, 1927), p. 39.
[3] *The Parliamentary Diary of Sir Edward Knatchbull, 1722–30*, ed. A. Newman (Camden Third Series xciv), pp. 15, 18.
[4] *CJ* xxiv, 685. In 1735 the time from which the passages to the House were to be kept open was altered from 10 to 11 a.m. (*CJ* xxii, 459). In 1742 the Lords altered the time for hearing counsel from 11 a.m. to 'first business after prayers' (*LJ* xxvi, 120).
[5] J. Steven Watson, 'Parliamentary Procedure as a Key to the Understanding of Eighteen-Century Politics', *The Burke Newsletter*, iii (1962), 114. This incident is in any case quite irreconcilable with the statement, *ibid.*, p. 116, that by 1760 the House did not meet till 4 p.m. The difficulty arises from a misunderstanding of Onslow's remark about King William dismissing his ministers to attend by 11 o'clock; this evidently means 11 a.m., not 11 p.m.
[6] *Precedents* (1818 ed.), ii, 184.   [7] *Clerical Organisation*, p. 121, n. 3.
[8] E.g. *CJ* xxx, 186, 234, 281, 316, 383. Dr Thomas has evidence that, by the 1770s, 'noon' is simply a synonym for 'first business', but presumably the earliest orders for this time may mean what they say.

4 p.m.[1] and from early in the next century the House did not meet until 3.45 p.m. which was the latest time to allow new members to take the oath, as they were statutorily obliged to do, before 4 p.m.[2]

By the eighteenth century, probably the most important stage (or stages)[3] in the passage of a private bill took place, not in the House, but in select committees, and according to the rules (though doubtless these were not always observed)[4] such committees were to meet only when the House was not sitting. The order of 15 November 1670 'that Mondays and Fridays be appointed for the only sitting of committees to whom public bills are committed and that no private committees do sit on the said days'[5] is not, therefore, the origin of the reservation of nights for government business in the House.[6] It was a sessional, not a standing, order[7] and was not renewed in subsequent sessions. At that time the House still maintained the civilised custom of adjourning for dinner, usually from 1 to 2 p.m. If necessary the House then met again, but if business permitted the regular routine to be observed the House as such did not meet again, but committees met in the afternoon at 2 p.m.[8] and continued as long as they pleased. The order of 1670 then, was an attempt to get more progress with public bills at the expense of private bills which had also reached the committee stage, but of course, to say 'public bills' is not necessarily to say 'government business'. The actual position at the time of the order in 1670 was that twelve bills had reached committee stage, ten of these being local or private. The two public bills were 'for regulating the making of cloth' and 'for planting of hemp and flax'. In

---

[1] Hatsell, writing in 1795, remarked that the practice had begun 'within these last two or three years' (*Precedents* (3rd ed., 1796), ii, 175 n).

[2] 13 Will. III c. 6, repealed by 29 & 30 Vic. c. 19.

[3] Committees on petitions for private bills were subject to the same rules as those for committees after second reading.

[4] *Liverpool Tractate*, p. 56 [5] *CJ* ix, 164.

[6] As suggested in *Parliamentary Practice* (12th ed.), p. 230 n. 6.

[7] As Watson has it, 'Parliamentary Procedure', p. 113.

[8] Committees might also sit in the morning before the speaker took the chair. In the sixteenth century this meant 6 or 7 a.m. (Neale, *Elizabethan House of Commons*, pp. 367–8). In 1711 and 1714 it was ordered that no committee should meet in the morning without special leave (*CJ* xvii, 3; *CJ* xvii, 476).

addition three select committees were in being to prepare public bills on expiring laws, the navigation act and corn imports. Many members were named to more than one of these committees so some sorting out of their time of meeting was essential. However, it is noticeable that on the 'private' days committees were repeatedly put off (e.g. *CJ* ix, 194–5). During this time the House was making progress with supply without afternoon sittings, but after the supply bills were presented to the King on 6 March 1670/1 it was resolved to meet at 8 a.m. (instead of 9 a.m.) go to public business at 9 a.m. rise at noon and sit again at 3 p.m., and the House did in fact meet most afternoons to the end of the session on 22 April.

By the mid-eighteenth century this sort of situation could not have arisen, because of the altered times of meeting of the House and particularly because it had become usual to take public bills in committee of the whole House,[1] so the committee stages of most (though not all) public bills would be amongst the orders of the day, since committee of the whole, on any subject, was invariably ordered, as was the report from it and reports from committees of privilege or secrecy.[2] From the point of view of the government's business, the most important matter was committee of supply and ways and means, which, being committees of the whole House, were always ordered, and by sessional orders had their own days fixed – Mondays, Wednesdays and Fridays. It was not until 1811 that it was found necessary to give supply priority on those days and the move was then immediately obstructed.[3]

---

[1] *Liverpool Tractate*, p. 7. Private bills for compounding debts due to the crown were also taken in committee of the whole by order of 24 February 1708, made a standing order in 1710. Divorce bills also were taken in the whole House, for reasons probably not quite so reputable: in the Duke of Beaufort's case, 1744, 'the fact was very clearly and circumstantially proved, to the great entertainment of a very well filled bench of bishops and a very numerous audience' (*Bedford Correspondence*, i, 18). But it is simply not true to say as Watson does ('Parliamentary Procedure' p. 123) that most bills were taken in committee of the whole: the great majority of all private and local bills went to select committee.   [2] *Liverpool Tractate*, pp. 11, 50, 58.

[3] J. Redlich, *The Procedure of the House of Commons*, 3 vols. (London, 1908), i, 93, misunderstood the incident that took place on 6 March 1811 when Creevey moved the first amendment to the motion that the speaker leave the chair for

It is clear that only a quite limited number of specified types of business normally became orders of the day. The remainder, a motley collection, were all unordered. These include first readings of all bills, public or private, petitions, addresses or orders for papers and their return, any other readings of uncontroversial bills, reports of committees on private bills, motions for leave for public bills, motions for leave of absence. Apart, however, from all these matters of business, any matter of policy might be raised in the form of a substantive motion or an address to the crown without being ordered.

Mr Watson claims for Onslow the establishment of 'the convention that notice must be given to the ministry of any first class motion' and believes that these would then be 'included in the Orders of the Day'.[1] It is important to realise that no amount of private notice to a minister can convert a motion into an order. The orders of the day consist of matters set down by order *of the House* to be taken on a certain day. When this is understood it can be seen that while the orders of the day include some of the government's important business, notably supply, they also include many other matters; and on the other hand the orders of the day do not necessarily include the business of the greatest political importance. To take a few examples at random: the Dunkirk debate in 1730,[2] the debate on the peace treaties in 1762,[3] and Dunning's

---

committee of supply. He relied on Erskine May's evidence before the 1871 committee on public business (HC (137) 1871, ix, *1*, p. 2, qu. 10) but misquoted him. May stated correctly that it was not the speaker, but Spencer Perceval as leader of the House who resisted any encroachment on the government's time. However, May's remarks give the impression that Perceval objected in principle to the amendment, whereas the report of the debate makes it clear that Perceval was again referring to the vexed question of motions without notice (see below, n. 1).

[1] Watson, 'Parliamentary Procedure', p. 116. If it is true that Onslow established the convention, it is much older than has been supposed and this is difficult to reconcile with the debates on the subject in 1806. Compare Redlich, i, 70 and *Parl. Deb.*, vi, 521. Dr Thomas has many instances of notice of motion being given from the 1760s onwards, but considers it did not become an invariable practice during the eighteenth century.

[2] *CJ* xxi, 469. Committee of the whole house on the state of the nation, Friday 27 February 1730.

[3] *CJ* xxix, 393. Motion that the treaties be taken into consideration, Thursday 9 December 1762.

motion in 1780,[1] were all orders of the day; Colonel Burgoyne's motion for a select committee on East India affairs,[2] and Pitt's motion for parliamentary reform in 1782,[3] were not.

To confuse notices of motion with orders of the day makes nonsense of the attempts to get progress with the orders, for the sort of 'first class motion' Mr Watson has in mind would almost invariably be hostile to the administration – why then should they strive to find time for it? A motion to take the orders of the day is by no means necessarily in the interests of the administration; nor is the opposite true. It is just one more manoeuvre – like the motion for the adjournment or for the previous question – which could be used by either side depending on the circumstances. In any case, even if on a particular day the orders contained only urgent government business and this business was put off to allow discussion of members' motions, it is unsophisticated to suppose that, provided they did get their votes that day, the administration really objected to taking them late at night, without debate, in a very thin house.

The increasing formality of procedure gradually reduced the speaker's influence over the order of business until, by 1903, the deposit of a printed copy of a bill at the Private Bill Office caused it, without more ado, to 'be deemed to have been read a first time and ordered to be read a second time or referred to the examiners as the case may be … and shall be recorded in the Votes as having been so read'.[4] Formality can scarcely go further. The change to this state of affairs is difficult to date, but Dr Thomas has evidence from the diary of James Harris that already, by 1762, the speaker kept a private business list and called members in that order, and this was certainly the practice in the early nineteenth century.[5]

As early as 1698, an attempt had been made to have second

---

[1] *CJ* xxxvii, 763. Committee of the whole house on the Yorkshire petition on economical reform, Thursday 6 April 1780.

[2] *CJ* xxxiii, 691. Burgoyne had given notice, but since it was a Monday, the orders of the day, including supply, were taken first. 13 April 1772.

[3] *CJ* xxxviii, 987. Tuesday 7 May 1782.

[4] *Private Bill Procedure*, ii, 212.   [5] *Parliamentary Practice* (1844 ed.), p. 400.

readings of all private bills made orders of the day.[1] This had not succeeded and from that time members simply told the speaker that they were ready to proceed and moved the next stages of their bills whenever time served.[2] Officially, stages of private bills were not to be taken after the time fixed for the beginning of public business, but one could always get leave of the House to move another stage immediately, during intervals in, or after the end of, public business. According to Hatsell, Onslow introduced a rule that leave for a new motion was not necessary while any of the orders of the day remained to be taken, presumably on the ground that members were still in the House, waiting for the last order, and so could not be taken by surprise.[3] This was not a ruling likely to add to regularity of business, and as soon as Onslow retired, a small reforming experiment was tried.

The new rule of 4 December 1761, stated that leave was not to be given to take private business in public business time unless the House had been warned, the previous day, that such a motion for leave would be made.[4] This rule seems to have worked fairly well, but it was usually only invoked for the week before the last date for receiving private petitions and the week before the Easter recess, so it was found to be unnecessary and abandoned. But already, before 1761, and without any formal ruling, it had become customary to order stages, especially the report stage, of opposed private bills. Instead of receiving the report from the committee and immediately ordering the bill to be ingrossed, the report is ordered to be taken into consideration, usually the following day; it is thus brought formally to the attention of the House, as an order of the day. This practice began about 1757 and continued when the new rule of 1761 lapsed.[5]

The motive behind the order of December 1761 may have been to ensure that, if encroachment of private business upon public business time could not be prevented, at least some

[1] *CJ* xii, 45.   [2] *Liverpool Tractate*, pp. 6, 23, 26.   [3] *Precedents* (1818 ed.), ii, 184.
[4] *Liverpool Tractate* p. lxxvii and Watson, 'Parliamentary Procedure', p. 114. Watson considers Grenville was the prime mover in the matter, but Thomas suggests, convincingly, that the King himself may have been behind it.
[5] E.g. *CJ* xxvii, 674; *CJ* xxviii, 454, 518–19, 744, 785, 800.

warning could be had of the amount of disruption of the programme that was to be expected. But it seems more likely that the intention was only to get a more orderly method of handling private business, in the face of the great increase of such measures then taking place. In practice, there was little difficulty in finding time for the stages of bills, whether public or private, and little need for regulations on the subject. It was not yet customary to 'massacre the innocents' at the end of every session.[1] The clerks were not yet complaining of late nights, caused by there being 'a cessation of business, in consequence of the House being in debate for many hours'.[2]

Technically speaking, bills in the Commons were supposed always to be prepared by members, but although occasionally the committee appointed for the purpose may have finalised the draft of a controversial bill, it is evident that preparation by named members is usually a parliamentary fiction, since the speed with which the bill is produced makes it clear that the leader of the named band already had the copy in his pocket;[3] this applies even to finance bills, which regularly appear the day after the official members are named to draw them. That is, in general, proceedings in the House are started only after the bill is ready, not before.

From very early times most bills were drawn by lawyers and no doubt lawyer members drew most of the bills of a public nature which they personally, or like-minded members, wished to promote. Also, Hakewill explained, 'Private Bills are usually drawn by Councellors at Law, not being of the House, and sometimes by those of the House (and that for their fees) which howsoever it hath been held by some to be lawful, yet it cannot be but very inconvenient, seeing they are afterwards to be Judges in the same cause.'[4] This was a very

---

[1] Certainly throughout Harper's life time, there is scarcely an instance of a private bill being lost for lack of time. [2] HC (520) 1828, p. 64.

[3] In 1733, Sandys tried to gain a little extra notoriety for his pension bill by rushing it into the House without previous leave. Speaker Onslow warned him that even if the House would agree to this sudden introduction 'decency requires' an interval for the ostensible preparation of the bill. Sandys dutifully waited until committee of supply was over. (*Parl. Hist.*, viii, 1182–4.)

[4] *The Manner how Statutes are enacted in Parliament by passing of Bills* (1671 ed.), p. 133.

old problem and Pollard was optimistic in assuming it was solved by the ordinance of 1372,[1] for this was never enforced except for the 'unlearned' parliament of 1404.[2] In 1621 Crewe echoed Hakewill's comment with the dictum 'That no member of the howse ought to drawe a private bill, for he is a judge and ought to be indifferent.'[3]

The thought was not new and the rule was not observed: it was not until 1830 that a resolution of the House finally prohibited members from having any interest in parliamentary agency.[4]

However, all bills were ostensibly promoted and introduced by members, and it was certainly essential for any outside group to obtain the interest of some members, at least to the

---

[1] A. F. Pollard, 'The Clerical Organization of Parliament', *English Hist. Rev.*, lvii (1942), 50 n.4. The ordinance reads 'That men of Lawe who pursue divers peticions for singular persons with whom they are procureing and cause to be exhibited many peticions in parlement in the name of the Comons which nothing touch them but onely the singuler persons with whom they are procureing be not hereafter returned nor accepted knights of the Counties . . .' (*Rot. Parl.*, ii, 310).   [2] W. Stubbs, *Constitutional History of England* (1896), iii, 47.

[3] *Commons Debates, 1621*, v, 57. The editors comment, 'Crewe was upholding a new and high parliamentary code. Only a generation earlier men had received large fees for promoting ("following") certain measures in the Commons.' The references they give for the comparison are tautological: all in the end come back to Hakewill's statement quoted above. As long ago as 1937, Mrs Sims pointed out (*The Liverpool Tractate*, p. lii n. 77) that H. L. Gray in *The Influence of the Commons on early Legislation* (1932) had confused Ralph Starkey's tract, BM Add. MS 36, 856, ff. 3–22, which he ascribed to Richardson, with the next one in the volume, ff. 30–46, which is Hakewill's, so that almost all the statements which Gray confidently ascribed to Richardson are in fact by Hakewill. When a treatise was actually published in his lifetime by a man of Hakewill's eminence, and that with the full authority of the House of Commons (see the preface to the 1641 edition and *CJ* ii, 166, 168, 190, 198) it is misleading to quote from an eighteenth-century copy of the manuscript. Gray's attribution of Starkey's tract to Richardson arises from the following note in the front of Add. MS 36,856: 'This is a Copy of Serjt Richardson's MS who was chosen Speaker of the H. of Commons Jan. 30 1620. 18 Jac. The Original is Sir John Trevor's the master of the Rolls. 1710.' Gray assumed that this refers to the first item, whereas it refers to the whole manuscript which is one original book with a contemporary index to the whole. The implication is not that speaker Richardson was the author but that the volume was his property – the speaker's *vade mecum* – which was at this date (1710) copied for speaker Bromley. In addition to Starkey's and Hakewill's tracts it contains a copy of Glanville's notes of election cases, and an additional chapter by Hakewill on order in the House, which has been published by Mrs Elizabeth Read Foster, 'Speaking in the House of Commons', *Bulletin Inst. Hist. Res.*, xliii (1970), 35–55.

[4] *Parliamentary Practice* (1844 ed.), p. 399.

extent of going through formal procedures in the House, if a bill were to succeed. Members themselves had private interests coinciding with those of outside groups; many had causes they sought to promote; some had hobby-horses which they rode when opportunity offered.[1] For the most part we have little definite information about the promoters of bills concerning trade or social matters, or all the mass of public bills affecting, and probably promoted by, private interests.

Minority religious groups found it advisable to retain a solicitor permanently to watch their interests in parliament.[2] If these minority groups wished to promote legislation they were inclined to do their own drafting, by committee,[3] but this might not be advisable. The Quakers found it very difficult, and when they had found a member willing to support their interests he advised them to have the bill drawn by counsel 'which Counsellor Smith did accordingly'.[4]

The Trustees of the Colony in Georgia employed a solicitor who assisted them with parliamentary business,[5] and since Egmont and Onslow were close friends, they also had the benefit of the speaker's advice on procedural matters. In 1734 when legislation was contemplated, Egmont thought it could be introduced as a public bill and would thus cost them nothing, though some of his fellow-trustees disagreed.[6]

---

[1] In the war years, when there was parliamentary time to spare, there were some attempts to legislate against 'mad and mischievous dogs'. The first was counted out, the second defeated by thirty-four to twenty-six. On 25 February 1762, sixty-four members divided on the dogs bill and the serjeant was sent with the mace to give warning for the committee stage of the militia bill. Next day forty-four members were in the chamber for the dogs bill, following which 225 divided on the Bridgewater canal bill. *CJ* xxvii, 165–6, 274; *CJ* xxviii, 534, 579; *CJ* xxix, 96, 198.   [2] See the Presbyterians, above p. 45 and the Jews, below p. 83.
[3] N. C. Hunt, *Two early political associations* (Oxford, 1961), for the Quakers, pp. 75, 84, and the Presbyterians, p. 149.   [4] *Ibid.*, pp. 86, 88.   [5] Above, p. 14.
[6] The proposal was to investigate a charitable collection for the Palatines and, if abuses could be proved, to have the money transferred to the Georgia trustees. This explains the statement by some of the trustees that 'they had known private bills cost £1,400': it is a piece of gross, if pardonable, exaggeration, made in the heat of debate. The sum named is that which it was hoped to raise, and the implication is only that it was not worth while to pursue the matter because of legal costs. Egmont replied that he 'never understood private Bills cost more than a hundred pounds', and that even if they did not succeed in making it a public bill, 'the Speaker said he would give up his own fees, and Mr Douglas [the solicitor] said he would undertake to satisfy the remaining charges for £30'. (H.M.C. *Egmont Diary*, ii, 44.)

The Society of Gentleman Practisers in the Courts of Law and Equity was consulted by a member who contemplated a measure for the recovery of small debts; a small committee was appointed which met several times to discuss and amend a draft; but the tone of pleased surprise with which the Society received the request shows that this was a rare event.[1] The Society itself naturally feed counsel to settle its bills. In 1749, when the revision of the act for regulating attorneys and solicitors was under discussion, the Society decided to offer a clause to safeguard its interests and the secretary was twice instructed to 'attend Mr Harper thereupon'. In June it was reported to the committee that the 'clauses had been perused and settled by Counsellor Harper' and had been successfully included in the revising act since passed.[2]

Another small measure of law reform, the revival in 1748 of the acts of 12 Geo. I and 5 Geo. II against vexatious arrests, was promoted entirely on the initiative of the Society of Gentlemen Practisers.[3] They got a group of London members to put the bill through the House.[4] It passed without difficulty and was enacted right at the head of the year's statutes,[5] where one least expects to find a privately promoted bill: the first five or six public acts in any session are usually purely official measures – the land, malt and mutiny acts and such things as quarantine or trade embargoes according to circumstances.

Thus, though often of course it is obvious that a muncipality like London or Exeter, or an organisation like the College of Physicians is promoting a bill, in many cases it is not nearly so clear, especially as one approaches what would be thought of in modern times as the truly public domain. Certainly one must not, without detailed investigation, lump together bills on which there happened to be divisions and ascribe them all to opposition harrassment of the ministry.[6]

---

[1] *Records of the Society*, pp. 8–10. [2] *Ibid.*, pp. 34, 35, 37.
[3] *Ibid.*, pp. 25–6. [4] *CJ* xxv, 428. [5] 21 Geo. II c. 3.
[6] This is done by A. S. Foord, *His Majesty's Opposition, 1714–1830* (Oxford, 1964), pp. 97–8, with four bills in 1721–4. One of these, the drugs bill of 1724 was a purely private measure of the College of Physicians, even introduced on petition, though of course it had public consequences. It passed the Commons without incident of any sort; the divisions occurred only on the Lords amendments and were purely technical. By contrast the very title of another, to permit the Crown

The Treasury, of course, took care of the finance bills proper. After the Restoration, the clerk of the House received a payment of £50 a year in connection with money bills, but this payment, which ceased in 1699, seems to have been for agency rather than drafting.[1] In 1699 William Lowndes had been four years in office as secretary to the Treasury and so was experienced in the work; he was qualified by legal training and official experience to prepare all the legislation required – no doubt with the assistance of Treasury clerks. John Scrope, who succeeded on Lowndes' death in 1724, was equally competent and soon made himself equally indispensable; Scrope was also very active in the House, and in 1733, a Treasury clerk, Christopher Lowe, who had served under Lowndes, began to receive an additional salary of £100 a year 'for his extra care and pains in preparing for the House of Commons as well the Bills for raising the supply granted to his Majesty as all other public Bills relating to the revenues, making breviates thereof for the use of the Speaker and other services'.[2]

That there was some change in procedure at this time seems likely in view of Pulteney's complaint in 1734 that 'the Gentlemen of the Revenue ... have lately taken upon them a sort of exclusive authority to draw and present all Money-Bills to the House,' but Scrope certainly remained in full charge, and when in 1742 the Duke of Bedford wished to replace him, Pulteney himself, now in office, was compelled to reply that it was 'absolutely impracticable. Mr Scrope is the only man I know that thoroughly understands the business of the Treasury, and is versed in drawing money bills.'[3] Up to this time, then,

---

to issue letters patent of incorporation, is enough to send shivers down the spine of anyone who remembers the seventeenth century. It was introduced by the most formal method possible – royal message.

[1] *Clerical Organization*, pp. 24–8, 43.

[2] *Ibid.*, pp. 160, 162. Williams suggested that Lowe was appointed because there had been a technical error in the Excise Bill, so as to prevent such mistakes for the future, but the dates do not fit – if anything it was Lowe, in his first year, who made that mistake. I am inclined to think that Grover's allowance on the printer's account may be connected with this change (above p. 43).

[3] P. G. M. Dickson, *The Financial Revolution in England. A Study in the development of Public Credit, 1688–1756* (London, 1967), pp. 20, 220.

this area of government business had been handled by the (effectively permanent) secretary to the Treasury, with the assistance of a Treasury clerk. The second joint secretary to the Treasury, from the first appointment of Harley in 1711, had been rather a political appointment, the holder changing with his patron and the longest period of tenure being that of Horace Walpole.

At the time of Scrope's death in 1752 the second secretary was James West, who had held the post for six years and according to later practice, he, as 'elder secretary' would have taken over the 'parliamentary business of the department', that is, 'the preparation of bills and materials for their defense, and probably also the consideration of the estimates',[1] but it is not certain that this practice was established as early as 1752. West had legal training and had practised as a barrister, but he was, although very diligent, a wealthy man whose interests apart from politics were in science and antiquities. Hardinge, who joined him as secretary, had a legal education, but little experience; his background is best summarised as 'Eton and King's' – 'a brilliant classic and ... the most elegant composer of Latin verse of his day';[2] and it was Hardinge who had succeeded to the 'permanent' secretaryship. Obviously neither was in the class of Scrope or Lowndes as a financial draftsman.

From 1752 we find Robert Yeates obtaining an additional allowance of £100 a year 'for drawing up and preparing sundry bills to be laid before the House'.[3] Yeates was a Commons, not a Treasury clerk.[4] The Treasury clerk, Lowe, continued to draw his £100 to his retirement, though it is possible that the nature of the allowance had been forgotten and the post was already a sinecure, since Hardinge soon took an opportunity to pass the payment over to his nephew, Hardinge

[1] Dora M. Clark, 'The Secretaries to the Treasury in the Eighteenth Century', *Amer. Hist. Rev.*, xlii (1936), 41.   [2] *Clerical Organization*, p. 62.
[3] *Ibid.*, p. 332 n. 5. The date is a little obscure. He petitioned July 1755 and was paid in October 1755 in arrear for either 'five sessions' or 'three years'. If the former is correct he began in the session 14 November 1751 – 26 March 1752, before Hardinge's appointment to the Treasury. But the payment also covered some committee work, so perhaps the bills work began only in 1752.
[4] See above, pp. 45–7.

Stracey, two years down from Cambridge, who acted as confidential secretary to his uncle.[1]

Yeates drew his £100 annually in 1756 and 1757 but in the following two years he attended the important committees on Weights and Measures, for which he received special allowances;[2] since, however, one cannot imagine that these took up all the time of a man of Yeates' abilities, there are probably still some gaps in the story. Hardinge died in April 1758 and was succeeded as joint secretary by Samuel Martin, who had already held the post briefly, with Hardinge, when West had resigned with Newcastle in November 1756. West was reinstated in July 1757, and he and Martin served together for four years. In 1759 Yeates recovered the £100 for assistance with bills on the Commons account which, like Lowe's allowance, had been passed to Hardinge Stracey, and he was also appointed a principal clerk in the Treasury, 'to write all letters ... and references, according to directions given by their Lordships' minutes, and to do all the parliamentary business'.[3] We do not know precisely what business Yeates did that subsequently earned him an annuity of £750 a year,[4] but that it included all the Treasury drafting may be surmised from the rearrangement that took place on his death. The Treasury minute reads:

My Lords are pleased to appoint Danby Pickering Esq., to do the parliamentary business of this office performed by the late Mr. Yeates with a salary of £600 a year ... My Lords likewise appoint John Rosier Esq., to assist Mr Pickering in the execution of the said business at a salary of £100 ...[5]

His concentration on the Commons officers led Dr Williams to emphasise the assistant at the expense of the principal in his account of Treasury agency in the House. He made no other reference to Pickering except to index him as 'Treasury Clerk', which is to do less than justice to Pickering's attainments and is anyway inaccurate, for he was not appointed a clerk at all. Yeates was succeeded in his treasury clerkship by

[1] *Clerical Organization*, pp. 164–7.   [2] *Ibid.*, pp. 167, 333.
[3] *Ibid.*, p. 165.   [4] Above, p. 46.   [5] *Clerical Organization*, p. 169.

Thomas Pratt,[1] and the post that Pickering held was that of Parliamentary Counsel to the Treasury.

The son of Danby Pickering of Hatton Garden, gentleman, Pickering entered Westminster School, aged ten, in 1728. He was admitted to Gray's Inn in 1737, called in May 1741 and was subsequently bencher, 1769, and Treasurer, 1770. In 1753 when the Inn attempted to revive something like legal education for the young men in its care, Pickering was appointed law lecturer, at a fee of £60 for forty lectures and in the first year was awarded an extra £20 'for a piece of plate as a mark of their esteem for his having so well discharged himself in his office of Reader'.[2] Between 1762 and 1766 Pickering prepared for the Cambridge University Press the edition of the statutes which bears his name,[3] for a set of which the Society of Gentleman Practisers subscribed, sight unseen, because of their 'High opinion of the great learning and abilities of Danby Pickering Esq.' and because they wished to mark their approval of the efforts of the Press to reduce the 'present exorbitant price' of the statutes by breaking the King's Printer's monopoly.[4]

Pickering died on 24 March 1781,[5] and was succeeded as Parliamentary Counsel by Francis Hargrave. Hargrave was a member of Lincoln's Inn, called 1771, Recorder of Liverpool 1797, K.C. 1806. He was called to the bench in 1802 and subsequently served all the offices of the Inn – imbecility being no bar.[6] Hargrave was Thurlow's protégé and 'devil', the editor of *Coke upon Littleton* and many other learned works. He is said to have owed his appointment to Lord North and his dismissal to his attitude to the Regency question, although he was charged with negligence and 'inattention to Treasury Bills'.[7]

Whatever the immediate occasion, Pitt had determined to put in a protégé of his own in the person of William Lowndes,

---

[1] PRO T. 29/40 p. 102.   [2] Holdsworth, xii, 80–1.   [3] *Ibid.*, xi, 306.
[4] *Records of the Society*, p. 103.   [5] *Gentl. Mag.*
[6] John, Lord Campbell, *Lives of the Chancellors*, v, 519 n, 528. Hargrave's mind broke down in 1813 and as a result of his wife's petition his library was bought for the nation for £8,000 to provide a maintenance for him till his death in 1821.
[7] *D.N.B.*

one of the innumerable great-grandchildren of the great
William, former secretary to the Treasury. Lowndes was
educated at Charterhouse and Cambridge, and joined the
Middle Temple. He was a pupil of Edward Law, Lord Ellen-
borough, and succeeded to part of his practice as a special
pleader and draftsman under the bar. Having been employed
by the Stamp Office to draw a bill, he was recommended to
George Rose, then secretary to the Treasury, by whom 'he was
frequently employed in the public service and introduced to
Mr Pitt' with whom he formed a friendship.[1] He became
Parliamentary Counsel in 1789 and was soon in need of
assistance, 'Mr Pitt intending to take up some very serious
measures for the abolition of tithes and a complete revision
of the Poor Laws'.[2] William Harrison, a special pleader
under the bar, was appointed without salary but with the
promise of the reversion of Lowndes' place when he should
be promoted. The domestic reforms were laid aside because
of the war, but Harrison drew the tax bills and, being also
counsel to the War Office, all the army and militia bills.[3]
In 1798 Lowndes was appointed chief commissioner of
taxes, but presumably because of his close association with
Pitt and no doubt partly also because of the increase of business
caused by the war Lowndes continued to draw bills; after
Pitt's death he did less of the general work but still drew some
bills relating to taxes and to Ireland; he died in 1828.[4] Harrison
described in 1833 how in addition to his Treasury work, he
drew measures for other departments; in fact 'Bills have come
to me from all departments of government who have not a
Counsel of their own'.[5] Nevertheless, his successor was not a
Treasury official. Melbourne allowed Lord John Russell to
make the Home Office counsel, Bethune, the government's
chief draftsman, and this situation continued until the then

[1] *Annual Biography and Obituary for the year 1829*, xiii, 99–104.
[2] HC (648) 1833, xii, *179*.
[3] J. R. Torrance, 'Sir George Harrison and the growth of bureaucracy in the early
nineteenth century', *English Hist. Rev.*, lxxxiii (1968), 70–1.
[4] *Annual Biography and Obituary.*
[5] Sir C. P. Ilbert, *Legislative methods and forms* (London, 1901) printed Harrison's
evidence, pp. 80–2, and suggested that he exaggerated the importance of his office;
but this is only because Ilbert knew nothing of the pre-history of the post.

Home Office Counsel, Thring, was given a proper establishment as Parliamentary Counsel in 1869. Just before this, in the 1860s, 'it was found that as the number of Bills increased, different departments employed independent Counsel to draw their Bills ... the cost was great; for barristers employed "by the job" were entitled to charge fees on the scale customary in private Parliamentary practice'.[1] In so doing, the departments were reverting to the practice of the eighteenth century.

Throughout this time, the parliamentary counsel's assistant continued his work in the House. This has been amply described by Dr Williams who shows that the assistant's salary increased from £100 in 1769 to £800 plus £300 for Irish business in 1817, by which time the salary of the Parliamentary Counsel had increased from the original £600 to £1,000.[2] The work done by Rosier up to 1796, and by his successor Dorington, included the drafting of all routine revenue bills, the more difficult ones being 'settled' by the Counsel, and the supervision of the passage of approved bills through parliament, preparing the necessary resolutions for committee of supply, and so forth. The department, originally known as the Fees Office, became the Public Bill Office.

Insofar as there was any central supervision over legislation, this was exercised by the Treasury. Individuals who wished to compound crown debts had first to apply to the Treasury for permission to seek a private act.[3] Individuals who obtained parliamentary votes,[4] or even special acts promising them cash rewards,[5] still had to apply to the Treasury for the money. Petitions of merchants for relief from restrictions on trade were referred by the Treasury to the appropriate board for comment before permission was given to proceed with legislation,[6] and sometimes permission was refused.[7] Subsidiary departments put in proposals for reforms which might even be rejected on the ground that they would need legislation.[8] When a department reported difficulties, such as the Commissioners of Taxes had with the house duties, they might be

[1] Ilbert, *op. cit.*, p. 83. [2] *Clerical Organization*, pp. 170–7.
[3] *Cal. T.B.P.*, 1731–4, p. 216. [4] Above, p. 25 n. 2. [5] *Cal.T.B.P.*, 1731–4, p. 306.
[6] *Ibid.*, pp. 18–19, 217, 227; *Cal.T.B.P.*, 1735–8, pp. 8, 9, 288, 302–3, 362.
[7] *Ibid.*, p. 312. [8] *Cal.T.B.P.*, 1731–4, pp. 66–7.

directed to prepare legislation for next session,[1] and sometimes the law officers were consulted about such departmental legislation.[2]

The Treasury wrote regularly to the revenue departments to find out what measures should be included in the expiring laws bill. A committee to consider expiring laws was usually appointed by the Commons early in each session, and had a semi-permanent chairman.[3] It was concerned principally with laws concerning criminal offences and with matters in which the Customs and Excise departments were interested; but it might consider any type of act. The committee made a report to the House, upon the basis of which leave would be given to bring in one or more bills. One of these would usually be what is often scornfully called a 'hotch-potch act',[4] but it should be remembered that although these do contain 'provisions upon the most heterogeneous topics' they are not (or ought not to have been) original enactments, but only extensions of the term of existing acts. Usually this is the case, and the acts contain only extensions of time or small and truly technical amendments. In the absence of any serious attempts at codification, expiring laws might as well be continued in one act as in twenty individual ones. But even so, the necessity to continue a large number of laws, relating to a great variety of topics, and which were re-enacted on each occasion for another limited number of years, took up a good deal of parliamentary time and cluttered up the statute book alarmingly.[5] Apart from the main act, which concerned measures of consequence

---

[1] *Cal.T.B.P.*, 1735–8, p. 169.   [2] *Cal.T.B.P.*, 1742–5, pp. 32, 46, 544.

[3] Edward Bacon, afterwards chairman of the Committee of Privileges, often served as chairman of the expiring laws committee. This committee deserves serious study for the seventeenth, as well as the eighteenth, century, but the subject cannot be pursued here.

[4] There is an example in Holdsworth, xi, 373.

[5] This first attracted Charles Abbot's reforming attention. The 1802 report on Expiring Laws, First Series, xiv, 74–84, contains an interesting table of the laws then about to expire, with their pre-history. The sail-cloth bill, mentioned in the text, was originally enacted in 12 Anne and was renewed thirteen times up to 39 & 40 Geo. III. Nor was this a rare occurrence. In the 1796 report, First Series, xiv, 39, the committee remarked that there appeared to be no less than 150 original statutes, continued by nearly 300 subsequent acts; but the position was really much worse than this suggests, for many of the 150 originals were quite recent acts that had not yet been renewed.

to the administration, and which was often put through the House by the chairman of ways and means or the secretary to the Treasury, individual interests might also proceed through the expiring laws committee. The procedure was slightly simpler and cheaper than the normal method, since a formal motion for leave was unnecessary. The Corporation of London used this method in 1718 for the Act concerning assize of bread.[1] They paid £2 8s 8d in committee fees for 'getting the Bill reported as fitt to be continued'.[2] The clerks complained that the expiring laws committee was used to smuggle through, as if they were public, bills that ought to have paid fees,[3] and no doubt this is why individual bills were often introduced from the committee instead of 'hotch-potch' bills. The method might also be of some use in dodging opposition in the early stages, but once a bill had started on its way it had to face normal hazards. Harper's Yorkshire cloth bill [No. 70] was petitioned against in the Commons; the Lords ordered it to be printed and heard counsel; finally it dropped in the Lords for lack of time.

The Treasury solicitor was the officer through whom parliamentary business in the House was carried on, and some of his activities are rather surprising. In 1735, Sir John Barnard (not a favourite son of any government) moved for a bill to limit playhouses; 'At this motion many in the House seemed to smile', but Walpole finally came round to the idea. In the end the bill dropped because the opposition disliked any extension of the lord chamberlain's powers.[4] But although it was Barnard's bill from first to last, the government paid the Treasury solicitor's bill for the drafting.[5]

In 1732, following a select committee investigation, an

---

[1] The committee reported in favour of bills for this, sailcloth, and tobacco (*CJ* xix, 33). Bread and sailcloth together became 5 Geo. I c. 25 and tobacco passed separately as c. 7.

[2] *Clerical Organization*, p. 317.   [3] *Precedents* (1818 ed.), ii, 286–7 n.

[4] *Parl. Hist.*, xi, 945–7.

[5] *Cal. T.B.P.*, 1735–8, p. 11. The City of Exeter had petitioned to be included in Barnard's bill (*CJ* xxii, 477), and they found the act that was passed in 1737 (10 Geo. II c. 28) to limit theatres and playing for hire, ineffectual for they had 'a parcell of Fellows here that will play in spite of the Magistrates' teeth, pretending they don't play for Hire' (H.M.C. *Exeter MSS*, p. 172). It was in this context that they enlisted the aid of Zachary Hamlyn, above p. 40.

impressive body of legal experts were ordered to bring in a bill to void the sale of the Derwentwater Estate. Lord Gage, who had originally discovered the fraud and received the thanks of the House for so doing, saw the bill through the Commons.[1] It was a troublesome business. Dr George Paul, the King's advocate, represented the Crown when counsel were heard, his fees being paid by the Treasury solicitor, who acted as agent.[2] But the bill had been drawn by Robert Harper [No. 67]. The same session Harper also drew the two bills for sorting out the involved affairs of the Charitable Corporation [Nos. 68, 69] which the Crown took over while the bills were in the Lords. Since the Treasury solicitor was 'unable to instruct counsel in an affair of such intricacy' with no previous acquaintance with the details, the Corporation's solicitor continued to act and was paid his bill of £115 10s plus counsel's fees of £253,[3] but since the details of the Treasury solicitor's accounts have not survived we do not know whether Harper was any further concerned in the business than as the draftsman.[4] In this case too a Commons clerk, John Burman, received the huge sum of £1,200 for the expenses of the committees of investigation.[5]

On the whole, all these examples suggest that governments, through the Treasury, took a much more active part in legislation than is generally supposed.[6] In addition, some departments had legal assistance of their own,[7] and others employed Commons clerks as agents.[8]

Opposing Townshend's militia bill in 1756, lord chancellor Hardwicke complained that

[1] *CJ* xxi, 870, 883, 884, 890–904 *passim*.

[2] PRO T. 27/25 p. 102. *LJ* xxiv, 135. Gage also received reimbursement of legal expenses which did not satisfy Samuel Allen, an attorney he had employed. (*Cal.T.B.P.*, 1731–4, pp. 564, 566, 618.)

[3] *Cal.T.B.P.*, 1731–4, pp. 262, 264, 351; and PRO T. 27/25 p. 132; T. 1/281 no. 11.

[4] His papers include copies of some of the papers laid on the table of the House during the investigation: BM 357. b. 12(54, 55).

[5] *Clerical Organization*, p. 333.

[6] These sort of payments continued and indeed became more common, later in the century. For Gilbert's Poor Act, 22 Geo. III c. 83, which is cited by Holdsworth, xi, 371 as an example of private initiative in legislation, the Treasury paid for George White's agency. (*Clerical Organization*, p. 182.)

[7] Holdsworth, xii, 11–13.   [8] *Clerical Organization*, pp. 179–80.

every member of the other House takes upon him to be a legislator, and almost every new law is first drawn up and passed in the other House, so that we have little else to do, especially towards the end of the session, but to read over and consent to the new laws they have made: nay some of them are sent up so late in the session that we have hardly time to read them over ... the other House by their being so numerous, ... are too apt to pass laws which are either unnecessary or ridiculous, and almost every law they pass stands in need of some new law for explaining and amending it.[1]

Hardwicke looked back to a period when bills originated in the Lords and were drawn on the advice of the judges. That golden age, if it had ever existed, had gone for ever. Lords amendments were not always models of accuracy, though the judges could still be called into consultation.

At bottom, of course, Hardwicke's speech was political; the militia bill was an independent, opposition measure.[2] Newcastle took notice of the complaint to the extent of asking Hardwicke who should draft a bill for next year since some proposal could not be avoided.[3] There were amending bills in each of the following three years and in 1762 a long struggle over the proposal to make the militia perpetual. None of these was, in the strict sense, a government bill, yet in 1757 and in 1762, but not in the other years, Newdigate Poyntz, a Commons committee clerk, received a payment of no less than £350 'to reimburse his expenses and in reward for his service and attendance during the time the Bill for the better ordering of the Militia Forces was preparing and depending in the House of Commons'.[4] The bills were very troublesome; they were petitioned against; there were many amendments; they were ordered to be printed. But naturally they did not go to select committee, but were taken in committee of the whole House,

---

[1] There are two versions of the speech in *Parl. Hist.*, xv, 724–39. This passage does not occur in the version Hardwicke published. Complaints of this sort go on into the nineteenth century. John Tyrrell, a leading draftsman, complained bitterly of the manner in which bills originally perfect (his own) were mauled by amendments offered by 'junior common-law barristers' in the Commons. (HC (540) 1834, qu. 624.)

[2] For full details see J. R. Western, *The English Militia in the Eighteenth Century* (1965), especially pp. 127–93. For the earlier movement, in 1746, see B. Kemp, *Sir Francis Dashwood* (London, 1967).

[3] Western, *op. cit.*, p. 134.   [4] *Clerical Organization*, pp. 332–3.

where a committee clerk should not have been on duty. So one would dearly love to know what Poyntz did for his money, which was paid on 'a representation by several members of the committee'.[1] From at least the late eighteenth century both the War Office and the Admiralty regularly employed a Commons' clerk as agent for the mutiny bills,[2] but these payments are not on the same footing as those to Poyntz.

Hardwicke had his way about drafting by the judges for the Habeas Corpus bill of 1758,[3] and the judges also quite often attended the Lords for minor matters.[4] In 1731, George Robinson absconded while his wife's petition for judicial separation was being heard in the Lords.[5] The judges were ordered to prepare 'heads for a Bill, for making Process in Courts of Equity effectual against Persons who absent themselves and cannot be served'. Nothing was done that year, but the following session the committee on the proposal was revived and after long consideration a bill passed both Houses.[6] A copy of the 'Heads' as they were originally read before the Lords committee in 1732 is amongst Harper's papers.[7] The document is not in any of the hands associated with Harper's office and it is not on his list of 'Acts drawn' but he noted upon it two amendments proposed by the solicitor general and prepared a draft preamble (which, however, was not finally adopted), so that he evidently was consulted on the matter.

The law officers, as well as the judges, consulted outside practitioners. The bills for settling and disarming the Highlands after the rebellion of 1745 are quite naturally regarded by Holdsworth as fairly isolated examples of truly government-sponsored legislation demanded by an emergency,[8] and we

---

[1] *Clerical Organization*, p. 332 n. 7. Williams assumed that the bills of 1756 to 1762 were all of the same nature and that Poyntz' fee was tantamount to 'agency for the government' (p. 181) but this is hardly a sufficient explanation in view of the political history of the bills. [2] *Ibid.*, p. 180.
[3] Holdsworth, xi, 374–5. [4] Below, p. 115.
[5] *LJ* xxiii, 651, 664, 675. It is believed that only two separation acts were passed on the wife's petition: the Countess of Anglesey, 1700 and Lady Ferrers, 1758 (Clifford, i, 432). Mrs Robinson's plea failed.
[6] 5 Geo. II c. 25. *LJ* xxiv, 13, 179–85. Com. Bk. 26, 28 Jan. and 4 Feb. 1732.
[7] Vol. 8 no. 64. BM 356. m. 2(76). [8] Holdsworth, x, 78–81; xi, 371.

have no new information about them, but the amending bills of 1748 were drawn by Robert Harper [Nos. 318, 319], despite the fact that the lord chancellor presented the former to the Lords and the attorney and solicitor general were ordered by the Commons to draw the latter.[1] The amending bill for disarming the highlands contained provisions for the registration of attorneys and solicitors;[2] perhaps this is why Harper was consulted about it. But we see, from these examples, that the Treasury might be behind measures apparently quite privately promoted, and on the other hand, private attorneys and agents might be employed upon matters of state.

Even a subject so basic to any government as the nationality of its citizens, and the conditions under which aliens are permitted to obtain that privilege, was in the eighteenth century, hardly a matter of governmental regulation at all.[3] By the Act of Settlement, 1700, it was provided that even naturalised aliens might not hold public office, receive grants of land from the Crown, or become members of parliament or of the Privy Council.[4] In 1715, to make the matter more certain, it was provided that these disabling clauses should be written into every private naturalisation act.[5] As if this were not enough, attempts were made in 1705 and 1706[6] to disfranchise aliens, who, on being naturalised, were able to obtain property carrying an electoral qualification. The number of aliens being naturalised at this time was very large, though scarcely sufficiently so to arouse these somewhat hysterical political fears, the average being something over one hundred in each of the years 1701–8.[7] In 1709 a general naturalisation

---

[1] *LJ* xxvii, 173; *CJ* xxv, 562. [2] 21 Geo. II c. 34.

[3] The best discussion of the law of nationality and the history of naturalisation is by Clive Parry, *Nationality and Citizenship Laws of the Commonwealth and of the Republic of Ireland* (London, 1957), ch. 2, hereafter cited as *Nationality Laws;* this is based upon the same author's 'British Nationality Law and the History of Naturalisation', *Comunicazioni e studi* (Milan, 1953), v. 1–107, which contains a little more detail on some points.

[4] 12 & 13 Wm III c. 2. [5] 1 Geo. I c. 4.

[6] *CJ* xiv, 497, 528, 575, 578. *CJ* xv, 174, 177.

[7] See above p. 35. Dr Parry suggests that a proportion of the people concerned were naturalised unnecessarily. The law concerning foreign-born children of British parents was particularly obscure and was not improved by enactments on the subject in 1708, 1711, 1730, 1752 and 1773. (*Nationality Laws*, pp. 63–4.)

act, promoted by the whig government, provided that any aliens might be naturalised provided that they were communicants of any protestant church and took the statutory oaths.[1] The repeal of the act three years later was due, not to the clerks' petition complaining of loss of fees,[2] but to an outcry from the districts where immigrants had congregated, of the sort with which we have become familiar in recent times, fomented for party ends.[3] Early in 1711 the parishioners of St Olave, Southwark, petitioned against the refugees from the Palatinate who 'continued together in one Place several months ... that the Petitioners are extremely fearful some contagious Distemper may happen thereby'.[4] The petition was referred to a select committee who called for a mass of papers,[5] and produced a report containing such 'evidence' as that the house 'was become very nauseous' and 'the Palatines have no subsistence but what they get by their Wives begging for them in the streets'.[6] Without even waiting for the committee a repeal bill was rushed in and passed by 31 January,[7] only to be rejected in the Lords; next year, however, it passed very easily.[8]

Thereafter, private naturalisation acts were left to be managed by the clerks, and governments interested themselves only in minor measures to meet practical needs, leaving the struggle for a more general liberalisation in the hands of private members. Attempts made by these members in 1747, 1748 and 1751 to reintroduce a general measure failed in face of the same general prejudice,[9] the St Olave's petition of 1711

[1] 7 & 8 Anne c. 5.   [2] Above, pp. 33–6.
[3] G. S. Holmes, *British Politics in the Age of Anne* (London, 1967), pp. 69, 105–6.
[4] *CJ* xvi, 456.   [5] *Ibid.*, 458, papers printed 464–74.   [6] *CJ* xvi, 596–8.
[7] *Ibid.*, 457, 464, 468, 470, 472.   [8] 10 Anne c. 9.
[9] Thomas W. Perry, *Public Opinion, Propaganda and Politics in Eighteenth-Century England. A study of the Jew Bill of 1753* (Harvard, 1962), hereafter cited as *Jew Bill*, discusses the bill of 1751 and what he calls a bill of 1747 (pp. 35–7). This is in fact the bill of 1747–8. Perry does not mention the similar bill of 1746–7 which was introduced by Nugent, Hampden and Lord Baltimore, and read a first time on 16 December. It was petitioned against by the City of London in almost exactly the same terms as the following year, and also by the inhabitants of Westminster. In committee of the whole House, with Hampden in the chair, it was once counted out, and at the report stage, after being printed with the amendments, was finally lost by 78–50. (*CJ* xxv, 195, 258, 269, 275, 287, 295, 301, 313, 334.)

being actually read in the House on the last occasion,[1] despite its obviously complete irrelevance to the circumstances of forty years later.

Although the advocates of general naturalisation were not active in 1752, its opponents kept up the struggle. On 11 March some merchants of London complained that foreigners obtained private naturalisation acts, simply to avoid the alien duties, and then returned to live in their native countries.[2] Members supporting this attitude set out to make an example of the nearest alien, one Johan Meijbohm, who had the misfortune to be half-way through his bill at the time. On report of the committee a clause was offered to prohibit his living outside the British dominions. Witnesses, including merchants and representatives of the Russia company (but not Meijbohm himself) were examined on 23 March when the clause was adopted by fifty votes to nineteen.[3] The Lords, more generously, asked the victim of this very unusual procedure what he thought of it, to which Meijbohm replied 'that he was desirous that the Bill might pass with the said restriction rather than lose the benefit of the said bill';[4] and so it passed, but the precedent was not afterwards followed in private bills. In 1774 a public act provided that naturalised subjects trading abroad should not obtain the benefit of protective treaties unless they had lived in Britain for seven years.[5]

The attempt made in 1753 to permit naturalisation of Jews differed from the general naturalisation measures since Jews (like the Roman Catholics against whom the provisions were really directed) were prevented from obtaining naturalisation by private act and would have been unable to obtain any benefit even from a general naturalisation act, so long as these acts required the taking of the sacrament according to the rites of a protestant church. The government gave this bill at least moral support, but then again bowed to a public outcry and immediately repealed it, but it is interesting to observe that an attempt made at the same time to repeal the plantation act of 1740 was rapidly thrown out, by a vote of 108 to 88.[6]

[1] *CJ* xxvi, 171. [2] *Ibid.*, 488. [3] *Ibid.*, 500, 503. [4] *LJ* xxvii, 702.
[5] Parry, *Nationality Laws*, p. 68. [6] *CJ* xxvi, 861.

This was one of the small liberalisation measures designed for a practical purpose – to assist in peopling the American colonies.[1] Similarly, after the outbreak of war in 1756, the King was empowered to grant commissions to foreign protestants serving in the army in America,[2] and towards the end of the war an act was passed to naturalise those who had so served.[3] The Lords attempted to extend naturalisation under this bill to all army officers, but the Commons objected that the provision was 'far too extensive and important to be introduced by way of amendment to a bill of so limited extent as the present'; moreover the Lords amendment was technically faulty, if not completely illogical and drew upon their Lordships' heads a very justified rebuke from the Commons.[4] The lord chancellor's tirade against Commons drafting reads rather wryly after this incident.

We may conclude this chapter with the story of the Jewish naturalisation act of 1753, since it provides a useful example of normal procedures on a simple public bill,[5] needing neither expert draftsmen nor parliamentary agents. A public bill was introduced, not by way of petition, but by motion in the House. This bill began in the Lords, was read twice and committed, routinely, to a committee of the whole House. The amendments made in committee, again as usual, are not set out in the Lords *Journal*. What these amendments were Dr Perry deduced from the text of the Act on the assumption that all the clauses in the form of 'provisos' were introduced in committee.[6] In general, whether a clause in an act begins

---

[1] Parry, *Nationality Laws*, pp. 53–7.   [2] 29 Geo. II c. 5.   [3] 2 Geo. III c. 26.

[4] *CJ* xxix, 307. 'Secondly because if the establishment of such a method of naturalization could, with any propriety, be inserted in this bill, yet, for want of such a provision, for enabling the crown to grant commissions to the persons who are the subject of the amendment, as was made by the act of 29 Geo. II with respect to those who are the subject of the bill, the amendment proposed must be ineffectual; unless indeed it could be understood to convey, indirectly and by implication, to foreigners at large, a capacity of holding military commissions: which we fully persuade ourselves, your Lordships would be as unwilling to propose as the commons themselves to admit.'

[5] Dr Thomas has listed all the possible variations of procedure that might occur during the passage of either public or private bills and discusses them in detail. The passing of the Jewish naturalisation act of 1753 has been described at length by Dr Perry who misunderstood many procedural points.

[6] Perry, *Jew Bill*, pp. 46–9.

'provided that' rather than 'be it further enacted' depends simply on the context and meaning of the clause in question. In this particular case, the bill had been drawn by Thomas Sewell, a barrister,[1] and was very short and simple, but a glance at the original paper bill in the House of Lords Record Office shows that three of the four provisos were in the bill from the first, and the manuscript minute book of the House of Lords makes clear what happened to it thereafter. The Lords committee met on the 10 and 12 April with the Earl of Warwick, as usual, in the chair. The preamble, the first clause stating that Jews might be naturalised by private act, without receiving the sacrament, and the first proviso declaring that such acts must contain the usual disability clauses,[2] passed without amendment. The second proviso had a blank for the time of residence to be required before naturalisation, which was filled with 'three years'. Technical amendments as to the manner of proof of practising the Jewish religion were made to the third proviso. The only clause added by the committee was the fourth proviso, prohibiting Jews from presenting to church livings, which was offered by lord chancellor Hardwicke. The bill was then reported and read a third time without further alteration.

When the bill got to the Commons, the 'lack of haste' Dr Perry noticed in bringing on the second reading does not so much 'bespeak the confident attitude of the managers of the Bill' in allowing it to 'lie dormant for three weeks' while opposition developed,[3] as the intervention — rather comically in the circumstances — of the feast of the Resurrection of our Lord. The bill came from the Lords on 16 April and was read a first time next day; the House rose for Easter on the 19th and met again on the 30th; on 3 May the second reading was ordered to be taken on the 7th. So the interval between first and second readings was the perfectly normal one for a public bill, of seven sitting days. The bill was ordered to be printed, which suggests, in spite of Horace Walpole's remarks,[4] that there was some opposition about even at the first reading.

[1] Perry, *Jew Bill*, p. 22.   [2] Above, p. 77.
[3] Perry, *Jew Bill*, pp. 49–50.   [4] *Ibid.*, p. 50.

Although printing was becoming much more common, it was still normally ordered for public bills only if they were controversial.

Dr Perry makes a dramatic story of the presentation of petitions for and against the bill after the clamour against it had broken out. He describes how the government, who were evidently backing the bill, since Dupplin, Barrington and Hardinge all spoke for it at second reading,[1] got wind of an opposing petition being arranged by merchants trading to Portugal and determined to 'box it in' with two petitions in favour. 'The first part of the plan was put into effect shortly after nine-o'clock Monday morning, May 21, when the first favorable petition was laid before the House of Commons ... it was done at about the earliest possible moment on Monday: for the Journals show that the House had got through only a few matters of detail before the petition was presented.'[2] So early, indeed, that one wonders if even the cleaners would have been there to receive it! Of course, the House did not meet at nine o'clock,[3] and this petition was presented in the ordinary way, during private business time, before the orders of the day were taken, whereas the City exercised their invariable privilege to present their hastily concocted petition against the bill at the bar of the House the same evening.[4]

Complaint was made that the City petition was disrespectful to the House because it was presented so late in the proceedings, whereas the similar petitions of 1747 and 1751 had been offered soon after the bill was introduced.[5] But this is simply polemic. The City petition was late because this bill, unlike the earlier ones, had come down from the Lords without attracting much attention. The *Liverpool Tractate* is emphatic that there can be no impropriety in petitioning against a bill at any stage.[6] This bill, having gone through the committee of the whole House unamended, was ordered for third reading on 22 May. The petitions were presented on the 21st and 22nd and the petitioners were heard at the bar after third reading (a very unusual procedure at this time and a tribute to the

[1] Perry, *Jew Bill*, p. 52.   [2] *Ibid.*, p. 57.   [3] See above, pp. 56–7.
[4] Perry, *Jew Bill*, p. 62.   [5] *Ibid.*, p. 64.   [6] *Liverpool Tractate*, p. 35.

amount of trouble the petitioners had stirred up), but still petitions could not stop the bill. The division was taken as one would expect, not on a substantive motion, but on a motion to adjourn the debate for a month, after which the motion that the bill do pass was carried without a division.

Dr Perry quotes the text of the act from the *Whitehall Evening Post*;[1] even though this was a government organ, and it was P. C. Webb, the lord chancellor's assistant (acting in his private capacity as solicitor to the Sephardic community),[2] who published the text with a commentary,[3] a newspaper report is hardly a source upon which to rely for the wording of a document central to one's study. As it happens, the text was accurate, and it is interesting to note that Webb was careful first to get the consent of Thomas Baskett, 'who is the proprietor', to this breach of his patent as King's Printer.[4]

---

[1] Perry, *Jew Bill*, p. 46. He deduces the Lords amendments from the same source. The act is 26 Geo. III c. 26.
[2] *Ibid.*, p. 125. [3] *Ibid.*, pp. 128–9. [4] *Parl. Hist.*, xiv, 1431.

5

PRIVATE BILL PROCEDURE

The private bill procedure was used not only for those bills that subsequently became private acts, but also for all bills affecting private or local interests. Before 1720, some road and harbour bills, having gone through the private bill procedure, were classified by the King's Printer as private acts, but after that date, although they followed the same procedure in parliament, they were classified and printed as public acts at the end of it.[1]

All these bills of course paid fees, but fees were also payable by parties taking benefit from any act whatever, and it was in this area that disputes arose as to whether fees should be charged. As the order of 1751 clearly states, 'every bill for the particular interest or benefit of any person or persons, whether the same be brought in upon petition, or motion, or report from a Committee, or brought from the Lords, hath been and ought to be, deemed a private bill, within the meaning of the Table of Fees.'[2] It is not possible to have a more comprehensive definition than this. The list printed by Hatsell,[3] is not a list of private bills, but a list of bills on which fees had been paid, which is not at all the same thing.[4] Similarly, the sections of the *Liverpool Tractate* dealing with private bill procedure refer not at all to private acts as such, except for one very slight reference

---

[1] See below, pp. 173–7.   [2] *Private Bill Procedure*, ii, 273.
[3] *Precedents* (1818 ed.), pp. 284–5.
[4] Clifford, ii, 731 n. 1 quotes Hatsell's list with the comment 'The way for exacting fees upon Bills of this character ... had been paved by a Standing Order of February 15, 1700 [*sic*] dividing private Bills into three classes; the third comprised measures which, though not strictly of a local or personal character, affected some special trade or interest.' This statement is complete nonsense. It arises from a misunderstanding of George Bramwell's attempt to classify public and private bills, which specifically is not an attempt to say which bills have paid fees (*The Manner of Proceedings on Bills in the House of Commons* (1823), pp. 4, 6). The orders in question are those of November 1699, repeated on 15 February 1701, *CJ* xiii, 333: three days between readings; introduction on petition; chairman to report allegations; a week's notice of committee.

to inclosure,[1] but to those public acts which were required to pay fees and to go through the private bill procedure. The examples used make this perfectly clear:[2] trade of the kingdom, police of Westminster, amending highways, cleansing harbours, making rivers navigable, twopence Scots rates, building bridges and building chapels.

Williams' *History of Private Bill Procedure* and Clifford's *History of Private Bill Legislation* are similarly concerned principally with this type of public act. By far the greater part of Clifford's two huge volumes is concerned with the nineteenth-century development of local authorities by means of acts which by that time were separately classified as 'local'. Apart from a brief section on inclosures,[3] he gives only two short chapters to the whole history of private acts as such[4] and dismisses from this section all the eighteenth-century estate acts on the ground that they are 'too technical to be dealt with here';[5] almost all the rest of his eighteenth- and nineteenth-century examples are in fact of public, not private, acts, although they follow the private bill procedure. Legislation of this sort might affect the trade and transport of a wide area, or the whole system of rating and policing a city; or it need not be locally restricted at all, but might affect a branch of trade or manufacture throughout the nation. Inevitably legislation of these sorts would be controversial. It was for this type of legislation that new safeguards were introduced from the latter part of the eighteenth century and that the multiplication of possible stages in private bill procedure might be used for obstructive ends. Apart from inclosure bills, private bill procedure in the strictest sense – that which resulted in private acts – took place for the most part very quietly in the House of Lords and has received almost no attention from historians. The Lords standing orders governing private bills were made at the opening of our period.[6] They provided that a private bill must begin on a petition signed by all the parties concerned (S.O. 95, 103). All such petitions were referred to

---

[1] Pp. 24, 49. [2] Pp. 8, 24, 29, 33, 49. [3] Clifford, i, 13–28.
[4] *Ibid.*, 342–452. [5] *Ibid.*, 378.
[6] The orders are cited from the roll as printed in H.M.C. *House of Lords MSS*, x, 1–27.

two judges (S.O. 104) who were to examine witnesses upon oath (S.O. 108). Printed copies of bills had to be delivered not only to the House but also to the parties concerned (S.O. 101). There were no special regulations as to the time of proceeding on bills before the committee stage, but private bills were not to take precedence over judicial proceedings in the House (S.O. 102). Fourteen days' notice had to be given of the sitting of a committee (S.O. 91) the chairman of which was to have a copy of the private bill orders (S.O. 107). The consent of parties concerned had to be proved in person or by affidavit before the committee (S.O. 90). Trustees appointed under a bill had also to appear personally to accept the trust (S.O. 106). Committees had to take care that the orders of the House were complied with (S.O. 106) and that in the case of exchange of settled lands the values were fully made out and the proposed purchase properly made (S.O. 105). The chairman was to inform the House fully of the true effect of any amendments made in committee (S.O. 110). These orders, almost unaltered, governed Lords procedure for half a century. In 1762 the Lords repealed S.O. 105 (then numbered 100) concerning the exchange of lands and substituted more detailed provisions for the supervision of the purchase of new lands.

The Commons private bill orders have been described in great detail in O. C. Williams' *Private Bill Procedure*[1] and need only be briefly summarised. As in the Lords, private bills had to start by way of petition. Any petition might be committed and those involving local taxation were always so treated. As in the Lords, after leave was given, a bill had to be printed before it could be read a first time. Any bill for the confirmation of letters patent had to have a copy of the patent annexed. Public notice had to be given before any bill concerning estates in Ireland was read a first time. Three days had to elapse between the first and second readings of a private bill; for Irish bills this interval was extended to thirty days. The bill then went to a committee, of whose sitting a week's public notice was required.

---

[1] It should be noted that the standing orders listed in the 'Calendar', *Private Bill Procedure*, i, 262–3, are all given, rather inexplicably, in old style dates.

Before the publication of the standing orders and the *Method of Proceedings* an attorney with a large parliamentary practice, like Robert Harper, compiled his own list of standing orders[1] and made detailed notes on the procedure to be followed for the use of his office. As we have seen,[2] the first four volumes of Harper's collection were not made up currently, but were put together, perhaps in 1728, and it is clear that volume 1 was subsequently altered from its original form before it reached the Museum. Volume 1 now begins with two items numbered 1, the second being a copy of a petition of 1702 for a member of parliament to waive his privilege in a case of debt, which is entered as 'vol. 1, no. 1' in the index of special cases. The first item number 1 is a manuscript of one sheet, written on both sides, headed 'Memorandums relating to passing a private bill'[3] containing a detailed, step by step account of the procedure necessary to pass a bill first through the Lords and then the Commons, the account being corrected by marginal additions and comments. The manuscript is undated and since there were no material alterations to standing orders after 1708 internal evidence provides no clue. But a separate memorandum on procedure for a naturalisation bill, in the same hand and with every appearance of having been written about the same time, can be dated from its position in Harper's volume 8 to 1732.[4] Harper's handwriting is not easy to identify and several of his clerks wrote very similar hands, but by 1732 Harper was well established in his profession, drawing more than a dozen bills a year, so it is safe to assume that the memorandum and the comments were made under his supervision.[5]

Memorandum's relating to passing a private bill

	1st	Draw the bill
The petition must be signd by the parties before it be carryed in		Then draw the petition setting forth the most materiall Allegations in the Bill & the reason of applying to the parliament
		Get the Clerk or one of the Lords to carry the

[1] BM 357. b. 1(4).   [2] Above, p. 6.   [3] BM 357. b. 1(2).
[4] BM 356. m. 2(104) misbound at the end of volume 356. m. 3.
[5] Peniston Lamb's handwriting, which is luckily distinctive, does not appear anywhere in Harper's collections.

petition into the house, & a Lord to move
that the petition may be read
Then the Lords will refer it to the Judges
Call of one of the Clerks for the Order of
Reference, &

They may be sworn
at the side door
when a Cause is
hearing [illeg.]
must be carryed in
at the bottom by
the Usher
Costs 2s a Witness,
Cert. 6.8

Get all the witnesses who are to prove the
allegations in the Bill sworn at the bar of the
house,
And Let the Clerk give you a Certificate of
their being sworn
Carry all these to the Judges Chambers &
Let each Judge have a fair copy of the Bill

The judges must
sign ye bill but
the parties need
not

When the Judges have settled it & approved
it draw a Report for the Judges to sign, that
they are of opinion the Bill may pass into
a Law

But it any of ye
pties sign a prin-
ted Bill after tis
passd the Judges,
or sign an amendmt
tis lookd upon as
plain proof of
their Consent &
may sometime dis-
pense wt their
attendance

Get as many of the parties concerned in the
Consequences of the Bill as you can to
attend the Judges & give their Consent
Annex the petition, Order, Report & the
Bill signed by the Judges alltogether, and
either get the Judge or one of the Clerks of
the house of Lords to carry them into the
House

Or you may carry
it your Self & get
a Lord to move for
the reading

And carry a Short Breif of the purport of
the Bill, both as to recitalls & the enacting
part, for the Ld Chancellor to open the Bill
to the house

Memdum they
made me pay once
for an Order to
being ye bill in
NB there is an
authority for this
Committee may sitt

Get one of the Lords to move that it may be
read a first time
It will be read cursorily & ordered to be read
a second time in a day or two, & is commonly
read the next day
Upon the second reading it will be Orderd to
be referd to a Comittee who cannot report the

tho' ye House do not	Bill to the house till after 14 days from the Committment
Order of Comittmt cost abt 15s	Get a Copy of the Order of Committment & the names of the Committee and attend on them to get them to fix a day for the Sitting of the Comittee, who must be 5 in number at least
	[Two lines deleted. Mutilated]
[illeg.] a paper referring to the folios of the Bill to fill up the blanks for Trustees names by	The Allegations of the Bill must be proved before the Committee as they were before the Judges & all the Witnesses & as many of the parties as you can get must attend
The Committee may sitt tho' the House do not	Get the Lord in the Chair to report to the house that the Comittee has gone through the bill, and then they will order it to be ingrossed
	When it is ingrossed the Clerk will bring it into the house & you must get a Lord to move that it may be read a third time & passed, & Then they will Order 2 Ma^{rs} in Chancery to carry it to the Comons, which may be done altho' the Lords be not sitting the day it is carryed
Printed bills must first be delivered & the blanks filled up	Then get a Member to move to have it read a first time And it will be read a 2 time in iii days Exclusive & Comitted to a Com^{ee} who are not regularly to make their Report till after 8 days from the Order of Commitment The Comittee must be 8 in No at least The Allegations of the bill must be proved over again as before, but they are not so strict as the Lords
Comittee can't sitt during an Adjournment of ye house without a Spiall order	The Chairman of the Committee must be desird to report the Bill to the house & somebody must move to have it read a third time
	When it is read & passed, the Chairman commonly or some other member is orderd to carry it up to the Lords to acquaint them the Commons have agreed to the same
	And then it waits only for the Royall assent

Harper's memorandum is soundly based upon the standing orders but it is evidently the product also of experience. Like the *Method of Proceedings* it differs from the *Liverpool Tractate* in being much more concerned with procedures to be followed outside parliament. After 1706 when the Lords began to refer estate bills to the judges, it gradually became the usual practice to start such bills in the upper House. Both the memorandum and the *Method* are concerned chiefly with this type of bill, but the framework of procedure applies to any bill beginning in the Lords.

Harper leaps over the preliminary proceedings there to begin at the beginning: 'ist Draw the Bill.' The *Liverpool Tractate* advises the drawing of the petition first, with the assistance of the lawyer who is to draw the bill, but this advice relates, as we will see,[1] to controversial local bills, where there might be a contest even at the preliminary stages which might necessitate modifications to conciliate opposing interests. The *Method* follows the strict rule in putting the petition first, but it is obvious that if a petition were to be referred to the judges in the House of Lords (a matter with which the *Liverpool Tractate* does not deal at all) the bill had to be ready before the judges could proceed, since they were to satisfy themselves that the bill was so drawn as to carry out the intention of the petition and they were to approve and sign the bill.

Harper and the *Method* agree that once the judges had approved (and both agree that the judges' report should be drafted for them by the party's lawyer), the lawyer himself could carry the papers to the House and 'get one of the Lords to move that it may be read a first time'. The *Method* advises deferring printing to this stage, though mentioning that strictly this should be done before first reading;[2] Harper makes no distinct statement about printing for the Lords but suggests it should be done immediately after the judges' report. Nor does Harper mention the payment of fees, either those of the House, which, as the *Method* states, were payable at second reading, nor the committee fees thereafter, although Harper does refer

---

[1] Below, chapter 8.
[2] This is no longer accurate in 1767. It was the rule from 1705 that the bill be printed before first reading, but in 1742 the Lords altered their rule so that printing did not take place until after first reading. (*LJ* xxvi, 120.)

to an extra expense for the order of commitment which is not mentioned in the *Method*.

The most striking omission from the accounts of procedure given in the *Method of Proceedings* and in Harper's notes is that of any reference to the Lords Chairman of Committees; nor are his functions mentioned in the *Liverpool Tractate*. Whereas we know that, at least by the end of the century, he played a very important part in private bill procedure.[1] The function of the Lord Chairman was primarily to take the chair at committees of the whole House. John West, Lord Delawarr seems to have performed this function in the 1730s and was followed by the Earl of Warwick, Lord Willoughby of Parham, Lord Sandys and Lord Boston. The post, once obtained, was usually held for life, irrespective of changes of ministry.[2] The early history of the office is obscure and, since not even the most diligent chairman can be expected to be invariably present, it is not until the post becomes salaried that one can be quite certain who is holding it. In 1758, for instance, Sandys, Warwick and Willoughby of Parham all reported from committee of the whole on different occasions.[3]

By 1780 the Lord Chairman was receiving a salary of £1,500 a year from secret service money.[4] But although the comparable payment of £500 a year to the Commons chairman appears in Newcastle's secret service accounts, the Lords payment does not appear there, so one must conclude it had not reached £1,500 a year by 1762.[5] The Earl of Warwick received £500 a year from secret service money from at least the beginning of Newcastle's administration,[6] in addition to

---

[1] The best account of the office is in F. H. Spencer, *Municipal Origins* (London, 1911), pp. 95–113. The description by Edmund Gosse, originally a letter to *The Times* of 24 June 1911, reprinted by Spencer, pp. 327–9 and discussed by H. Burrows, 'Standing Orders of the House of Lords relative to Private Bills, etc.', *Journal of the Society of Clerks-at-the-Table*, xvii (1948), 75–7, should be ignored. I am grateful to Mr J. C. Sainty for permitting me to read his paper on this subject.

[2] In 1778 the opposition peers attempted unsuccessfully to put their own nominee in the chair for a debate on the state of the nation (*Parl. Hist.*, xix, 650–4).

[3] *LJ* xxix, 213, 220, 221, 253.

[4] John Norris, *Shelburne and Reform* (London, 1963), p. 190.

[5] Sir Lewis Namier, *The Structure of Politics at the accession of George III* (2nd ed. London, 1957), p. 228.

[6] *Ibid.*, p. 222. The payment continued to Warwick's widow.

a civil list pension of £800 which he had received from first inheriting his impoverished honours.[1] Willoughby of Parham received £400 a year from secret service from 1755 as well as £200 civil list pension. Sir Lewis Namier classified both men simply as impoverished peers, and had these been payments of salary to the Lord Chairman the going rate would hardly have been reduced from £500 to £400 when Willoughby succeeded Warwick, nor would the difficulty about the continuation of the former's allowance on the change of government have arisen.[2]

So, in the absence of further evidence, we may take it that the office of Lord Chairman was not fully established in the 1760s. Although one peer did normally act as chairman of committee of the whole House, and the same person frequently took the chair at select committees, he was not the sole chairman. Even after the payment of salary is vouched for in 1780, there is little evidence that the Chairman had yet extended his functions to include the very active supervision of private bills which became the rule at the end of the century, and this development may have been an invention of Walsingham's who took office in 1794 and whose position was made official by resolutions of the House on 23 July 1800.[3] Thereafter, although a chairman was ostensibly nominated at the commencement of every session, the holders of the office served for life and received their salary from public funds.

In 1799 Charles T. Ellis, himself a solicitor, published *The Solicitor's Instructor in Parliament, concerning Estate Bills and Inclosure Bills*. Ellis makes it clear that by that time even a bill beginning in the Commons had to be submitted to the Lord Chairman before beginning its parliamentary career and if a bill began in the Lords he was to be consulted before the committee stage. In 1809 the Lords made it a standing order that the judges' report on an estate bill must be referred to the

---

[1] Payment is recorded as £1,000 a year in the civil list accounts for 1721–5, printed *CJ* xx, 535, but payments of £200 quarterly can be traced in the *Calendars of Treasury Books* from 1729.   [2] Namier, *op. cit.*, pp. 222, 224.
[3] *LJ* xlii, 636. In Dec. 1797, the speaker was discussing a new plan 'for arranging the matter of Inclosure Bills in the Lords' (Abbot's MS Journal, P.R.O. 30/9/32 f. 154).

Lord Chairman before the bill was read a first time.[1] An anonymous handbook published in 1827 amplifies this, stressing that even in the case of a local bill, the petition for which had been committed in the Commons, the Lord Chairman would 'arrange the clauses', and later he was to be supplied with a printed copy with the blanks filled, 'when his Lordship adds to or expunges from it whatever he thinks proper' before the meeting of the Commons committee on the bill.[2] In 1833 John Dorington described the procedure at some length and, being asked whether he had not 'heard repeated complaints' of the nature of the directions given by the Lord Chairman replied, diplomatically, 'I have heard complaints of them'.[3] The following year, John Tyrrell, a leading parliamentary draftsman, was less reticent. He complained: 'I have several times heard that parties and solicitors have been told at the House of Lords that any person of common sense can draw an Act of Parliament and that they had better not apply to counsel.' Tyrrell disapproved of the standing clauses which the Lord Chairman required to be inserted in various classes of bills and told an anecdote of the Chairman's refusal to permit the alteration of one of these clauses even though the amendment had been drawn by the Lord Chief Justice.[4]

C. T. Ellis appended to his *Solicitor's Instructor* two sample bills of costs which illustrate these complaints. The first of these is a composite of the types of charges that might arise on an inclosure bill. It includes the instance which Ellis mentioned in his evidence before the 1800 committee on inclosures[5] when he was compelled to make a special journey to Durham, at a cost of over £40, to obtain the signed consent of one proprietor. The bill of costs shows that Ellis consulted Lord Walsingham,

---

[1] *LJ* xlvii, 104.

[2] *Practical Instructions on the Passing of Private Bills through both Houses of Parliament . . . By a Parliamentary Agent* (London, 1827), cited Spencer, *Municipal Origins*, pp. 107–8. I have not seen this book, the British Museum copy having been destroyed by bombing.

[3] Report of committee on establishment of House of Commons, HC (648) 1833, qu. 2362.

[4] Report of committee on private bill fees, HC (540) 1834, qus. 601, 618. He voiced similar criticisms six years later, HC (520) 1839 qus. 51, 53.

[5] First Series, ix, 236.

then Lord Chairman, to try to persuade him to accept instead a letter of attorney; Walsingham referred Ellis to Mr Arnot, Reading Clerk of the Lords, upon whose judgement the journey to Durham had to be undertaken.[1] The other bill of costs, although supposed also to be a composite, is very closely based on a real case.[2] Ellis did not see the Lord Chairman until after second reading and then at Walsingham's own request. Although the bill had been settled by Lancelot Shadwell, a leading parliamentary counsel, and had already passed the judges, Walsingham suggested alterations which Shadwell had to approve. Walsingham then raised difficulties about the consents of the remainder-men, with the result that the bill was three days in committee, at an additional cost of at least £12 in fees and attendances; and after all this havering, Walsingham 'at last' agreed to the opinion already expressed by the judges that the interest of the remaindermen was so remote it should be barred.[3]

The Lords committee books, though very detailed, are not sufficiently so to bear out all the minutiae of Ellis' description, but the latter is accurate where it can be checked. It is not possible to tell from the committee books that the Lord Chairman was solely responsible for the alterations; to all appearances a real committee might be at work; so the committee books do not help us to discover when the Chairman began to extend his functions. Both the *Method of Proceedings* and Harper's memorandum hint at some difficulty about the assembling of the Lords committee. In accordance with the practice of that House, a committee was formed of all the members present in the chamber when the motion was put;[4] but already in 1767 it was up to the agent to 'get such Lords as you can to attend';[5] luckily only five were needed for a quorum. In 1799 Ellis remarked that 'unless you request two or three peers to attend it is not easy to form a committee', so he thought it right to charge in his account for 'attending

[1] *Solicitor's Instructor*, pp. 113 ff.
[2] *Ibid.*, pp. 97 ff. The bill is that for Sir John Honeywood's estate 38 Geo. III pr. c. 40.   [3] On this point see below, pp. 122–3.
[4] Spencer, *Municipal Origins*, pp. 91–2.   [5] *Method of Proceedings*, p. 16.

Sir John in Upper Grosvenor Street to request that he would use his influence with some Lords to attend the committee'.[1]

The committee books do not show the numbers present except in the rare case of a division in the committee. One occurred in 1798 on the question of consents to an unopposed inclosure bill which had started in the Commons. The Lords committee was appointed on 27 March in a very thin house, so only seven peers qualified for the committee; the division was 2–2 on the motion to report, the clerk noting that five peers were present but one abstained. Walsingham got out of the difficult by reporting the whole proceeding of the committee to the House (though it is hard to see by what authority he did so); as a result the committee was opened and the enlarged body reported the bill without amendment.[2]

Clearly, even in 1798, the Lord Chairman did not yet have everything his own way. What had happened certainly by 1833 was that the intervention of the Lord Chairman had caused all necessary amendments to unopposed bills starting in the Commons to be made in committee of that House, so that the committee procedure in the Lords was a formality.[3] Similarly, for an estate bill begun in the Lords 'the evidence taken in the committee of the house of Lords is considered sufficient' in the Commons.[4] By 1837 the Lord Chairman with his counsel alone adjudicated upon unopposed bills, even if they had started in the Commons; opposed bills only were referred to a semi-judicial Lords committee of five.[5]

Being concerned with unopposed private bills beginning in the Lords, both the *Method of Proceedings* and Harper's memorandum treat Commons proceedings as a formality. The *Method* states simply 'you must have your printed Acts as passed the Lords, and give two to a Member to move to take the Bill off the Table to be read the first time; one he gives the Speaker, and the other he keeps himself. The Bill being read at two different Times is committed', and then leaps straight to report stage.[6] Harper remarks that although the allegations of the bill

---

[1] *Solicitor's Instructor*, p. 53.
[2] Bozeat Inclosure 38 Geo. III pr. c. 26. *LJ* xli, 515, 516, 517.
[3] HC (648) 1833 qu. 2336.   [4] *Ibid.*, qu. 2348.   [5] *Private Bill Procedure*, i, 91–3.
[6] *Method of Proceedings*, p. 23.

must be proved again before the Commons committee 'they are not so strict as the Lords'.

Certainly the case would be different with a bill beginning in the Commons. But if there were nineteen different stages to a private bill and if 'the tendency was *not* to reduce these stages to formalities'[1] these lawyers were not aware of it. They anticipate little difficulty in getting progress with their bills. If we look at what actually happened in the House of Commons, we will see that orders do not always mean what they appear to say; procedure was altering very gradually into a machinery for the efficient handling of an increasing mass of legislation.

The requirement that private bills should be printed was a pre-requisite for any proper consideration of them if the House was to have time for any other business at all. This requirement was introduced at the very beginning of our period, but although it would take 'a man of more than common penetration'[2] to discover it from the wording of the order, the rule was understood not to apply to name, naturalisation and Scottish rate bills. Similarly, in the Lords, petitions for all private bills were ordered to be referred to the judges, but in practice only estate bills were so treated.

A Commons committee on a petition had first to hold a preliminary meeting to arrange for its first formal sitting, and this meeting, we know, did not take place at all by the time of the *Liverpool Tractate*. Indeed it was often impossible that it should have done so; many times eight, ten or even more committees each of thirty or forty members, were ordered to meet that afternoon 'at five o'clock in the Speaker's Chamber'.[3] Instead, the member in charge of the bill simply spoke to the clerk who was very willing to accept such notice without more ado 'provided he is allowed to charge the ... Attendance'.[4]

Commons committees on petitions and on bills after second reading consisted of anything from twenty to fifty or more

---

[1] Watson, 'Parliamentary Procedure', p. 122.   [2] *Liverpool Tractate*, p. 24.

[3] That this was simply a formula is clearly shown on an occasion in 1765 when leave was given 'near 8 p.m.' for the appointment of a committee on an inclosure bill, which was nevertheless ordered to meet at five that afternoon (*CJ* xxx, 276).

[4] *Liverpool Tractate*, p. 26.

named members, apart from the members for the locality or other classes of members who were often added. Such huge committees were appointed even for the naturalisation of a single person. How the names were chosen we do not know. About 1800, the speaker prepared lists of members by counties to facilitate the addition of local members, and presumably some lists of this sort were in existence before that date, but this does not affect the problem of the named members. The *Liverpool Tractate* mentions, as a quaint survival, that the regular method of naming committees was for each member to stand up uncovered and make his nomination, 'but they now name committees without any such ceremony'.[1] When special select committees were appointed by ballot, each member was supposed to put an independent list of suggested names into the glass, but in fact, both opposition and administration arranged prepared lists beforehand, so that all their followers made the same nominations.[2]

By 1825, the member in charge of a bill himself named the rest of his committee,[3] and it may be significant that in 1768, the names of committee members are abruptly dropped from the *Journal*. Thereafter we are given the name only of the member in charge of the bill and one other. What is quite certain is that, as the number of bills increased, it was physically impossible for eight or ten committees, each of twenty or more members, to have been named in the House and the names written down by the clerk, in the hour or so allotted to private business. Written lists must have been given to the clerk,[4] though additional names might be added by the House if anyone was paying any attention.

There is good evidence from the latter part of the century

---

[1] *Liverpool Tractate*, p. 40.   [2] H.M.C. *Egmont Diary*, i, 365.

[3] HC (457) 1825, p. 2. In 1796, a new member, wishing to have a committee appointed, consulted the speaker, who himself dictated the list of those to be named. The member then spoke, or wrote, to each asking whether they were willing to accept nomination; when they had agreed, the member named them in the House. This is Charles Abbot's committee on temporary laws (see below pp. 180-1) and no doubt procedure was a good deal more punctilious for an important select committee of enquiry than for a routine committee on a bill.

[4] It may be significant, also, that from 1765, the names of the committee of privileges are given in the Journal in alphabetical order (*CJ* xxx, 42).

that routine business, whether public or private, was transacted round the speaker's chair, while the rest of the House chatted and moved about to speak to friends.[1] The best description of the actual procedure comes from a very suspect source – John Horne (Tooke)'s libel on speaker Norton – but it has a splendid air of verisimilitude:

Mr De Grey's petition was then received and some members crying out 'Hear, hear' and one part of the House beginning to give attention; the Speaker turned round to them and said 'It is only a common petition for a common inclosure', upon which wilful falsehood and premeditated trick of the Speaker, the House (as is usual when mere matters of course are going forward, only preparatory to the business of the House) began talking again and heard no more. The moment Mr. De Grey's petition was read, the Speaker instantly muttered in a low voice, and as hastily as possible, 'all you that are for the question say Aye; all you that are against it say No; the Ayes have it. Now bring up the other'.[2]

In the ensuing debate, the members all agreed that there had been nothing unusual about the speaker's behaviour on this occasion; no one troubled to deny Horne's description.

Nine years later, speaker Cornwall defended Burke against the accusation that he had privately altered his Pay Office bill after it was ingrossed. The speaker explained that the alterations had been made, nominally, by the House at report stage reversing the decision of the committee on the bill; three clauses had been expunged and another altered. The speaker explained that:

As he understood that the parties concerned were all agreed, and that no opposition was to be given, he had put the question in a low voice, merely loud enough to be heard by the parties themselves, who were at the time round the chair, attending to what was going forward; in a word, the question had been put just in the same manner, as in all cases, where the parties were perfectly agreed.[3]

Though they did not quite believe that Burke was blameless,

---

[1] Thomas has many examples of this sort of mild disorder.
[2] *Parl. Hist.*, xvii, 1009. As to the substance of the Tottington Inclosure bill, to which the libel related, the errors and misrepresentations (to use no harsher term) contained in Horne's charges are so numerous and so double-dyed that the subject is not worth pursuing.   [3] *Parl. Hist.*, xxiii, 989.

no member in the subsequent debate challenged the speaker's description of the normal procedure.[1]

Whatever the actual method of naming committees it is clear that a relatively small number of members were regularly named to a large number of committees and many were scarcely ever asked to serve. How many of those named actually attended is a virtually insoluble problem. Edward Knatchbull was one of those very frequently named, yet his diary contains no reference to these activities. Moreover, Knatchbull was one of the country gentlemen who made a habit of going home as soon as the major business of the session was over, anything from two to six weeks before it formally ended.[2] Yet one finds him named to committees on several occasions after his diary has ceased, and once at least on the day he left London.[3]

In 1824, the quorum for Commons committees was reduced from eight to five yet, even after that, it was known that in fact the member in charge met alone with the committee clerk who selected the names of four other members from the list 'and enters them on his minutes as present'.[4] The Commons formally recognised the distinction between opposed and unopposed bills when the method of appointing select committees was reformed in 1839. The quorum for an unopposed bill was then formally fixed at one, and even that number could not always be obtained.[5]

But long before this there are hints that attendance was not normally large. Much attention has been paid to the packing

[1] The doors of the House were supposed to be closed before any question was put (whether or not there was to be a division), but apparently this rule was not observed for unopposed business of any sort. Dr Thomas quotes the diary of John Clementson, which he is to edit, for the Serjeant at Arms' rules about fastening the door.
[2] *The Parliamentary Diary of Sir Edward Knatchbull, 1722–30*, ed. A. Newman (Camden Third Series xciv), pp. vii, xi.
[3] One cannot make too much of the point since it is always possible that Knatchbull attended the House without making a diary entry. The details are:

Diary ends	1 April 1726	Knatchbull named to committees to 13 April.
	26 April 1727	Knatchbull named to committees to 29 April.
	7 May 1728	Knatchbull added to a road bill, 11 May.
	23 April 1729	He was named to a committee that day and can have had no intention of taking part in it.

[4] John Halcomb, *A Practical Treatise of passing Private Bills* (London, 1836), p. 53.
[5] *Private Bill Procedure*, i, 81–3, 92.

of committees on opposed bills and the scandal of opening committees with the motion that 'all have voices' so that questions might be decided by huge committees on party lines. But the great majority of private bills were unopposed and it is a question how far the committees which sat on them were ever real bodies. Even in the Elizabethan parliaments members had to be persuaded to attend committees on private bills.[1] In the late seventeenth century, Courthope's minute book contains, not minutes, but draft reports for unopposed bills. For the controversial River Weaver bill of 1727, the agent got twelve copies of the list of the committee and gave these to friends to persuade members to attend, but he prepared only twenty copies of the bill for the use of the committee.[2] By the end of the century, an agent should 'request a member or two' to attend, since 'there should be eight members to form a committee but the number is not rigidly observed'.[3]

We have evidence of the number of members attending a Commons committee in only one instance before the last decade of the eighteenth century, and this is not a committee on a bill, but George Cooke's select committee on bankrupt laws of 1759. The minutes as printed are not quite complete,[4] but twenty meetings are noted. On five occasions, perhaps ominously, the presents are not entered and on three more a bare quorum was present. Yet this was a committee which attracted a good deal of interest. Initially forty-two members were named to it, with all the members of the long robe and all the merchants and all who come to have voices; thirty-five members were later added by name. Of the forty-two originally named, only seventeen ever served and only six of these attended more than twice. Of the thirty-five additions, three were duplicates – they had already been named amongst the original forty-two – but still in fact never attended. Of the remaining thirty-two some were certainly lawyers, and so need not have been named, and only five ever served. Twenty-six unnamed members attended occasionally, most only once or twice. Two were more diligent – William Hammond who

---

[1] Neale, *Elizabethan House of Commons*, p. 391.   [2] Below, p. 160 n. 4.
[3] *Solicitor's Instructor*, pp. 20, 35, 42.   [4] *CJ* xxviii, 473, 544, 602–23.

attended eight meetings at two of which he acted as chairman, and P. C. Webb who was professionally interested as secretary of bankrupts in Chancery. He had easily the best record of attendance with thirteen of the fifteen recorded meetings, whereas the nominal chairman, Cooke, scored only nine. Thus for a reasonably interesting and controversial committee, which all might have attended and to which seventy-five were particularly named, only fifty ever appeared, the great majority of these on only one (nineteen) or two (twelve) occasions; the largest number present on one day was eighteen. There is no reason to think this untypical of the eighteenth century. For the controversial public accounts committee, appointed by ballot in February 1763, it was necessary to move the House, on 28 March, to have the quorum reduced from eight to five.[1]

As usual, all the criticism of committee procedure comes back in the end to nineteenth-century select committee reports.[2] It is by no means certain that these were accurate as evidence even for their own time,[3] and they are no evidence at all for the eighteenth century.[4] The *Liverpool Tractate* treats the motion for 'voices' as a normal procedure, without sinister implications. Moreover we do not know the practical effect of the motion in the eighteenth century. It is supposed that if 'voices' are ordered any member may speak and vote as a full member of the committee, but that the quorum must still consist of the named members, or those in a category such as lawyers or merchants.[5] If this were not so, the practice of adding more named members after voices had been ordered, which happened to the bankrupt laws committee and also to private bills on innumerable occasions, would be quite incomprehensible. But if this is the correct view of the situation, the rule was ignored at least by the bankrupt laws committee,

[1] *CJ* xxix, 617.
[2] In this case the Second Report of the committee on private bill procedure HC (468) 1824, vi, *501–6*; the report on committees on private bills HC (457) 1825, v, *103–6*; and the committee on private business HC (679) 1837–8, xxiii, *405–80*. Holdsworth, xi, 341–50, Clifford, ii, 824–33, Spencer, *Municipal Origins*, pp. 52–63, *Private Bill Procedure*, i, 49–50, all cite only these sources.
[3] Peel, receiving the resolutions of the 1825 committee, 'did not believe the committees on private bills to be that mass of corruption which some members asserted them to be', *Parl. Deb.*, xvi, 161.
[4] For example, see above p. 37.   [5] *Liverpool Tractate*, p. 55

who had a quorum from amongst their seventy-five eligible members on only two occasions.

In the 1760s it became usual to order voices for any private bill committee if opposition appeared, thus distinguishing between opposed and unopposed measures and ensuring a hearing for the opposition. The practice developed gradually.[1] On the other hand, I suggest that the addition of named members to a committee need not mean anything more than the difficulty of getting a quorum. On the last two sitting days of January 1760 members were added to committees on petitions for no less than eight bills and voices were ordered for four of them. Edward Smith (who is not known to have spoken or voted after 1754)[2] was added by name to the members to prepare and bring in ten of the eleven Leicestershire inclosure bills then pending. Being county member, Smith would be invited, as a matter of ordinary courtesy, to bring in all such bills. Since none was presented immediately, and he in fact brought in only two of them, the normal reason for adding a member to bring in a bill – that the person originally entrusted with the duty is not available on the right day[3] – cannot apply. Therefore it appears that Smith, and probably many like him, had come up from the country only on the 29th, when the last day for receiving private petitions had been 26 January.

Amongst the members regularly appearing while we still have the names of private bill committees, before 1769, are the chairman of ways and means and the two joint secretaries to the Treasury. During his tenure of the latter office, Nicholas Hardinge frequently took the chair of committee of the whole House on public bills and also picked up and saw through the lower House uncontroversial private bills, particularly naturalisation and name bills coming down from the Lords. He was thus fulfilling all the functions exercised at that time in the

---

[1] In 1760 voices were ordered for the Tamworth Road bill, 33 Geo. II c. 41, though no opposition had appeared, but not for the Kidderminster Road bill 33 Geo. II c. 50 which was petitioned against and for which counsel were ordered.
[2] *The House of Commons, 1754–90*, ed. L. B. Namier and J. Brooke (London, 1964).
[3] On two occasions in 1758, members were added to the gentlemen who were to invite a preacher to deliver a sermon or return thanks for one! (*CJ* xxviii, 26, 260.)

upper House by the Lord Chairman of committees. But it was
the chairman of ways and means who was ultimately recognised
as the Commons equivalent of the Lord Chairman. From at
least 1754 the chairman of ways and means had received a
secret service salary of £500,[1] which by 1840 had increased to
£1,000; he was then awarded an addition of a further £500 and
the assistance of counsel in order to take on the duty of scrutinis-
ing all private bills. He was to be chairman of all committees
on unopposed bills and he, together with one of the members
in charge of the bill, were to constitute a quorum.[2] Thus the
Commons achieved a situation similar to that obtaining in the
Lords from at least the late eighteenth century. But it may be
that the orders of 1840 regularised a procedure that had
previously existed informally, and which perhaps had been lost
sight of during the extreme congestion of business in the early
nineteenth century. In 1797, the speaker was lamenting 'the
great want of an efficient Chairman of Ways and Means to
look at the Public Bills'.[3] The chairman of ways and means and
the secretaries to the Treasury were accustomed to working
together: 'The proper officers bring in the estimates; it is taken
for granted that they are necessary and frugal; the members go
to dinner and leave Mr. West and Mr. Martin to do the rest.'[4]
One wonders how often these three found themselves alone in
the private committee rooms, as well as in the House.

A Commons committee on a bill, after second reading, was
required by standing order to give seven days notice of its
meeting. (Here again, as with the order for printing, the
requirement was never applied to naturalisation bills.) By the
end of the century, proceedings on an unopposed bill could be
speeded up by arranging for the clerk to prepare the report
during the necessary seven days before the committee met, so
that the report might be made to the House the same day.[5]
We do not know when eighteenth-century committees met, so it
is not possible to tell how often this device was used. But again

[1] Above, p. 91.   [2] *Private Bill Procedure*, i, 93 and ii, 133.
[3] *Diary of Charles Abbot, Lord Colchester*, i, 116.
[4] Lord Chesterfield, 1759, cited in Henry Roseveare, *The Treasury* (London, 1969),
pp. 89–90.   [5] *Solicitor's Instructor*, p. 44.

we remember that Courthope's minute book of 1696 contains two different types of entry – some are real minutes and some simply draft reports.

Another way of speeding up proceedings in use at the end of the century was to ask the ingrossing clerk to begin work before the bill was reported; this made it possible to take third reading the day after the report was made.[1] This we can check from the *Journal*. At least a dozen private bills received this treatment in 1763. It is also noticeable from the 1760s that ingrossed bills from the Lords are sent straight from the Commons committee back to the other House in one movement, unless they had been amended in committee, thus not only speeding up but actually eliminating three stages – that the report lie on the table, that the bill be read a third time, and that it pass.

Thus in very many ways the procedure of both Houses changed gradually during the eighteenth century, without any change in standing orders and without any formal motions for the purpose. Purely personal bills were always exempted from the formalities of printing and notice of committee. Other unopposed bills gradually developed a less cumbersome procedure of their own, although the rules could always be invoked if opposition appeared. We shall see that similar developments in the practice of the house occurred, unannounced, to safeguard parties affected by more controversial measures, long before standing orders were made for the purpose.[2]

Perhaps typically, in spite of all these changes, one really ancient ritual was still regularly enacted. We have seen that Ellis, writing in 1799, was very little concerned about getting the correct quorum for a committee; by contrast he did worry about getting the bill carried up to the Lords. It was essential to 'procure the attendance of eight members' at third reading if the bill was to go up the same day.[3] This ancient rule had been relaxed only to the extent that if the member in charge of the bill was not able to carry it, it was no longer necessary to get a special order of the House to substitute another name;

---

[1] *Solicitor's Instructor*, p. 45.   [2] Below, pp. 141–2.   [3] *Solicitor's Instructor*, p. 51.

even this relaxation had not come about in the 1760s when such orders are frequent. In the upper House, the lord chancellor still went through the ritual of tramping up and down the chamber to receive each bill from the Commons individually. In 1847 it was calculated that, in receiving fifty-one bills on one day, the chancellor walked 1,670 yards, taking forty-four minutes to do so, although 'he walked as quickly as he could'.[1]

Before turning to a more detailed examination of some of the subjects dealt with by private bill procedure, it is necessary to say something of the nature of the evidence of the bills themselves. We have seen that, by standing orders of the Houses, private bills, including all local bills, were required to be printed at the expense of the parties at an early stage in the parliamentary process. Public bills were not to be printed except by specific order of either House; the practice of printing controversial public bills became common from about 1740 and the number of orders to print increased steadily thereafter. Copies of private and public bills so printed by standing or special order, are to be found in local record offices and in the great libraries. Estate and inclosure bills have survived in great numbers; the British Museum set of this category, though wrongly called 'Private Acts', is complete from 1728. Local bills, those for roads, rivers and so forth, are not nearly so commonly found; I know of no complete series.[2]

Many printers, both local and metropolitan and the King's Printer himself, shared the work of printing private bills.[3] The House printer, Luke Hansard, naturally engaged in this work in the nineteenth century as Richardson had done in the eighteenth.[4] After the bills had become acts, however, the

---

[1] HC (705) 1847, qu. 2485.

[2] A list of extant printed copies of bills for the first half of the century is to be found in my *List of House of Commons Sessional Papers, 1701–50* (List & Index Society, 1968), but no attempt is there made to establish what stage the printed bills represent.   [3] Lords committee on fees, 1827, *LJ* lix, 568, 573.

[4] *Clerical Organization*, p. 183. W. E. Tate referred to Hansard as King's Printer (*The English Village Community and the Enclosure Movements* (London, 1967) p. 103; hereafter cited as *English Village Community*). This Hansard never was, but on the contrary had a long-standing feud with that gentleman. Hansard was the last man in the world to infringe the King's Printer's prerogative of printing acts; to have dared to do so would most seriously have jeopardised his moral position in their running fight. See P. and G. Ford, *Luke Graves Hansard, His Diary*, passim.

position was quite different, for the King's Printer was emphatic that his patent gave him the exclusive right to print acts of all kinds 'the copyright being vested in him' and insisted that 'our Grant gives us the exclusive right to sell as well as to print'.[1] Under the terms of his patent the King's Printer issued the texts of all truly public, and of some local, acts, but private acts were never printed at all before 1798.[2] No official text of them exists except in the original acts in the House of Lords Record Office. But they were printed as bills, perhaps at more than one stage, and these printed copies are often entitled 'Acts'.

Such printed copies may be unique pieces of evidence, for any bills beginning in the Commons. They are not so important for bills beginning in the Lords since in that case the original paper bill may be among the Lords 'main papers'; if not, the Lords committee book will usually show what changes were made there; and the ingrossed bill will show any changes made in the Commons. But if a bill began in the Commons, the original act will show the text of the bill as it was ingrossed, after report stage in the Commons, and any amendments made thereafter, but it cannot show amendments made before ingrossment: that is, at the most important stage – in committee of the house of origin. Since amendments made in committee are not set out in the *Commons Journal*, surviving bills printed at first or second reading stage are the only source for such amendments. It is therefore essential to the study of any particular piece of legislation to establish what parliamentary stage a printed copy represents.

The standing orders did not specify how many copies of private bills were to be printed. In 1717, 500 copies of the Duke of Rutland's bill [No. 1] were printed before the Lords committee met and this perhaps represents the usual practice at the beginning of the century. In 1794 it was ordered that canal bills must be reprinted as amended after the committee stage, and although this order was not extended to other types of bill until 1855,[3] it is clear that reprinting was becoming common long before that date. Of the River Weaver bill in

---

[1] HC (373) 1810, p. 205.

[2] For further details on the promulgation of the statutes see chapter 9.

[3] *Private Bill Procedure*, i, 44, 266; ii, 236.

Private bill procedure

1727, 300 copies were printed before second reading in the
Commons, and an unspecified number (from the price,
probably 450) were reprinted at third reading, to include the
copies needed then and also for the House of Lords and afterwards for the use of the commissioners to be appointed under
the Act.[1] Some of Harper's later copies are ominously marked
'last edition' and it is to be feared that the earlier printed versions
were destroyed. In the 1760s agents' accounts show that it was
usual to print only a small number of copies initially and to
reprint as required during the passage of the bill.[2]

The *Method of Proceedings* does not specify how many copies
were to be delivered for a bill beginning in the Lords but
remarks that most were wasted: 'as few Lords attend, few of the
Bills are disposed of, but kept by the Doorkeepers who sell
them in Lots every Session.'[3] By the end of the century, Ellis
states that only twelve copies need be given to the doorkeepers
of either House at first reading, but that fifty copies should be
given to each (not for the House, but as their perquisite) after
the act was passed.[4] Thus what had begun as the doorkeepers'
appropriation of unwanted copies had developed by the end
of the century to a regular system of perquisites of settled
amount.

The agents' accounts of the 1760s indicate that, by that time,
while controversial bills were reprinted many times and in
great numbers, it was usual to print only sixty or seventy copies
of most local bills for the Commons, and this probably only
when the copies were immediately wanted for the use of the
committee.[5] Later, 200 more copies were usually printed and
the other evidence suggests that some of these would be used
for the formal proceedings in the Lords and for the committee
stage there, some would be wanted for the use of commissioners
and others in the locality and 100 went to the doorkeepers of
the two Houses. The copies reprinted at this stage would be

[1] Below, pp. 157–60.
[2] Above, p. 48. The type was kept standing HC (648) 1833 qu. 1970.
[3] *Method of Proceedings*, p. 21.   [4] *Solicitor's Instructor*, pp. 51, 56.
[5] See above, p. 48. Not many of the accounts show dates of printing and one cannot rely very much on month dates only, but some of the bills had begun well
before the ostensible date of printing.

entitled 'Acts' not 'Bills',[1] and were so nearly perfect that the doorkeepers and some of the clerks built up a regular clientele to whom they sold what they quite improperly called 'Setts of Acts' each session.[2]

These printed copies of bills may therefore represent the correct text of the act as passed. If necessary, copies could be certified by the Parliament Office and would then be perfectly satisfactory for use by the commissioners appointed to execute them. They are satisfactory for the use of historians only if it is remembered how they came into being. It may be a counsel of perfection to say that such printed copies should never be used, as the texts of acts, except for 'the most casual reference';[3] by the end of the century many do embody reasonably correct texts,[4] but it is not possible to guess whether this is the case or not.[5] Strictly, all such printed bills should be checked with the original act in the House of Lords, or (for local bills), with an officially printed version,[6] before it is assumed that they do represent the act as passed.

---

[1] 'You must have your printed Acts as passed the Lords', *Method of Proceedings*, p. 23. 'The Bill, which is now entitled an Act, is brought up', *Solicitor's Instructor*, p. 52.

[2] Com. Bk., 5 July 1797. The King's Printer could not afford to offend the clerks, and since what they were selling were not really 'Acts', he would have had to wink at this encroachment.

[3] M. F. Bond, *The Records of Parliament* (London, 1964), p. 6.

[4] This no doubt misled W. E. Tate, who was willing to rely entirely upon copies of 'Acts' found locally and who gave much very unfortunate advice on how to find and use such copies. (*Nottinghamshire Parliamentary Enclosures* (Nottingham, Thoroton Soc. 1935), pp. 8–16, largely reprinted in *English Village Community*, pp. 93–104.) To deal briefly with the more important points: the statute roll ceased to exist in the reign of Edward IV and the texts of private acts are to be found in complete series only in HLRO. It is absolutely true that many private acts were never printed, the standing orders that *bills* should be printed being quite irrelevant to this point. It is only after 1815 (not 1798) that inclosure acts were officially printed in any considerable numbers and distributed to the clerks of the peace, but even after that a few remained unprinted. The only correct and convenient place from which to take the title of an unprinted act is from the Table of the Statutes attached to the King's Printer's sessional set of acts, which includes all titles, whether or not the texts are printed. The examples of parliamentary forms which Tate printed from the *Journals* are very inaccurate in detail.

[5] An examination of some sample years, near the end of the century, in the 'Salt Collection' of 'Private Acts' in the Cambridge University Library shows that, although the printed copies all look very much alike, some do, and some do not, embody the amendments made in the second House.

[6] An officially printed version will always carry the King's Printer's imprint.

To study any particular piece of legislation, it is obviously essential to have the correct text of the act as finally passed. If one can also find a printed copy of the bill as originally introduced, so much the better; even if the bill were introduced in the Lords, so that the paper 'house copy' of the bill survives in the House of Lords Record Office, a printed bill may contain variants; if the bill was introduced in the Commons, a copy printed before the committee stage will contain unique evidence of the intentions of its promoters. Such a printed bill will assist with understanding, and itself be illuminated by, the *Journals*, the original acts, and (if one is lucky) the Lords main papers and committee books.

6

ESTATE BILLS

Not unnaturally, the greater part of Robert Harper's practice was concerned with that 'most notable achievement of the conveyancers',[1] the classical strict settlement. Although the papers themselves have not survived, his indexes show that Harper drew innumerable agreements of this kind, as well as the attendant conveyances, wills and mortgages relating to his clients' lands. These agreements were protected by the courts and did not require legislation;[2] indeed, so well were they protected that legislation was often needed to unsettle them, and thus arose the eighteenth-century private estate acts. It says much for the conservatism of landed families that, just as they felt obliged to 'continue in the tradition of re-settlement',[3] they did not even more often resort to procedure by private act, which was cheap, expeditious and very effective.

Very little work has been done on the contents of these acts, although they contain information which must be of importance for local and economic history.[4] It is to be wished that they could be analysed in geographical groupings, taking into account the local and inclosure acts for the same time and place. It will often be found that a landlord intent on developing his own estate by private act will be taking the lead in inclosure and other measures in his locality. The petitioners cover a wide social range, from the greatest landowners to country rectors and small gentry; the condition of their lands, the state of their rent rolls and of their debts, and their relations with

---

[1] A. W. B. Simpson, *An Introduction to the History of the Land Law* (Oxford, 1961), p. 220.

[2] For an outline of the history of the strict settlement and the procedures usually followed see *ibid.*, pp. 213–24.

[3] G. E. Mingay, *English Landed Society in the Eighteenth Century* (London, 1963), p. 34.

[4] M. F. Bond, 'Estate Acts of Parliament', *History*, xlix (1964), 325–8. At the simplest level, the preambles to these acts frequently give comprehensive, and proven, genealogical information, which may be quite difficult to obtain from other sources.

their families all emerge from the evidence of the estate bill procedure. Very personal information concerning individuals otherwise unknown to history may be given in the petitions and the acts themselves: we know that Robert Harper became senile in his last years only because the fact was mentioned in a judges' report. We cannot here explore the question of the contents of the acts, but shall be concerned with the procedure by which they came into being, a matter that has also received no attention from historians.

Almost any difficulty arising in the management of a settled estate could be remedied by act: 'It would be utterly impossible to enumerate the variety of cases in which private acts of Parliament may be obtained.'[1] In the courts, an entail could be broken by a tenant in possession joining with his eldest son in the fictitious action of recovery,[2] but this was not possible if a tenant for life was childless; or, the family might miss a valuable opportunity to re-organise their property if there were a son but he was not of age when the occasion arose. Then, although the best-drawn settlements gave the life tenant wide powers to lease, exchange, or even to sell the settled lands, many were badly drawn and too restrictive to meet changing economic conditions.[3] All such restrictions could be set aside by private act in the interests of good management of the estate: land in the neighbourhood of growing towns might be sold for building; timber might be cut and minerals exploited; dispersed estates might be consolidated to facilitate inclosure.

If it was desired to continue a strict settlement, re-settlement usually took place on the marriage of the eldest son,[4] but if the son were under age at the time of his marriage he could not enter into a valid agreement. Similarly an infant or a lunatic in possession of an estate was not permitted to engage

---

[1] William Cruise, *A Digest of the Laws of England respecting Real Property*, 3rd ed. 6 vols. (London, 1824), v, 4. Cruise's volume v contains his 'Title 33. Private Act' which will be hereafter cited by paragraphs. Paras. 12–19 summarise some of the more usual reasons for estate acts. George Bramwell, *An Analytical Table of the Private Statutes* (London, 1813), supplies brief descriptions of all private acts, 1727–1812, with indexes.

[2] And as we shall see, below pp. 122–3, even in such cases procedure by act might be cheaper than procedure by recovery. [3] Simpson, *Land Law*, p. 223.

[4] On the vital importance of marriage settlements to the preservation of estates see Mingay, *English Landed Society*, pp. 30–2.

in many transactions which might otherwise have been permitted to a tenant for life under a well-drawn settlement. If an estate had run into debt to the extent that the income could no longer meet the interest, nothing could be saved from the wreck if there was no power to sell or mortgage. All these difficulties could be met by a private estate act and by that method only.

Estate bills usually began in the House of Lords and were there referred to the judges before their introduction in the House. This procedure was evidently important and real, even though the party's attorney was expected to draw the judges' report. In 1724 the judges appointed to consider Lord Barrymore's bill [No. 13] were changed because 'Lord Chief Justice King being made Speaker of the House of Lords would not have time to go on with the reference'. Harper's opinion of the judges was not always complimentary. On the Duchess of Portland's petition [No. 26] he observed that the Lord Chief Baron 'insisted that Lord George Bentinck (Tho' he was an infant and his Mother & Guardian was Petitioner on his behalf) should sign both the petition and the Bill. Yet he never objected that the Petition was for one purpose and the Bill for another.' In 1742, Harper angrily noted some changes in Bentley's bill [No. 205] which could not properly be inserted 'without embarrassing the sense and confounding the narration' but which were insisted on by Lord Chief Justice Willes and Mr Justice Fortescue Aland because they 'could not comprehend' the method Harper thought correct. In 1740 four printed pages of Conyers' bill [No. 169] were re-drawn by the judges, whose opinion was afterwards reversed in committee of the House.

The importance of procedure before the judges is emphasised by the number of acts finally passed which had been petitioned for but never introduced in a previous session. This applies to about forty of Harper's estate acts.[1] Probably most of them

[1] It is tempting, but probably unwise, to claim that most of these failed when they were not in Harper's hands and succeeded when he was given charge of them. There is some evidence to this effect. Harper's volumes, being made up currently, give the petitions for bills in the year in which he drew them, whether or not they passed. A very small number of bills appear twice in his list, having

had been started prematurely and had to be withdrawn because the necessary formalities could not be complied with in time, as for instance in the case of the Duke of Kent's bill [No. 33] in 1729 (though this bill did pass), when 'the Duke of Kent insisted that Lord Glenorchy should be a petitioner on the behalf of his Daughter. So the title of the petition was altered ... and because of this alteration we were forced to stay till Lord Glenorchy returned from Denmark and signed the petition. Tho' the Judges would have passed it upon the first petition.' Only once have we direct evidence of an alteration by the judges which caused the loss of a bill: in 1729 on Margaret Goddard's petition [following No. 38] to permit building leases of her estate, 'the Judges signed this Report and the Bill, But they declaring their opinion that the Leases made by the power should be for 60 years only, the petitioners thought no body would build on so short terms and therefore proceeded no further in the Bill'.

If a petition for a bill failed, or was withdrawn, at the stage of reference to the judges, it paid virtually no parliamentary fees, so it was probably worth while to proceed with a petition even if it was doubtful if all the necessary signatures could be got in time to proceed with the bill, rather than have to go to the trouble of petitioning for leave to proceed out of time. Moreover, if there were any doubtful points about a petition, the judges' opinion could be obtained at relatively little cost,[1] so improving the bill's chances of a smooth passage the next session.

The other forms of the House of Lords did not impede the work of an agent. As the *Method of Proceedings* puts it, if a bill

---

failed one year and been redrawn the next. Most of the bills which failed before the judges appear in Harper's papers only in the second session, when they were successful. In Bulstrode's case [No. 369] the first petition for leave to proceed out of time, in 1750, stated that he had employed 'an Agent to get the same prepared', but because of the agent's illness this had not been done. Harper's draft of this petition [following No. 357] shows that the 'agent' was in fact Benjamin Periam, who was Bulstrode's father-in-law. In spite of Harper taking over, this bill failed in 1750 but was reintroduced and passed the next year.

[1] From the evidence of the accounts in Ellis's *Solicitor's Instructor* and for the Duke of Rutland's bill [No. 1] the reference appears to have cost a little over £30 including the cost of three fair copies of the bill at £5 each.

any ways interferes with any standing order of the House that is usually dispensed with; you must draw a Case to shew the Reasons for Dispensation, and give it to a Lord, to move that the Lords may be summon'd to take the Matter into Consideration, which will be ordered for the next or some short Day, when upon reading the Order of the Day, the Lord who made the motion is called upon to give his Reasons for a Dispensation; upon which it is ordered accordingly, if the House thinks it reasonable.[1]

Towards the end of a session the standing order that there should be fourteen days notice of the meeting of a committee was frequently dispensed with. The Lords strict orders concerning exchange of settled lands were more rarely set aside, but no petition for such a dispensation was refused; the number of such requests increased markedly in 1760–1 which suggests that the revision of 1762 was caused by a breakdown of the system.

The sessional order setting a final date for the receipt of private petitions was usually observed but requests that petitions might be received out of time were freely accepted and for a wide variety of reasons: a cursitor of Chancery in Ireland was newly appointed [No. 426]; widows pleaded that their husbands had not died in time [Nos. 432, 450]; 'the great floods ... and violence of the season' prevented the signing of the petition [No. 131] or inundated the land to be exchanged 'so that a proper Survey could not be taken thereof' [No. 448]; the parties lived at a great distance from one another [Nos. 422, 479]; the party was ill [No. 405]; the agent was ill [No. 369]; or the petition was sent to the wrong address [No. 496]. The Onslow family were at one another's throats and there was no hope of 'preserving peace and Amity in the family' unless they could proceed at once with the compromise just laboriously arranged [No. 520]. The Earl of Powis [No. 363] and the Duke of Kingston [No. 518] did not deign to offer any excuse at all, and Samuel Harper, as agent, said simply that he had not received his client's instructions in time.[2] In 1749 Speaker Sir William Lee ruled that a petition to proceed out of time must include the recital of the petition for the bill itself;[3]

[1] Pp. 21–2.   [2] *LJ* xxix, 255.   [3] BM 357. d. 5 (p. 20).

it is not clear that this could serve any real purpose except to increase expense, but Harper was careful to observe the rule thereafter [e.g. No. 432].

Once past the judges and given a first reading very few estate bills failed – only ten out of Harper's total of over 400 estate bills suffered this fate. Five of these dropped in committee of the Lords [Nos. 41, 105, 147, 226, 376] and one in committee of the Commons [No. 300]. Since these bills dealt with very personal matters, a party's circumstances might be changed by domestic events so that the bill was not proceeded with. In Garrard's case, for instance [No. 293], Thomas Garrard, one of the parties, died while the bill was before the judges. His sons obtained leave to proceed with the bill, but there must have been occasions on which a death in the family made it unnecessary or undesirable to go ahead with the original scheme.

We know that Delahay's bill of 1743 [No. 226] was dropped because the party changed his mind, and this may have been the case with other bills also. This bill was to enable the sale of settled lands in Herefordshire pursuant to a decree in Chancery. Mr Clark, one of the parties, tried to include in the bill some pieces of land belonging to his family under the will which were not covered by the decree, but since the clauses were

offered within a few days before the end of the Session. And it was doubtful whether the Committee of the Lords (for it was proposed to be offered to the Committee by way of amendment) would receive such an amendment unless it had been previously referred to the Judges. And as Mr. Clark would not give his Consent at the Comittee unless these Clauses were in the Bill, The Bill was dropt & never came before ye Comittee.

Lord Irwin's bill of 1756 [No. 479] was rejected on third reading after the judges had been summoned to attend the House, but a very similar bill passed without amendment the following year [No. 491]. Three bills were lost when opponents appeared asking to be heard by counsel [Nos. 6, 94, 395]. The first of these concerned the estate of John Addison, a lunatic, whose brother petitioned in 1721 for power to administer his estate. The judges did not report until very late in the session, whereupon four opponents claiming to be 'very much concerned in the consequences of the Bill' appeared and the bill dropped. The following session George Addison petitioned again, trying to avoid another reference to the judges by the ingenuous claim that the previous bill had dropped only 'by reason it was apprehended there would not be sufficient time in the session for the passing thereof'. However, the bill was referred to the same judges and passed very rapidly through the Lords by 20 December. In the Commons it had reached committee stage when the four sisters of George and John Addison appeared, claiming that there was no provision to save their right to the remainder of the estate in the bill, which had been introduced 'without their privity or consent'. Their petition was referred to the committee which nevertheless reported in favour of the bill without any amendment. The bill was then abruptly rejected at third reading, probably in a very thin house, and no more was heard of the case. Harper remarked that the decision was reached 'on the false supposition that the Fines and Recoveries suffered by the Lunatic did not bar the remainders in tail'.[1]

But although not many bills failed, the Lords committee investigated proposals with some care and sometimes made substantial amendments, for instance as to borrowing [Nos. 5, 14] or investment [No. 24] powers. The Earl of Warwick once adjourned a committee to consult the lord chancellor about the equivalent for certain settled lands [No. 313] and as a result the bill was recommitted to amend the preamble. Even bills coming from the Commons were scrutinised both by the judges and the Lords committee. In one case the judges found a misrecital [No. 82], and in another the bill was found to contravene the Lords standing orders on exchange of settled lands [No. 83]; so power under the bill to sell was reduced to power to lease only. But instances of substantial amendment are relatively rare. The majority of Harper's estate bills were not amended at all by either House, even though the necessary filling of blanks was counted as amendment for the purpose of reporting a committee.

[1] BM BS Ref. 2. bound following 7 Geo. I pr. c. 11.

If minor difficulties arose bills were not thrown out, but the Lords committee would adjourn, as they did for instance on 22 February 1725 on the Guy's Hospital bill, giving notice to the trustees 'to advise with Counsel in the mean time'. An adjournment was sometimes allowed to an objector even though he had not gone through the proper formalities [No. 369]. The *Lords Journal* sometimes gives the impression that committees were dilatory in dealing with bills, but the committee books show that this was often the fault of the parties: Westby's bill [No. 52] was adjourned several times because the necessary consents were not ready. Moreover, the benefit of an act could be felt even before it was passed. Edward Bulstrode, himself solvent, became heir to an encumbered estate; he hastened to introduce a bill [No. 369] but meanwhile the vultures gathered so that while the bill was in committee 'the Petitioner is apprehensive of being arrested by some of his creditors, the Fear of which will prove a Hindrance to him in prosecuting the said Bill'. The privilege of freedom from arrest for debt was promptly extended to him.

A case whose interest is chiefly its unusual features and that we for once have a fairly full account of it from various sources, nevertheless illustrates several of these points [No. 30].

Sir John Wittewronge in the year 1721 had the misfortune in a Sudden quarrel with one Joseph Griffith at the Saracen's Head Inne in Newport Pagnell in the County of Bucks to give the said Joseph Griffith a Wound with a sword of which Wound he soon after dyed. And the said Sir John Wittewronge shortly after the said accident left the Kingdom and still resides in foreign parts.

This Sir John, the fourth baronet of the name, was the son of the late M.P. for Wycombe, the eldest of five legitimate and two illegitimate brothers.[1] At the time of this unfortunate 'fact' as our papers call it, Sir John was twenty-six; he had served in the army. His victim is variously described as 'a mountebank' or 'a Surgeon of Chatham'. After some years Sir John returned to England and died, unmarried, in 1744, in a debtors' prison, of wounds received in a drunken brawl.[2]

[1] *Notes & Queries*, 8th ser. ii, 13.
[2] George Lipscombe, *A History of Buckinghamshire* (4 vols. 1847), iv, 347. *V.C.H. Bucks.*, iv, 464.

Some six months after the murder of Griffith, occurred the death of Sir John's father, the third baronet, and it is from his will that the need for a private act arose. The first baronet, a creation of Charles II, was the son of a brewer from Ghent, but was brought up in London by his stepfather, Alderman Sir Thomas Midleton. The first baronet married his own half-sister, became member of parliament and sheriff of Hertfordshire and purchased the estate of Stanton Berry in Buckinghamshire.[1] The Stanton property was strictly settled and was twice re-settled, the second time upon the marriage in 1696 of the second baronet. At the time of the murder, perhaps because of it, the fourth baronet could no longer hope to live in England, he joined with his father in suffering a recovery to bar the entail, and the third Sir John left the estate in his will to trustees to be sold for the payment of debts of £12,000 and legacies to his children of £8,000. A decree in Chancery of 1725 confirmed the sale of the estate to the highest bidder, who turned out to be Sarah, Dowager Duchess of Marlborough, Sir Matthew Lamb making, on her behalf, a bid of £21,600 'having a deduction for all outgoings' – a net sum of £20,714. But unfortunately, the words of the third baronet's will did not vest the fee simple of the property in his trustees, so that they could not convey a good title, and the duchess, very rightly, would not proceed without one.

So a private act was necessary and here the murder introduced a difficulty, for all private acts contained a clause saving the King's right, and although the fourth baronet 'hath not yet been indicted outlawed or attainted for the said fact But as the same was committed before the said Recovery was suffered It is apprehended that in case he should hereafter be attainted That part of the Estate which was comprized in the Recovery may be forfeited to your Majesty'. The King agreed that the bill might contain an exception to the general saving. Harper's office worked hard on a draft speech for the Duke of Newcastle to use when he conveyed this information to the House on 11 April.[2]

[1] *V.C.H. Herts.*, ii, 36.

[2] This was rather late, since the bill was already in committee. The King's consent to any bill affecting royal estates or interests was usually signified at or before second reading. Lords committees would not report without it. But by the end of the century it was often treated as a formality and not given until third reading.

The petition for the bill had been introduced in the Lords on 12 March 1728 and referred to Mr Justice Price and Mr Justice Denton. Leave was given on the judges' report on 22 March and the bill immediately read a first time. On 25 March it was committed for 9 April, the presents being thirty-nine members including ten bishops. The committee met, as ordered, on 9 April with Delawarr as usual presiding, and various documents mentioned in the preamble 'were perused by the Lord in the Chair, and found to be truly recited'. But the Lords were not satisfied that the errant fourth baronet had been properly informed of his position as to the tithes of Stanton, which it was proposed were to pass with the property but which had not been included in the recovery and so might be held to belong to Sir John. One of the Wittewronge brothers and 'another Witness' who had gone with him to Brussels to obtain Sir John's consent to the bill, were not able to say upon oath that 'Sir John was apprized of the State of this Case'. The committee broke off because the House was sitting and next day William Dixon[1] informed the committee 'of an agreement that was drawn up at his Chambers whereby the several Legatees had agreed to give Sir John a consideration for consenting to the Bill'. This turned out to be £500, and 'Mr Middleton Receiver of the Estate Acquainted the Comittee that the Value of the Tythes were not above £40 or £50 a Year, and that £30 yearly was paid to the Vicar, and that he thought £500 was a great deal more than they were worth.' But yet it had not been shown that the compensation was in any way connected with the tithes, or that Sir John understood the position; so the committee left the clause out of the preamble and instructed the parties to adapt the rest of the bill to the preamble before the next meeting. This would not do at all. The committee did not meet pursuant to this adjournment, probably at the request of the parties who were trying to sort out the problem. It was formally revived on the 6th for the 8th of May when one of the brothers, George Wittewronge,

---

[1] Of Lincoln's Inn, admitted 8 March 1699, died 1737. Since he was also a trustee of [No. 4] in which another branch of the Wittewronge family was involved, he presumably was acting for the family. He received a mourning ring in Peniston Lamb's will, above p. 9.

attempted to offer a petition. He was told he must first petition the House, but was asked whether he intended to oppose the bill, since he was nominally a petitioner for it; he said not, but it had occurred to him that he also might get some consideration for his consent. The meeting adjourned to give George time to petition. By Friday of the same week the matter had been cleared up. It had been agreed to compensate George (for what is not clear, and the amount was only 50 guineas) and to buy off Sir John with an increase of £300 on his compensation. Harper had drawn a new form of consent which 'one Salesbury' and 'one Sturgeon' had rushed over to Brussels; they were present at the committee to prove Sir John's signature to the instrument. So the bill went through as it had been drawn, passing the Commons without amendment, and William Dixon and Robert Harper became trustees under the act.

The accounts of their stewardship are not quite complete, but they show that the matter was settled in about twelve months after the act passed. The Duchess of Marlborough paid up on 20 July, and the major debts of the estate, consisting of three mortgages amounting to nearly £9,000, were immediately discharged. Some smaller debts are specified and some £2,000 was reserved to pay petty debts remaining to be proved in the country and in London. The total came to very little more than the £12,000 specified in the Act and the balance of £8,115 was distributed to the legatees in instalments.[1] Sir John's share came to nearly £1,000 in addition to his £800 compensation; he received £500 in December 1728 and the balance at the rate of approximately £100 a month.

The two trustees naturally figure in the account:

Mr Dixon his Bill of Costs of Suites & Disbursements about the Act of Parliament £419. 8. 0.

Mr Harper his bill for the Act of Parlt. & other charges £259. 15. 6.

[1] There is one curiosity in the accounts of Martha and George Wittewronge. £75 and £52 10s respectively of the amounts due to them were paid in cash to Orlando Hamlyn, Zachary Hamlyn's younger brother, filacer of the Court of Common Pleas. Unfortunately we have no information on the reason for these payments. On Zachary Hamlyn see above, pp. 39–40.

These sums cannot be considered excessive in view of the trouble involved; amongst other things they must somewhere include the cost of the various journeys to Brussels. Yet even so, taken together they represent hardly more than 3% on the capital value of the estate.

It is clear that if the formalities were complied with and the parties in agreement, the House of Lords was an efficient machine for private estate legislation. In matters for which the courts could provide no remedy, if the parties agreed, parliament would rubber-stamp the agreement, making possible a good title to land to be conveyed. The procedure was swift as well as efficient. The Archbishop of York got his son's marriage settlement through from first petition to royal assent in precisely six weeks [No. 9]. While this is, understandably, exceptionally quick, no parliamentary session lasted eight months and most were less than six; to anyone accustomed to Chancery cases this must have seemed almost indecent haste. In 1737, the first three of Harper's nine estate bills [Nos. 123–31] were petitioned for on 9 and 16 February; the first of them went to the Commons on 30 March and received the royal assent on 22 April despite a ten-day Easter recess. The others, started between 21 February and 24 March were assented to on 21 June. This rate of progress was normal in Harper's lifetime and speeded up later in the century.

A private act once passed bound only the parties consenting to it and those claiming under them who were mentioned by name; the rights of all other persons were unaffected. Since these were quite private matters it was possible to identify all the parties concerned, and the rules of the House of Lords made certain that all were consulted and had an opportunity to voice opposition. If parties legally incapable of giving consent were concerned, the Lords ensured that their interests were protected. But if parties with very remote interests could or would not give consent, the Lords, like the courts, would set aside such claims in the general interest of those more nearly concerned.

By standing orders it was strictly required that all remaindermen, however remote their interests (who might be many and perhaps not even identifiable), should attend and give their consents to a private bill, but this requirement was dispensed with if it could be shown that their rights could be barred by a recovery. An opinion given by James Booth in 1764 is held to have settled this question. The Duke of Kingston wished to sell lands vested in him by his agreement with Lord Gower, confirmed by a private act of 1759 [No. 518].[1] The prospective purchaser raised objection to the title because the remaindermen had not given consent before the House of Lords.[2] Having emphasised that non-observance of standing orders could not affect the validity of an act once passed, since either House could dispense with its own orders at any time, Booth maintained that there was in fact no irregularity in this case. Since the parties were

obliged to go to Parliament, they were advised, and rightly advised, that to suffer four recoveries (for the lands lay in four counties) would be to go to a needless expense: for that in a case where parliamentary assistance was, on other accounts, absolutely necessary, there the Parliament would so frame their words, which were to become a law, as to have the same force and operation and to bar all rights that would be barred by a common recovery. 'Frustra fit per plura quo fieri potest per pauciora' is the rule of equity, reason and good sense; and it is no wonder that the gentleman whom these noble lords thought fit to consult upon this occasion should govern himself thereby, especially as in his own experience, which is known to be very great, he had seen frequent instances of the parliament's having passed bills of this kind.[3]

Booth[4] has been described as 'the father of the modern school of conveyancing',[5] but in parliamentary matters he relied upon Robert Harper. The precedent Booth mentions for the Duke of Kingston's case is an act with which he was himself con-

[1] A summary of the details of the transaction may be found in Cruise, *Digest*, para. 34.
[2] Harper made a note of the objection inside the docket of his copy of the bill, BS Ref. 2.
[3] Anon. *Cases, with Opinions of Eminent Counsel* (2 vols., 1791), ii, 412. The allusion is certainly to Robert Harper.
[4] James Booth, d. 1778. He practised as a conveyancer because, as a roman catholic, he could not be called to the bar. His conveyances set a fashion for a great part of the century, their fault being that they were 'remarkably prolix'. (*D.N.B.*)   [5] Anon., *Law & Lawyers* (2 vols., 1840), ii, 84.

cerned, for the sale of the Earl of Stamford's estate [No. 277] in 1747: 'that matter was, by my direction, laid before Mr. Harper first, and he drew a rough draft of the bill'.[1] But Harper had long since noticed the point and had precedents going much further back. The largest group of entries in his index of special cases refers to this very important point of 'A remote and all subsequent remainders in tail barred by Act of Parliament without a recovery'. The Duke of Kingston's case is the last of ten such precedents, the earliest being in 1732 [No. 58].

Booth's opinion was confirmed by Lord Chancellor Apsley in 1771 in the case of *Westby* v. *Kiernan*;[2] thus the development of procedure by private act, to some extent at least directly attributable to Harper's work, made this method superior to, and even noticeably cheaper than, existing procedure, even in those cases where the parties were in a position to proceed through the courts. As Booth remarked, 'who is aggrieved here? I know not, unless the clerk in the prothonotaries office, or the tipstaff of the court of common pleas, who may complain of having unjustly lost their fees.'[3]

Procedure by private estate bill can certainly not be considered unduly expensive. The 1732 committee on fees aired the complaint that 'the extravagant payments for Bills which pass in Parliament to Counsel, Solicitors and other persons without doors is equal to the charge of the fees, which in a Single Bill that passes without opposition amounts to about £60 ...'.[4] But a total of £120 can only be considered a small matter for the larger estates in comparison to the benefit to be obtained by, for instance, making building leases on the outskirts of a growing industrial city.[5]

---

[1] *Cases, with Opinions*, ii, 415.
[2] Cruise, *Digest*, paras. 35, 36. Westby's act was [No. 52].
[3] *Cases, with Opinions*, ii, 416.   [4] *Clerical Organization*, p. 307.
[5] It is not easy to make any estimate of the value of different estates without a minute study of the papers in each case. Figures more easily available are the schedules of debts appended to many acts. These must be used with some caution (see below, pp. 125–7) but as examples:

No. 203	£7,166	No. 243	£29,645
No. 235	£5,436	No. 287	£13,001
No. 240	£2,662	No. 309	£12,394

In fact it seems likely that many estate bills cost more than
£120. We have details of Harper's charges only for the Duke
of Rutland's Act [No. 1] for which he can scarcely have been
solely responsible.[1] The account, which was transcribed for
precedent purposes at some later date, totals £445 10s, made
up of £116 for fees of both Houses (the normal fees for a double
bill including incidentals), £35 18s for ingrossing, £16 15s
for printing 500 copies – the bill was a long one, making
twenty-three printed pages. £66 was charged for making
abstracts and other miscellaneous clerical work, twenty
guineas to counsel for 'perusing the bill' and ten to 'Mr
Jodrell's Clerk[2] for methodizing us being ye first we passed'.
The agent's own charges are itemised as £50 for 'drawing the
Act and perusing settlements in relation thereto', and £100
'for trouble and attendance on Mr Webb [Counsel] many
times to settle the Act & for attending Ld. Parker[3] the Judges
& both Houses of Parliament to get the Act passed'. The parliamentary history of this bill suggests that it was the simplest
possible business; it went through unamended. Some of the
high cost is due to its being a double bill, and some probably
to the exalted social standing of the parties.

In 1798, Honeywood's bill,[4] which was a single-fee bill,
cost £378, but it need not have cost more than £300. The basic
house fees and gratuities cost £76, additional small fees £6,
ingrossing £23, printing £22 and procedure before the judges
£31. It is not clear why counsel was employed, but this cost,
in fees and attendances, £40 and the solicitor's fees came to
about £100. So the total, if all had gone smoothly, would have
been £298. But the parties were dilatory and one of the judges
went on circuit; it cost about £10 to get new judges appointed.
Then the party changed his mind about the contents of the
bill and the petition had to be withdrawn; this cost about £8
in additional fees to counsel, £30 in solicitor's fees for re-
drafting, etc., and over £20 because four fair copies of the
first bill had to be scrapped. Finally Lord Chairman Walsing-

---

[1] Above, p. 9.   [2] Presumably Zachary Hamlyn, on whom see above, p. 39.
[3] Thomas Parker, later Earl of Macclesfield, was at this time Chief Justice of
King's Bench. I am not clear how he comes into the story.
[4] The account is printed in Ellis, *Solicitor's Instructor*, see above, p. 94.

ham havered for three days about consents, costing the parties at least £12 more.

The procedure did not escape criticism. In 1781 lord chancellor Thurlow delivered himself of a tirade on the manner in which private bills went through without proper consideration: 'there was a family of the name of Gardiner in Wales which had been stripped of its whole property by the compendious and certain operation of a private bill'.[1] We have seen that procedure in the Lords was in general very careful, but in so great a number of measures some undesirable things were bound to happen sometimes. The cases that are recorded are all of the same kind: the whole, or part, of an estate was to be sold, or mortgaged, to pay debts, the amount of which were falsely stated, so as to put cash into the hands of a life tenant to the detriment of the remaindermen.

The creditor who persuaded David Roberts that a private act [No. 81] was the best way to extricate himself from his embarrassments, first took over most of the debts, written up in a rather doubtful way, and had himself appointed trustee.[2] Most of the estate was sold to a Mrs Middleton, who evidently had good advice and was the only person to come safely out of the transaction, for she insisted that the debts assignable to the property she bought should be separately discharged and the balance only paid over to Richard Eadnell, the trustee. He, however, did not, as he was bound to do, pay

---

[1] *Parl. Hist.*, xxii, 59–60. The only case I can find to which this might refer is that of John Gardner Kemeys, who had added the name of Kemeys under the will of his father-in-law. He, 'having contracted very considerable debts, conceived a plan for extricating himself out of his difficulties' (*CJ* xlix, 269) and by false evidence concerning his estate in Monmouthshire, obtained a private act in 1772 (12 Geo. III pr. c. 93), which effectively disinherited his family. He managed to impose, not only on the legislature, but also on so shrewd an operator as Richard Rigby. His son was given relief by a public act in 1794 (34 Geo. III c. 66) and the dates do not fit very well with Thurlow's statement. Kemeys' son came of age in 1779 and perhaps he then became aware of what had happened and began to seek legal advice as to the remedy, which came to Thurlow's ears. Kemeys senior, the culprit, lived until 1793. The other example given by Thurlow is quite untraceable; even Holdsworth calls this 'another tale' (Holdsworth, xi, 344 n. 5).

[2] Richard Eadnell is described as of the Inner Temple, Gentleman, but although he is said to be a 'member' of that Inn he was apparently a bookseller by profession. (F. A. Inderwick, *A Calendar of the Inner Temple Records* (5 vols. 1896–1937), iv, 197, 402.) Eadnell died in June 1738.

from the balance a debt of £800 due to Mrs Ellen Godolphin who, four years later, petitioned the Lords for redress. A long investigation ensued.[1]

The root of the matter was the way in which the schedule of debts had been originally presented to the judges. The Lords committee on Mrs Godolphin's petition asked Eadnell 'who was the Sollicitor for the Bill' to which he replied 'that Mr Harper drew the Bill and attended the Judges, that he has been with Mr Harper and desired him to search his papers'. Mr Harper was not present but Samuel Harper was holding a watching brief and 'informed the Committee that his brother was at home, and that he was not concerned for Mr Roberts but imploy'd by Mr Eadnell to draw the bill'. Next day 'Mr Harper being present' he was asked 'whether he knows how that Variation happen'd between the Debts wch are mention'd in the Judges Report to be £5500 & the Debts in the Schedule which are £7416'. Mr Harper 'says he cannot tell, he do's not remember any of the particulars at this Distance of time, Since he heard of this Com^{ee} he has search'd among all his papers for the Original Draught of the Bill, but cannot find any, he has found the Original Draught of the Petition, and the foul Draught of the Judges Report with Blanks'.[2] The original paper bill was examined as to some words apparently altered and Mr Harper 'look'd upon the Bill, & said he believ'd the Words (thirteen hundred) are of his Hand Writing, he do's not remember how it happen'd, but says it must be from what appear'd in Proof before the Judges, he is very sure he did not make any alteration in the Bill after it pass'd the Judges'. The committee was apparently satisfied and Harper is not mentioned again in the proceedings. The Lords seem to have decided that there was not much to choose between the contending parties; it was shown that Mrs Godolphin had gone on to have some more rather questionable money dealings with Roberts after the act had passed, and in the event the matter was recommitted for a long day and heard of no more, so that the case does not appear among the legal precedents.

Indeed, it is hard to see what the House of Lords, sitting in

[1] Com. Bk. 29 April, 3, 4, 5, 10, 12 May 1737.   [2] We no longer have these.

its legislative capacity, could have done about it. Booth seems to have held that a grievance created by act of Parliament could be remedied only by another act.[1] This would be true of many public acts and there is at least one instance of the repeal of an inclosure act:[2] this was useful because it took some time to effect an inclosure after the act was passed. But it is hard to imagine a case in which the repeal of a private estate act would have been of any benefit to an aggrieved party; and if the property involved had already been dispersed, repeal could only have caused grave injustice to innocent purchasers. It would not have helped anyone in Roberts' case. In Kemeys' case the plaintiff was, in effect, relieved from public funds, since the only money remaining was by that time absorbed in Richard Rigby's enormous debts to the crown. Consequently the procedure had to be by public act: the repeal of the original private act would have served no purpose at all.

A remedy could, however, be obtained through the courts if money remained in the hands of trustees appointed under an act, the leading case being that of Sir James Mackenzie,[3] decided in 1754.[4] In his act of 1739 [No. 157] Sir James included in the schedule of the debts of his estate two which were 'fictitious and fraudulent' and thus 'misled both the remaindermen and the Legislature'. On appeal to the House of Lords, the trustees were required to repay the amount of the fictitious debts to the estate,[5] and this precedent was afterwards followed in Biddulph's case.[6] None of these families was 'stripped of its property by ... a private bill': they were defrauded by perjury. No method of procedure can give protection if a man, and even a judge, is willing to give false evidence on oath in order to enrich himself at the expense of his heirs.

These estate acts represent more than half of all the private acts passed in the middle third of the eighteenth century and

---

[1] Cruise, *Digest*, para. 49 and see the discussion in Holdsworth, xi, 354–9.
[2] Below, p. 130 n. 2.
[3] Sir James Stuart Mackenzie (1671–1744) was Lord of Session (as Lord Royston) and Lord of Justiciary from 1710, his uncle Roderick having resigned office in his favour. (*The Scots Peerage*, ed. Sir James Balfour Paul (Edin., 1906), iii, 72, 76.)
[4] Holdsworth, xi, 356.   [5] Cruise, *Digest*, para. 51.   [6] *Ibid.*, para. 53.

more than a fifth of the total legislative production, public and private. There is no evidence at all that they took up more than the necessary minimum of time in the Houses or in committee. Nor is there one instance of questions being multiplied beyond those necessary for the basic procedure by three readings, or of any form of obstruction.[1] Although the procedure went on very smoothly the number of acts is of course very great, and one could wish that parliament had found better things to do with its time. One must remember, however, that all the real work of estate legislation was done in the Lords by a procedure essentially judicial and not involving the time of the House.

Some small attempts were made to reduce the number of acts required by general legislation empowering infants, lunatics and married women to deal in property in certain very restricted ways.[2] The clerks were afraid that the first act of this sort would reduce their fees,[3] but none had any very marked effect on the number of bills required. The reasons for estate bills were as various as the petitioners for them, and experience had to be gained before reform could be expected. The slow and halting process by which reforms were achieved, which gradually eliminated the need for private estate bills in the nineteenth century,[4] is sufficient evidence that no such development could have been looked for a century earlier.

---

[1] The same is true of the 357 strictly personal acts which make up more than a quarter of the private and more than 12% of all acts in the same period (1732–62). Divorce bills were the only exception and these form only a tiny proportion of the whole. These and name bills will not be further discussed; on naturalisation bills, see above, pp. 36–9. [2] Holdsworth, xi, 590.
[3] *Clerical Organization*, p. 290. [4] Simpson, *Land Law*, pp. 252–61.

7

INCLOSURE BILLS

The merits or otherwise of the movement to inclose open fields and common land by private act of parliament, which began in the eighteenth century, is still the subject of controversy.[1] The most extreme writers of the anti-inclosure school,[2] notably the Hammonds, based much of their comment on evidence given before parliamentary committees in the nineteenth century, a source which must always be used with caution. They all ignored, or perhaps refused to see, the extent to which the procedure of both Houses, in the eighteenth century, did offer protection to parties affected by proposed inclosures and the attempts made to improve that procedure. Both critics and advocates of inclosure have been inclined to exaggerate the parliamentary costs of inclosing by act.

The Lords, in 1706, promulgated the standing order that private bills were to have a preliminary hearing before the judges, which, as we have seen,[3] had an important effect on estate bills and seems both to have made it certain that the interests of all parties were consulted and also to have avoided charging applicants with parliamentary fees in doubtful cases. But in 1706 inclosure bills had been almost unknown, and although the wording of the order appears to apply to all private bills, it was never in fact applied except to estate bills.[4] At first, all inclosure bills began in the House of Lords, the parties no doubt thinking of them as a sort of extension of

---

[1] The most judicious full treatment remains that by E. C. K. Gonner, *Common Land and Inclosure*, of which a new edition (London, 1966), contains an excellent bibliographical introduction by G. E. Mingay. A good modern study is that by J. D. Chambers and G. E. Mingay, *The Agricultural Revolution, 1750–1880* (London, 1966), especially chapter 4.

[2] Some of the more violent statements are briefly summarised in W. E. Tate, *The English Village Community*, pp. 96–7.   [3] Above, pp. 112–13.

[4] Harper, being so used to the procedure before the judges on his estate bills, noted with surprise on his second inclosure bill [No. 31] that it had not been subjected to this scrutiny.

estate bills, and leave was granted by the House immediately upon the reading of the petition. However, the Lords were not completely indifferent to the development of the inclosure procedure. In 1721, when only four such bills had been offered since 1706, a committee was appointed to consider the procedure,[1] but it failed to meet. In 1733, when a party claimed that he had not had notice of an inclosure affecting his interests,[2] the Lords made an order that, in future, notice of the sitting of their committees should be given in the *London Gazette*,[3] and this order, though not universally observed, was obeyed in some cases without discovering any new opposition to the bills involved.[4]

But meanwhile there had been a new development. In 1727, for the first time, an inclosure petition was offered in the Commons[5] and from 1729 such petitions were for a time offered indifferently in either House. The Commons had long insisted that any bill imposing a charge on the subject must originate with them, and after a test case in 1661 the Lords acquiesced in this arrangement.[6] In 1717 the Commons ordered that petitions for such bills must be committed for investigation before leave was given for a bill, and in 1734 this was made a

[1] *LJ* xxi, 408, 416.
[2] *LJ* xxiv, 226. Richard Powys complained that the Aldham inclosure act, 2 Geo. II pr. c. 25, 'was obtained when the said Richard Powys was a Minor, and out of the Kingdom, neither had he or his guardian Notice of the then intended inclosure'. The act was consequently repealed in part by 6 Geo. II pr. c. 24.
[3] *LJ* xxiv, 226.
[4] The sets of the *Gazette* to which I have access are incomplete, so I have been able to check only a few years. In the three sessions 1739–41 notices appeared in only four cases, out of fifteen inclosure bills

Shipton Moyne	12 Geo. II pr. c. 32	*Gazette* no. 7794
Gt Driffield	14 Geo. II pr. c. 11	*Gazette* no. 7982
Sherston Magna	14 Geo. II pr. c. 13	*Gazette* no. 7985
Chawton	14 Geo. II pr. c. 12	*Gazette* no. 7986

The Driffield and Chawton bills originated in the Commons and passed the Lords without amendment. The other two were amended in the Lords but there is no sign of active opposition.

Notice was given of two of the three inclosure bills that got to the Lords in 1746: Ripon, pr. c. 9 and Kelfield, pr. c. 10, both in *Gazette* no. 8515.

Sherston, Ripon and Kelfield were Harper's bills [Nos. 183, 266, 267]. He also noted the *Gazette* advertisement on [No. 76] and filed *Gazette* no. 7280 with his copy of [No. 91].

[5] Hucklecott, Glos., 13 Geo. I pr. c. 13. *CJ* xx, 779, 792, 797, 802, 811.
[6] *Precedents* (1818 ed.), iii, 115–16.

standing order.[1] It is possible that inclosure bills may 'by construction be considered as imposing a burden on the people',[2] and if they were so regarded they should all have begun in the Commons, the petitions for them being committed under the 1717 order. From 1729 to 1740, without exception, petitions offered in the Commons were so treated,[3] but bills begun in the Lords continued to be accepted and agreed to by the Commons. However, there are signs of tension between the two Houses on the subject of private bill initiation in general.

A bill for building a chapel at Wednesfield, which seems certainly to come within the rules for local acts, was nonetheless passed by the Lords in 1746, only to be rejected at second reading in the Commons; the following year it was introduced in the Commons [No. 301] and became a public act. In 1752 Harper noted that a bill concerning tithes [No. 394] was 'rejected by the House of Commons, because it began in the Lords', but although Harper's note continues 'And the bill as it now stands amended was begun in the house of Commons and passed in 1753' he was in error. Hatsell correctly noted[4] that the second bill [No. 396] 'respecting the very same place and matter', also originated in the Lords. In 1753 the Commons rejected even an estate bill [No. 402] on the ground that it should have begun with them because lands granted by the crown were involved.

Several of these instances are referred to by Hatsell in his long section on matters deemed by the Commons to represent improper 'interference' by the Lords,[5] but he does not isolate the problem of inclosure bills. In 1736 leave was given in the Commons for a Stallingborough inclosure bill [No. 122] but it was not proceeded with; next year it was introduced in the Lords and passed without trouble [No. 132]. In 1744 petitions for the Langton inclosure bill [No. 232] were offered in both Houses within five days of each other, presumably as a precaution on the part of the promoters; the Commons won, and

---

[1] *Private Bill Procedure*, i, 263.   [2] *Ibid.*, 142 n. 4.
[3] Dr Williams is in error on this point, *ibid.*, i, 29.
[4] *Precedents* (1818 ed.) iii, 136–7.
[5] *Ibid.*, pp. 110–57. Dr Thomas believes that speaker Onslow was actively leading the House against Lords encroachments.

the bill beginning there passed without difficulty. In 1749 leave for the Nether Heyford inclosure was given in the Lords but was not proceeded with; the following year the bill was introduced in the Commons and passed [No. 354]. A decreasing proportion of inclosure bills continued to originate in the Lords until 1752, but thereafter almost all began in the Commons. Between 1753 and 1774 only nine such bills began in the upper House and on the last occasion, Ashburnham's precedent [No. 402] was read in the Commons, the bill was laid aside, and a new bill ordered.[1]

But, meanwhile, the Commons had changed their own procedure. Up to 1740 petitions for all inclosure bills were committed in the Commons; in 1741 this practice was abruptly dropped and thereafter leave was given (as in the Lords) immediately upon reading the petition.[2] I can offer no explanation of these developments. The two aspects of the question are probably connected but their meaning would seem to pull in opposite directions: if inclosure bills were not to begin in the Lords[3] because they included an element of taxation, then petitions for the bills should have been committed in the Commons; but that practice was dropped just at the time that the Commons began to claim the right to initiate. The clerks of the House of origin had an advantage over those of the second House in the matter of fees,[4] and this may have had some influence. Whatever the reason, it is clear that the Commons had successfully claimed the initiation of inclosure bills before the inclosure boom really got into its stride, and despite Hardwicke's complaints there is little evidence at this time of the chief drawback of Commons initiation[5] – a House of Lords with nothing to do at the beginning of the session, but

[1] *CJ* xxxiv, 733, 745.
[2] W. E. Tate held that petitions were committed if opposition was expected or if the standing orders had not been complied with (*English Village Community*, p. 95) but such question-begging reasons could never be the basis of any Commons procedure. From 1741 to 1763 inclusive no inclosure petition was committed in the Commons; later a few were so treated; what these have in common is that they included drainage provisions involving local taxation. See John Halcomb, *A Practical Treatise of passing Private Bills* (London, 1836), p. 47.
[3] And why were a few still allowed to begin there?
[4] *Clerical Organization*, p. 290.   [5] Clifford, ii, 785–6.

with extreme congestion of Commons bills, to which they could give no proper consideration, at the end of it.

It is clear from what has been said above that the years 1729–40 were the time of strictest parliamentary control over inclosure bills in the pre-standing order period. During those years, if a bill began in the Commons, the petition was committed for investigation, and no matter in which House a bill originated, notice of the meeting of the Lords committee should have been given in the *Gazette*. It is believed that, in the first half of the eighteenth century, most of the inclosure bills represented simply a confirmation of an agreement already arrived at by the landowners concerned.[1] Agreements of this sort might be enrolled in Chancery to give them greater legal force, but if any of the parties were incapable at law, as for instance minors or lunatics, then, just as in the case of settled private estates, an act was necessary to validate the agreement. During the first half of the century very few bills failed.[2]

Inclosure by act became more common when it was realised that by this means a majority of landowners could compel an unwilling minority to accept the inclosure, a development impossible by any other form of proceeding. The proportion of bills that failed then increases. Between 1715 and 1774 of nearly 1,000 petitions, about 14% failed but more than one hundred of these attempts never proceeded beyond the petition stage – no bill was in fact introduced, though leave was given.[3] It may be that the majority landowners threatened the minority with an act of parliament, which may well have been quite as effective as the threat of a lawsuit[4] in producing inclosure by 'agreement'. More than 800 bills passed without any counter-petition appearing, but a counter-petition did not necessarily stop a bill; of the seventy-two thus objected to, fifty nevertheless passed into acts.

[1] Chambers and Mingay, *Agricultural Revolution*, p. 78.
[2] If one eliminates duplication when a bill for the same place failed more than once, or if a bill passed at a second attempt, there are not more than half-a-dozen failures between 1720 and 1750 against 109 acts passed.
[3] In only three of these cases was an opposing petition presented. The analysis in this paragraph is based only on the *General Index to the Commons Journals*, so the figures are only approximate, but the proportions are sufficiently accurate for the purposes of the argument.
[4] Chambers and Mingay, *Agricultural Revolution*, p. 78.

But it should not be supposed that after 1741, when the Commons dropped the practice of committing all petitions, there were no safeguards. A Commons origin had one public advantage over the Lords in that the *Votes* of the lower House were published daily and contained the substance of all petitions received by the House. One is not suggesting that farm labourers or cottagers read the *Votes*, but like the notice of Lords committees in the *Gazette*,[1] they at least gave an oppotunity to absentee landlords and owners of adjoining estates, to learn what was going on. If one regards parliament as the landowners' club, *par excellence*, members had plenty of opportunity to learn of proposals affecting land in which they or their friends might have an interest. Apart from the publication of petitions in the *Votes*, inclosure bills had to be printed and available in the lobbies. All members for the adjoining counties in the Commons and all active members of the Lords, were named to the select committees on the bills and members not included could see the notice of the sitting of the committees – one week in the Commons, two in the Lords – that had to be posted in the lobbies.

For landowners directly affected by an inclosure such notice was unnecessary, for the committee procedure in both Houses required that every party with a right to land to be inclosed had been personally approached to give his consent, and the committee had to be informed whether each individual was for, against or neuter. The expense of obtaining these consents was one of the things most complained of, as increasing the cost of inclosure by act, at the end of the century. Clifford assumed that notice of bills was normally given locally even though there was no particular order that this must be done,[2] and there is evidence to this effect in the similar case of local bills for roads or rivers.[3] If this is correct then, as in so many procedural matters, the standing order of 1774 that notice of an intended bill must be posted on the church doors for three weeks in the summer before the parliamentary session, simply

---

[1] The two publications had about the same circulation – up to 2,000 daily – and presumably their readership overlapped. Many petitions against local bills say specifically that the petitioners got their information from the *Votes*.
[2] Clifford, ii, 763.   [3] Below, p. 168.

regularised what had become a usual procedure. Indeed, in view of the consents required, some local notice must have been given; the inclosure process often began, long before the bill was drawn, with a public meeting, held in the village inn, the expense of which was also made a matter of complaint in 1800.

Undoubtedly amongst such a large number of measures, there may have been cases in which the rules were not observed and the bill somehow pushed through in spite of it; as with estate bills, there may have been sharp practice, or even fraud in a few cases. But in general it was quite impossible for an inclosure bill to be 'promoted entirely over the heads and without the knowledge of some of the proprietors concerned'.[1] The only source for this statement is a remark made, without evidence, in the report of the 1775 committee on the revision of the new standing orders relating to local and inclosure bills, which reads:

Many Members of your Committee cannot but remember the great Inconveniencies which were felt, and much complained of, before the making of these Orders; Persons residing at a Distance had their Estates cut through by a Canal, or were put to great Expences for an Inclosure, almost without any Notice at all, or at least too late to have an Opportunity of considering the Proposition maturely, and of laying their Observations upon such Bills before Parliament with Effect.[2]

It is to be noted that this statement does not claim that no notice was given, but only that the notice was inadequate, and that it refers *only* to absentee landlords. It was an absentee who obtained the repeal of the Aldham inclosure act;[3] in 1765 a group of absentee owners, living in London, petitioned against an inclosure in Durham because 'no proper notices' had been given of it[4] – yet somehow they had found out enough to present a counter-petition.

Whether parliamentary scrutiny of inclosure bills was adequate is still uncertain; that it was a great deal more careful than is commonly supposed can easily be shown. Once

---

[1] Tate, *English Village Community*, p. 129.   [2] *CJ* xxxv, 443–4.
[3] Above, p. 130.   [4] *CJ* xxx, 251.

again, all the criticism of the procedure rests on the evidence of nineteenth-century select committees,[1] and it appears that, as with estate bills too, at least in the early part of the century, parliament conceived its function to be to authorise agreements arrived at, rather than to arbitrate between parties. If opposition appeared, the parties were told, in effect, to go away, sort it out amongst themselves, and come back next year. Later in the century, parliament began to play a much more active part in regulating the content of the bills. But a great deal more study of individual bills will be needed before it will be safe to generalise in this way.

It is going much too far to say that bills 'were rarely subjected to any substantial amendment in their passage through either House'.[2] Amendments made at committee stage in either House are very rarely set out in the *Journals*. In the case of a bill beginning in the Commons (and most inclosure bills began there from mid-century), one can find out what these amendments were only by taking a copy of a bill as printed at first reading and comparing it with the ingrossed bill in the House of Lords. Until this work is done for a sufficient number of cases we simply have no idea what amendments may have been made in committee of the Commons.

Although Lords amendments made in committee are rarely set out in the Lords *Journal*, Lords amendments to Commons bills do usually appear in the Commons *Journal* and even without going to the Lords committee books and the ingrossed acts for full details it is clear that it is not true that 'the amendments introduced by the Lords were utterly unimportant' and concerned only with the 'correct style of reference to some exalted member of the Upper House' or clauses 'safeguarding the interest of the Church'.[3] In 1780 the Commons injudiciously attempted to extend their campaign against Lords 'interference' with inclosure acts to include a claim that the Lords had no

---

[1] Above, p. 101.   [2] Tate, *English Village Community*, p. 103.

[3] Tate, *Nottinghamshire Parliamentary Enclosures*, pp. 13–14. It is to be hoped that Tate did check at least his Nottinghamshire printed bills with the original acts (though there is no sign of it). If he did, one can only say that, whatever may be the case in the matter of the economic aspects of inclosure, the parliamentary aspects cannot be extrapolated from results taken from only one county.

right even to amend such measures. But the Commons own committee rapidly found that the precedents were all against them, and produced a very useful and lengthy list of no less than fifty-seven occasions on which such amendments had been accepted by the lower House.[1] Even a cursory examination of this list shows the Lords fulfilling the proper function of a revising House, by inserting usual clauses omitted from particular bills, dealing with misnomer (which is by no means necessarily a trivial matter) and sometimes making much more substantial amendments.

But there is much more evidence than this in the Lords committee books, which show that procedure there was very careful indeed. One of the earliest bills[2] has more than eight pages of minutes devoted to it. Harper's second inclosure committee [No. 31] was adjourned so that the Lord of the Manor and the rector might alter their agreement so as to provide for payment of land tax on the rector's compensation. His third [No. 38] ran into a great deal more trouble. This was a confirming act concerning lands at Thurnscoe in Yorkshire, and before it even got to the House the Archbishop of York refused to give his consent until a commission had investigated how the rector's lands had fared under the inclosure; when a petition for this purpose was presented to the Archbishop, Harper noted with exasperation that 'he refused to issue his commission except the petition was signed by all the parties ... though he might have received the same satisfaction from a return of the Commission issued upon the petition of Mr Benson'. Then, when the bill got into committee,[3] it was found that the petition for it was signed by two persons who had sold their lands since the inclosure had begun and so were no longer interested. The Lords insisted on having documentary proof of this, so the committee was adjourned while the 'agent' (unnamed, alas, but Harper and Charles Palmer of the Middle Temple had power of attorney to give consents before the committee, and the 'agent' had drawn the bill), obtained affidavits from Yorkshire. The Lords did accept the agent's

[1] *CJ* xxxvii, 820–32.
[2] Gratwood Heath. 6 Geo. I pr. c. 7. Com. Bk. 20–5 Jan. 1719/20.
[3] Com. Bk. 31 March, 16, 23 April 1729.

word for it that agreements mentioned in the preamble had not been reduced to writing, but then the committee found interlineations in the consent bill.

The Agent for the Bill acquainted the Com^ee that he drew the Bill from Papers that were sent him out of the Country, and when he had prepared the Draught he sent the same down into the Country to be signed by the Pet^rs and that they themselves made the Alterations and sent it up with those Interlineations, Whereupon the Person who prov'd the Pet^rs signing was examined as to the Interlineations being made in the Copy before the same was Sign'd and not being able to give the Com^ee Satisfaction in that particular 'Twas proposed to Adjourn till this Day Sennight.

This must have seemed nearly fatal, for it was already 16 April and the session could not be expected to last much longer. However, a new bill was sent into Yorkshire and somehow got back in time and the bill did pass.

The difficulties here were technical, but Lords committees sometimes made much more substantial amendments.[1] For the Buckland inclosure [No. 75] for instance, they provided that notice of the meeting of the commissioners should be given in two parishes, not one only; and that if new commissioners were required they should be chosen by the existing commissioners, not by the proprietors.

If there were opposition, the Lords committee might go to great trouble to promote compromise. The Slaughter inclosure committee [No. 50] was first put off for three days because the parties were not ready; then part of the bill was taken and some amendments made but the committee adjourned because the House was sitting.[2] On 30 March eight more clauses were agreed and to the next some words were offered and accepted to safeguard the interests of the copyhold tenants. The tenants' real objection, however, seems to have been to a proviso enabling the lady of the manor to lay piped water to the manor house. Evidence was heard on both sides and the clause amended so as to prevent the lady laying pipes through any one else's property or any pipes at all of more than an inch diameter, 'the Persons who made the Objection on ye behalf

[1] Com. Bk. 21 March, 3, 5 April 1733. [2] Com. Bk. 23, 26 March, 1730/1.

of the Tenants declaring that they were satisfied with those alterations'. Thus the tenants were safeguarded and it does not appear that they even had to fee counsel for the purpose.

In other cases, too, petitioners seem to have handled bills themselves, but such intrepid characters might run into difficulties. Mr Stanton, lord of the manor of Queeneborough, tried in 1730 to get an inclosure bill, but it was petitioned against and dropped after first reading. The next year Harper drew the bill [No. 53] and Stanton appeared before the committee[1] to ask for an adjournment because his witnesses had not arrived, to which the opposition objected, saying that they attended with their counsel and witnesses. To sort the matter out the committee deliberated in private and read the three petitions against the bill, one of which even cast doubt on Stanton's claim to be in fact lord of the manor. When Stanton was called in and asked about this he bumblingly repeated that his witnesses had not yet been sworn, but the Lords were patient with him and asked 'whether he had not Deeds to prove his Title' but 'he inform'd their Lordships that he had not brought his title Deeds with him'. The exasperated committee remained patient to the end and calling Stanton in again explained to him that 'considering his unpreparedness and the many difficulties that attended this Bill and the opposition that is made to it, are of opinion that there will not be time to go thro' it this session'; to avoid putting him to any further expense they offered to adjourn the committee for two months to which Stanton, as well he might, 'return'd their L^pps thanks for their Indulgence'.

A similar course was taken with the Bisley inclosure bill of 1733.[2] Here both sides had feed counsel and the committee went into minute detail about the precise nature of the population, common rights and number of cottages, but finally decided 'in regard of the many difficulties that have arisen in the proceedings upon this Bill, and that there is no likelihood of going through with it this session upon the foot it stands'

---

[1] Com. Bk. 8 April 1731.
[2] Not one of Harper's bills. Copy in BM 356. m. 5(6). Com. Bk. 19, 20 March, 1 May 1733.

to adjourn to a very distant day. But this was a very long session and when the distant day (1 May) arrived the House was still sitting and the parties appeared pursuant to the adjournment to say that they were making progress with compromises and asking for another week's grace to perfect the business; but they still did not succeed in completing it in time.

If the opposition employed counsel they did not always take care to instruct him adequately, for on the Chipping Warden inclosure [No. 74] when the opposition was said to be small in value and to have refused all offers of compromise, counsel for the bill[1] again offered compensation before the committee, but since counsel for the objectors had no instructions on the point the clause was withdrawn.

These examples are sufficient to show the great care taken by Lords committees and the great value of the committee books as evidence for individual inclosures. It is to be feared that they might not be quite so valuable in the later part of the century, when bills have begun in the Commons, but they should never be ignored. The Bishop's Tachbrooke inclosure [No. 47] was the first of Harper's inclosure bills to begin in the Commons, and although the Lords committee made no amendments they at least went through the motions of having all the facts proved formally upon oath.[2] The Lords power to amend was only a little restricted by constitutional rules, as for instance 'in inclosure bills, the Lords cannot alter the limits of parishes because it is altering taxable limits'.[3]

The need for certain sorts of amendment was gradually eliminated by the development of a common form of act.

---

[1] Com. Bk. 15 March 1732/3. Counsel for both this and the Bisley bill was John Strange, on whom see below p. 161 n. 4.

[2] Com. Bk. 24 March 1730/1. That the often lengthy documents said to be 'read' before committees were actually read is suggested by an entry concerning the Inkpen inclosure, 28 January 1746, when part of the preamble reciting a previous inclosure award was not read 'being very long' and the clerk informed the committee that he had compared it with the award itself which had already been proved. But see above, p. 119, for a case in which documents were simply 'perused by the Lord in the Chair'.

[3] *Precedents* (1818 ed.), iii, p. 155. Two clauses in [No. 50] were altered for this reason.

Gonner noticed this development[1] but more work is needed to show the precise ways in which the best practices of some draftsmen were made to apply to all acts. We can do no more here than point out some of the common-form clauses whose inclusion is obvious from a study of the *Journals*. The standing orders of 1774 relating to inclosure bills required, in addition to the order that notices should be given locally, upon which we have already remarked,[2] that commissioners to be appointed under the acts should be named in the bill and that the commissioners should be required to account for moneys raised towards the cost of inclosure.[3] In 1781 orders were made concerning the fencing and width of public roads across inclosures, with detailed provisions for the repair and maintenance of the roads.[4]

But long before these orders were made, provisions of these sorts were being inserted *ad hoc* in particular bills. The order that commissioners should be named was scarcely necessary, for they almost always had been named.[5] We have seen the Lords taking care of the situation that would arise if new commissioners had to be appointed;[6] the Commons did the same for the Pool inclosure in 1761.[7] Provisions about laying out of roads were also usually included in bills: the Commons added the provisions to one that lacked them in 1760.[8] In 1764 the Commons amended at least four inclosure bills so as to require the commissioners appointed by the act to take oaths to perform their functions correctly.[9] In 1765 the Commons went systematically through the inclosure bills, adding to any that did not already contain them clauses directing how the public roads should be repaired,[10] giving an appeal to Quarter Sessions in case of dispute;[11] and requiring trustees to keep down the interest on money borrowed for fencing or draining.[12] In one case when the Commons missed the last clause it was added

---

[1] *Common Land and Inclosure*, pp. 62–5.   [2] Above, p. 134.
[3] *CJ* xxxiv, 577, 608–9, 649, 684.   [4] *CJ* xxxviii, 224, 232, 288.
[5] In 1764 there was a division on the names of commissioners in a bill (*CJ* xxix, 744).
[6] Above, p. 138.   [7] *CJ* xxviii, 1086.   [8] *Ibid.*, 824–5.
[9] *CJ* xxix, 888, 913, 928, 930.
[10] *CJ* xxx, 252, 253.   [11] *Ibid.*, 277, 385, 391.
[12] *Ibid.*, 301, 312, 324, 325, 333.

by the Lords.[1] Thus there grew up, piecemeal and without any regulatory orders, a body of good practice in the drawing of these bills upon which parliament insisted, while the inclosure movement was still in its infancy and long before the Lord Chairman had taken over supervision of unopposed bills.

In the same period there was even general legislation on the subject, which has received very little attention. In 1756 a group of landowners in Surrey petitioned for leave to inclose several commons for the purpose of planting timber, with which some of them had been experimenting on their own lands. Instead of leave being given for a bill, these petitions were passed for investigation to a select committee chaired by Nicholas Hardinge, late Clerk of the House and now secretary to the Treasury, himself a Surrey landowner. The committee reported in favour of a general measure, which Hardinge piloted through the House as a public bill.[2]

In 1773 there was an even more extensive measure designed to permit a sort of experimental inclosure by agreement.[3] This public act 'for the better Cultivation, Improvement and Regulation of the Common Arable Fields, wastes and Commons of Pasture, in this Kingdom' was promoted and put through the Commons by Sir Richard Sutton and Sir William Dolben.[4]

At first it was intended to deal also with the vexed question of tithe compensation but this proposal was dropped until the Lords reintroduced it (along with proposals to keep rams off commons in order to improve the breed of sheep). The bill does not seem to have aroused much interest for, although it was printed, the division on the Lords amendments was attended by only fifty-two members.[5] The act provided that three-quarters in number and value of the occupiers in a

[1] *CJ* xxx, 331. We have evidence of these amendments in the Commons *Journal* either because they are amendments to Lords bills or, as in 1765, because they were made, not in committee, but at report stage or third reading. Why this was so I do not know, unless the parties were 'jumping the gun' by having their reports and ingrossments prepared in advance; on this see above, pp. 103–4.

[2] 29 Geo. II c. 36, amended by 31 Geo. II c. 41. *CJ* xxvii, 465, 573–4, 595–6, 600, 604–5, 606.   [3] 13 Geo. III c. 81.

[4] Both independent country gentlemen. Dolben was a reformer and slave trade abolitionist; he also chaired the 1781 standing orders committee. Sutton was interested in the welfare of the poor. (*The House of Commons, 1754–90*.)

[5] *CJ* xxxiv, 179, 183, 261, 266, 294, 314, 320, 387.

parish might make rules for the cultivation of common fields and for the ploughing of baulks which were to be in force for six years under the supervision of field reeves; the rights of commoners and cottagers were to be saved, those who did not agree being allotted some sections of common for their sole use.

The act is well summarised by Holdsworth, who thought it a pity that it 'failed to effect its purpose ... because it was a real attempt to deal fairly with the rights of all persons concerned'[1] as compared with private acts which Sir William considered (without any evidence at all) to be unfair. I have not found any discussion of this act by writers on agriculture and it would appear to have been a dead letter, but it remained on the statute book for over a century, and it would be interesting to know if the experiments it permitted were ever attempted locally. At least this act may be the source of the belief that the consent of three-quarters of the proprietors was necessary for a private act, the origin of which is otherwise obscure.

The attempts at general legislation made in 1796 and 1797, by contrast, contained some very drastic provisions indeed.[2] These arose from 'investigations' inspired and conducted by the officials of the newly formed Board of Agriculture.[3] They were the economic whizz-kids of their generation, all passionately convinced that inclosure was the only prerequisite for an economic miracle. The 1796 bill would have permitted a majority to compel inclosure, while that of 1797 would have permitted a minority, however small, to have withdrawn any lands determined to be theirs from the common holdings, thus completely disrupting the organisation of the community. Both failed.

One of the critics of inclosure has held that 'if the General Act of 1801 or better still that of 1836 had been passed a century earlier' inclosing 'could have been carried out more economically, more expeditiously and certainly more equitably'.[4] The 1801 act[5] was simply a model clauses measure, which did something to reduce the cost of drafting, printing and ingrossing

---

[1] Holdsworth, xi, 454–5.
[2] The period is well summarised by Gonner, *Common Land*, pp. 66–70.
[3] See below, p. 148. [4] Tate, *English Village Community*, p. 106.
[5] 41 Geo. III c. 109.

a bill, though probably not as much as the movers had hoped;[1] it did nothing to reduce the number of bills required. The 1836 act[2] permitted inclosure by consent of two-thirds of the interests by value, no safeguards at all being provided for the interests of the remaining third. Not surprisingly by 1844 it had been discovered that 'a good deal of enclosure had taken place in such a way as to dispossess small proprietors, and that often, for example in the matter of village greens, it had been conducted with total disregard for the general interest of the neighbourhood'.[3] Consequently the 1845 act appointed a body of Enclosure Commissioners who in fact dealt 'rather more drastically'[4] with open lands than the commissioners in the first half of the nineteenth century.

In general, the parliamentary cost of inclosure by private act has been much exaggerated. From the very beginning of the movement, neither House had applied to inclosures the strict letter of their standing orders requiring all parties affected to appear in person to give their consents (which were insisted on for estate bills unless good cause for dispensation could be shown), since 'if this order was to be complied with literally, it would put a stop to the passing of Bills for Inclosures'[5] by requiring virtually the entire population of the village to come to London to give consent before the House. Instead 'the Committees in both Houses in those cases accept of a Bill signed by the Parties and proved by a Witness'.[6] Obviously this proof of consent was one of the real safeguards built in to the inclosure procedure, but the cost of bringing witnesses to prove signatures was much complained of in 1800,[7] and the requirement was relaxed (before the really great increase in the number of inclosure bills) by an order providing that consents might be given by affidavit.[8]

It seems clear that the total cost of inclosure rose fairly steeply from the end of the eighteenth century. Mr Martin

---

[1] A solicitor before the 1800 committee estimated four-fifths of the length of a typical bill could be saved by standard clauses; a very experienced parliamentary agent disagreed and estimated only two-fifths. (First Series, ix, 235.)
[2] 6 & 7 Wm. IV c. 115.   [3] Tate, *English Village Community*, p. 135.
[4] *Ibid.*, p. 136. The act is 8 & 9 Vic. c. 118.   [5] *Liverpool Tractate*, p. 54.
[6] *Ibid.*   [7] First Series, ix, 231–5.   [8] *Private Bill Procedure*, i, 267.

has suggested as an explanation[1] that, apart from the effect of rising prices, the inclosures easy to effect – from the point of view of division, fencing, drainage and so on – had by then been completed and only those that were relatively difficult and expensive remained until rising prices made it economically worth while to embark upon them. The cases usually cited as examples of excessive parliamentary fees come from this period and they have in common either that the area to be inclosed was very small, probably having been left over from a previous inclosure, or, if the area were large, that extensive drainage works were needed to enable the inclosure to take place.

It is from the very small inclosures that the belief has arisen that 'notoriously'[2] the parliamentary costs of inclosure were so great as to be irrecoverable even by the sale of all the land involved.[3] If any instance of the sort had occurred, one feels that the very partisan committees at the turn of the century would triumphantly have produced it, in making their recommendation that in future very small inclosures should be deemed to be only single bills.[4] In the event the House went even further than the committee and removed this cause of complaint (again before the really great increase in the number of bills had begun), by ruling that inclosures of less than 300 acres should pay only a single fee and those under 100 acres only a half-fee.[5]

Most inclosure bills were charged a double fee because they concerned bodies of people, not individuals. The 1800 committee received evidence from the clerk of the fees that the total fees usually paid on a double fee bill, including ingrossing, but not printing, were £154 3s 6d. Before the same committee, John White, a member of one of the largest firms of parliamentary agents, gave evidence to the same effect: 'From £180

---

[1] J. M. Martin, 'The Cost of Parliamentary Enclosure in Warwickshire', *Univ. Birmingham Hist. Journal*, ix (1963–4), 144–62.

[2] Even Williams used this word (*Private Bill Procedure*, i, 47).

[3] This statement is normally cited from Clifford, ii, 733, but the only source given by Clifford is George W. Cooke, *The Acts for facilitating the Inclosure of Commons* (4th ed. 1864), and it is a remark made in passing in Cooke's preface. Cooke was employed by the inclosure commissioners under the 1835 act but he can have had no first hand information concerning the state of things before 1801, to which the remark must apply.   [4] First Series, ix, 227–38.   [5] *CJ* lvi, 663.

to £280 or £300 including all expences of both Houses; and sometimes with an opposition it does not amount to more than £200 or £240. It depends upon the particular circumstances of the case.' White's estimate included printing as well as all the costs in both Houses.[1]

One of the few detailed studies that have been made of the actual costs of inclosure bills in one county over a period of years confirms these figures.[2] It also illustrates the difficulty of isolating actual parliamentary costs from the other costs of inclosing under an act. In sixteen of Mr Martin's cases the item of 'Fees to Clerk and Solicitor' cannot be separated from 'Obtaining Act and Legal Expenses' and even in the remaining twenty-two cases the latter category may still include items other than parliamentary fees. Nevertheless, up to 1795, the highest figure is £342, and less than £200 is usual. Figures given to the Commons in 1834 show that the average cost had by then actually gone down; the usual amount of fees paid in the three preceding years, for thirty-eight inclosure bills, was only £120.[3] A solicitor specialising in inclosure bills was asked by the 1800 committee whether the payment of the usual double fee was 'any obstacle to great Inclosures'. His reply was 'Certainly not.'[4]

There is no doubt that in a few very exceptional cases the costs were very much higher than this. The table put before the 1800 committee by John Dorington, clerk of the fees, and which is undoubtedly authentic, gives the figures for the past fourteen years of the fees actually paid on all inclosure bills.[5] There is no reason to suppose that the fees charged before 1785 were any higher or the pattern any different.[6] Dorington's table shows that of 707 bills, 679 paid a double fee, twenty of the remainder paid 2-double (that is four) fees and just one was in the highest category of 4-double (or eight) fees. It is clear from the table that eight fees was the most that had ever been charged on one bill up to that time, and the cost was £483 0s 4d, not eight times the cost of a single fee because committee, ingrossing

[1] First Series, ix, 235. [2] J. M. Martin, 'Cost of Parliamentary Enclosure'.
[3] HC (350) 1834, xi, 321–4. [4] First Series, ix, 233. [5] First Series, ix, 237–8.
[6] See Williams' calculation that the average number of fees incurred 1776–88 was between 2 and 2½ (*Clerical Organization*, pp. 318–19).

and doorkeepers' fees were not increased in proportion. Dorington repeated the evidence given in 1800 before the Lords committee on private bill fees in 1827, and Walmisley, a House of Lords clerk and an experienced agent, said that he could not recollect an instance of an inclosure bill being charged more than a double fee.[1]

The bills upon which multiple fees were charged were those which included extensive drainage works. It was in such cases, which bear more resemblance to local bills for river navigations than they do to inclosure bills, that the House rules would require the payment of additional fees by each local authority that was given power to raise money towards the works. The two notorious cases are the Ely Drainage bill of 1810 and the Welland outfall bill of 1824 which paid thirty-two and ten fees respectively. These examples were cited by Dorington in 1827 as the greatest number of fees he had ever known to be charged; they have been cited ever since as if they were the norm. But in fact, from Dorington's evidence in 1827 in conjunction with that of 1800 one may readily deduce that ten was in fact the largest number of fees ever charged between 1785 and 1827 with the one exception of the Ely bill. The case considered by the 1827 committee was the similar one of the Nene Outfall, concerning which the country solicitor complained that they were to be charged twenty fees amounting to nearly £2,000. But a study of the evidence shows that this had not yet been settled, that the promoters were willing to pay twelve fees, and that the charge was in fact reduced to fifteen fees on appeal to the speaker.[2] Moreover Dorington's evidence contains a hint that if the bill had been better drafted, more of this expense might have been avoided.[3] Also, the total cost of the works involved was £130,000,[4] and the tonnage figures for the port of Wisbech trebled in twenty years as a result of the works.[5]

---

[1] *LJ* lix, 563–615.

[2] It should be remembered that by this time the clerks gained no personal benefit from fees on private bills, all of which were carried to the fee fund of the House.

[3] On another occasion, an agent gave evidence that Dorington's advice about drafting had saved his client a large sum in fees (HC (540) 1834 qu. 1013).

[4] *LJ* lix, 576, 580, 582, 612.

[5] H. C. Darby, *The Draining of the Fens* (2nd ed. Cambridge, 1956), p. 202.

We may dispose once and for all of the myth that a bill to inclose land where forty-seven parishes had common rights paid forty-seven fees. Tate[1] cited this case on the authority of Lord Justice Scrutton,[2] but Scrutton was quoting from the 1795 committee on inclosure.[3] This was one of the more scandalous examples of a select committee. It was set up at the instigation of Sir John Sinclair, president of the Board of Agriculture, who became its chairman. When it was appointed, on 11 December 1795, it consisted ostensibly of forty-five named members, all the lawyers, and all the knights of the shire, but on 15 December, five new members were added and the quorum reduced to five.[4] A week later it produced a lengthy report, consisting almost entirely of the text of a speech by Sinclair and snippets torn out of context from the Board of Agriculture's own county reports.

The reference to the forty-seven parishes comes from Thomas Stone's 'General View of the County of Lincoln'. Stone did not say that there had been any such act, but that the cost was a deterrent to inclosure because it 'might probably involve' the payment of forty-seven fees. Upon which William Marshall generously remarked, 'This can never be. The Parliament of England cannot have a usage half so irrational as this!'[5] Perhaps they might! But in this case Marshall's comment is certainly quite correct.

It would have been open to eighteenth-century landowners, gathered in their parliamentary club, to have passed legislation

---

[1] W. E. Tate, 'The cost of Parliamentary enclosure', *Econ. Hist. Rev.*, 2nd ser. v (1952), 259.   [2] *Commons and Common Fields* (1887), p. 144.
[3] First Series, ix, 199–215.   [4] *CJ* li, 225, 234.
[5] *The Review and Abstract of the County Reports to the Board of Agriculture*, ed. William Marshall (5 vols. 1811–18, reprint London, 1969), iii, 20. The alleged cost was only the second of Stone's four reasons why this inclosure had not been attempted. The first was that the principal landowner was not interested, the third that 'an equitable mode of dividing the commons is not yet agreed on' and finally 'the present scarcity of money'. None of these reasons, of course, was mentioned in the report of the parliamentary committee. For the real practical difficulties of inclosing the area – East, West and Wildmore fens – see H. C. Darby, *The Draining of the Fens*, esp. pp. 151–2. In spite of the difficulties, inclosure of the area was in fact begun as a result of an act obtained in 1801 (*ibid.*, pp. 233–7). Dorington carefully explained to the 1827 committee that it was only if parishes *did not* inter-common that an additional fee would be charged on that account (*LJ* lix, 576).

to enforce inclosure generally. They did not do so, but proceeded gradually to develop the form of private acts by the addition of clauses found to be useful by experience, more rarely enforcing these sort of rules by standing order, and removing causes of expense when these became burdensome. The private act may not have been the ideal method of proceeding, but one of the more obvious difficulties in the way of general legislation was that of finding a skilled and impartial body of inclosure commissioners. Charles Abbot wrestled with this problem when the 1796 bill was in committee, but the Master of the Rolls thought all the suggestions made quite impracticable.[1] Although a body of professional commissioners soon began to grow up as inclosure became usual, one cannot envisage any one in the eighteenth century being willing to endow these men with the powers conferred by the 1845 act.

It is not surprising that John Ley, the clerk assistant, 'was very decided in his opposition' to the 1796 bill, 'asserting that there was no protection for property in any other mode of proceeding' than that 'which had been so long the established custom'.[2] Arthur Young naturally attributed Ley's attitude to greed for fees, but Ley was certainly not alone in regarding the movement for such reforms 'as part of a general attack on the constitution, on the established government, and on Law and Order'.[3] The eighteenth-century parliamentary procedure, though cumbersome, at least provided a method of investigation and gave some opportunity to small interests to voice objections; the nineteenth-century legislation removed every safeguard.

[1] *Diary of Charles Abbot*, i, 45–52.
[2] *Autobiography of Arthur Young*, ed. M. Betham Edwards (1898), pp. 261–2.
[3] G. E. Mingay, *English Landed Society*, p. 267.

8

LOCAL BILLS

It is when one turns to local bills that parliamentary controversy is to be expected; it was with these bills that the time of
parliament was unnecessarily taken up; and it is they that
have given private bill legislation in general a bad name.
It is for local bills that the immensely complicated precautions
embodied in the nineteenth-century standing orders had to
be invented, which Dr Williams at such laborious length
explained.[1]

The content of these local acts has been discussed at great
length by Clifford[2] and the Webbs[3] who concentrated on the
nineteenth-century development of municipalities; that is,
the manner in which local authorities obtained powers to deal
with finance, sanitation, water supply and so forth. This type
of legislation in the eighteenth century is well described by
Spencer.[4] The acts relating to transport by road, river and
rail, are discussed by Jackman;[5] there have also been many
local studies of particular projects.[6] The nature of the materials
in the House of Lords manuscripts for the study of these
topics has been described by Mr Bond and Mr Cobb.[7] There
is no need to go over this ground again.

Both Clifford and Williams chose the Bridgewater canal

---

[1] *Private Bill Procedure.*   [2] *Private Bill Legislation.*

[3] S. and B. Webb, *English Local Government* (4 vols. London, 1906. Reprinted with
an introduction by B. Keith-Lucas, 1963).

[4] F. H. Spencer, *Municipal Origins.*

[5] W. T. Jackman, *The Development of Transportation in Modern England* (London,
1916. Reprinted with an introduction by W. H. Chaloner, 1962).

[6] See Jackman's immense bibliography, and, for recent work, Mr Chaloner's
introduction.

[7] M. F. Bond, 'Materials for Transport History amongst the Records of Parliament', *Jour. Transport Hist.*, iv (1959), 37–52.

H. S. Cobb, 'Sources for Economic History amongst the Parliamentary Records
in the House of Lords Record Office', *Econ. Hist. Rev.*, xix (1966), 154–74.
'Parliamentary Records relating to Internal Navigation', *Archives*, ix (1969),
73–9.

bill of 1762 as an example for a description of the outline
of procedure in the House of Commons.[1] Neither remarks
on one of its most striking attributes: it became a private, not
a public, act as was the case also with the Duke's three other
measures concerning his navigation.[2] But apart from this, the
Bridgewater canal bill was also unusually controversial.
As Dr Williams pointed out, this was because, for the first
time, statutory authorities already appointed under previous
acts came into conflict; we witness one of the first battles between new capitalist organisations. As a result, the matter was
taken out of the hands of the ordinary select committee, to
enable counsel to be heard in the House itself, and in public
business time, with more than 200 members present, as befitted the importance of the subject. The bill was reprinted four
times while still in the Commons, and the attendant pamphlet
literature was printed in quantities of up to 1,600 copies.[3]

The *Liverpool Tractate* assumed that members would themselves deal with all the procedural forms for local bills (we
have seen that these had always to begin in the Commons)
and indicated that it was unwise to introduce a petition
without first consulting 'the Sollicitor on whom your Chief
dependence is'.[4] But the implication is clear that this wise
precaution was not usually taken, and this perhaps is the
clue to the failure of so many local bills, especially in comparison
with the experience of estate and inclosure bills. In the view of
the *Liverpool Tractate* the function of the solicitor was simply
to draw the bill. This was before the days of standing orders
requiring notices in the locality and elaborate evidence of
precise technical proposals, and there was no real reason why a
member should not handle a local bill himself, without the
aid of a parliamentary agent, provided the parties were
sufficiently in agreement. If a local bill were much opposed
it would be necessary to employ someone, usually a solicitor,
who could negotiate with the different factions and draft the
necessary compromises. However, we will see that despite

[1] Clifford, i, 34–8; *Private Bill Procedure*, i, 35–7.   [2] See below, p. 175.
[3] George White was the agent. For his printing account see above, pp. 47–9.
[4] *Liverpool Tractate*, p. 28.

the evidence of the *Liverpool Tractate*, agents were very often employed for local bills.

Most local bills had an easier passage than the Bridgewater act. Had it not been so, the eighteenth-century House of Commons could never have got through its business. During the years of Robert Harper's prime, 1732 to 1762, 793 local acts passed and about one-third as many more were begun but lost along the way. Harper specialised in private estate acts and his practice in connection with local bills was by comparison small, but still, during his active career, he drew something like fifty such measures. These are not confined to any particular type of bill or any particular locality or promoter, but cover the whole range, showing that Harper's function was that of a parliamentary specialist, rather than attorney for the parties. What we do not know is whether he did more than draft papers in these cases; there is no evidence to show that he or his brother Samuel attended as agents in parliament – a much more time absorbing matter for local than for estate bills. The only hint that he may have done so, provided by the drafts remaining amongst his papers, is that he occasionally drew a report for a Commons committee on a petition [Nos. 121, 247] as he was accustomed to do with the judges' reports in the Lords. This function should, of course, have been performed by the committee clerk.

Harper drew the bill for the Sankey Brook navigation [No. 442A] which was connected with that of the River Weaver, and has been claimed as one of the first beginnings of the canal boom, of which the Duke of Bridgewater's enterprise is a much more famous example. It has also been suggested that the bill would have been opposed had not the promoters concealed the fact that their intention was to make a new canal, not simply to make Sankey Brook navigable.[1] Unfortunately Harper's papers throw no new light on this point. Curiously enough, although Professor Barker's account of the parliamentary history of this bill is completely erroneous, because he confused the committee on the petition with that on the bill,

[1] T. C. Barker, 'The Sankey Navigation', *Trans. Hist. Soc. Lancs. & Cheshire*, c (1948) 121–55.

this does not make any difference to the validity of his story.[1] The only difference between procedure on an inclosure bill and on a local bill was that in the latter case the petition for the bill was always considered by a committee before leave to introduce a bill was given. The Sankey petition was committed on 16 December 1754 and the report received on 17 January; it is this report which contains the 'encouraging evidence from ... the surveyors'. The bill was introduced on 31 January and committed after second reading on 4 February. It is this committee, not that on the petition, which reported on 21 February. Petitions in support of the bill were received on 17 December from the merchants of Liverpool and from proprietors of saltworks at Northwich, both of which, like the bill, had been drawn by Harper. On 7 February a petition of coalmine proprietors on the upper Sankey asked that the navigation should be extended by some 800 yards in each of its three branches. This petition was separately committed and reported on, with favourable evidence from the engineers, on 11 February, and the bill completed its career in the Commons without incident. Since the bill was not opposed, the entry in the Lords committee book is very brief and formal.

Although it is not a bill with which Robert Harper was concerned, it will be worth while to look again at another well-documented case, that of the River Weaver, which is more typical than, because not quite so controversial as, the Bridgewater canal bill. The history of the Weaver navigation illustrates some of the difficulties involved in using parliamentary material for the study of local history, gives very complete details of the cost of local bill procedure, and throws more light on the subject of parliamentary agency, including the activities of the clerks of the House. The story of the navigation has been told at length by Professor Willan,[2] and we shall be concerned here only with its parliamentary aspects.

[1] T. C. Barker, 'The Sankey Navigation', *Trans. Hist. Soc. Lancs. & Cheshire,* c (1948), p. 136. Compare *CJ* xxvii, 53, 55, 102, 115, 133, 137, 144, 148–9, 169.

[2] T. S. Willan, *The Navigation of the River Weaver in the Eighteenth Century* (Manchester, 1951), hereafter cited as Willan. For more detail on the general background and economic interests involved see Edward Hughes, *Studies in Administration and Finance, 1558–1825* (Manchester, 1934), pp. 249–65, 357–432, cited as Hughes.

The agitation for the improvement of the River Weaver began in 1699 but because of conflicting local interests it was not until 1721 that the first act was passed. In 1699 the promoters were the rock salt proprietors, led by Thomas Slyford, and the opposition the local landowners, led by Sir Willoughby Aston. In 1709, Thomas Slyford was allied with Sir Thomas Johnson, M.P. for Liverpool, and Richard Vernon an attorney, who did business for Lord Rivers, owned an estate near Middlewich, and was proprietor of a salt works at Winsford.[1] Sir Willoughby Aston's son, Sir Thomas, obtained the assistance of Peter Shakerley, M.P. for Chester, who was to organise the opposition to the project until his retirement in January 1715. Shakerley organised local petitions against the proposal and tried to obtain the support of the county members, John Crewe and Langham Booth, who were unseated at the general election of 1710 and replaced by Sir George Warburton and Charles Cholmondeley, both opponents of the navigation. When a bill was at last presented to the House by Sir Thomas Johnson in 1711 it was defeated on second reading.[2]

In May 1715 a bill presented by the now county members Booth and Warburton was heavily petitioned against and lost in committee.[3] The true promoters of this bill are not identified, though they are said to have complained that it cost them £400. On this occasion the opposition, still led by Sir Thomas Aston, employed William Watts, a Middlewich attorney, who organised local petitions and also went to London to watch over the parliamentary proceedings. Aston heard that Watts' charges were 'very extravagant' and complained of his having employed other persons without authority.[4] Nevertheless, Watts, although he had not been paid for his services in 1715, was still acting for the opposition in 1720 when yet another abortive bill was introduced. This time there were even more petitions and counsel were heard for and against the bill, which was lost in the Lords.[5]

[1] Willan, pp. 9–10, 24–5, 144.   [2] *Ibid.*, pp. 10–11.
[3] *Ibid.*, pp. 14–15, 154. If it is seriously meant that the vote in the committee was 4–2 only, the proceedings were invalid for want of a quorum.
[4] Willan, pp. 154–5.   [5] *Ibid.*, pp. 17, 20.

On the evidence of the Weaver bills of 1715 and 1720 Professor Willan not unnaturally assumed that what is needed to pass a bill is a large number of petitions in favour of it.[1] This is not the case at all. Not more than one or two petitions in favour of a bill were normally presented, as in the case of the Sankey navigation, and often none at all except the original petition for the bill, unless opposing petitions were presented.[2] The amount of petitioning that went on in the Weaver affair was quite unusually great. The best way to make sure a bill passed was to get agreement amongst the contending interests outside the House, as was done when the Weaver act finally passed in 1721 and not a single petition for or against it was presented.[3]

The success of 1721 has been ascribed to the bubble mentality.[4] On 1 March 1720 William Watts had reported: 'I find the present disposition of the House of Commons is for passing all manner of Bills for navigation', so that opposition, however well-founded, could not obtain a hearing, even though the opposition in this case had been lucky enough to find evidence of what seems to have been a clear and serious breach of privilege on the part of the promoters.[5] Seymour Cholmondeley, Charles' brother, wrote on 16 April that the 'combination of the projectors for 6 Bills of this nature had worked up the temper of both Houses to such a love of navigation that, I assure you, it is a mark of peculiar favour to be suffer'd to speak against any Bill with that title'.[6] On 10 May he reported that 'we could only throw out this Bill upon a promise that we would bring in a good one to the same effect next sessions'.[7]

Hughes maintained that, with the passing of the 1721 act 'the new commercial forces had at last triumphed' and that

---

[1] Willan, pp. 15, 19.

[2] Peter Shakerley's advice 'The more petitions the better (for one petition will not be so advantageous), but the words of each must be varyed' (*ibid.*, p. 145), refers to petitions against a bill, not in favour of it.   [3] Willan, p. 20.

[4] *Ibid.*, p. 17.   [5] *Ibid.*, p. 157.

[6] *Ibid.*, p. 158. Four river acts passed in 1720 for the Derwent, Derbyshire, the Douglas, Lancs., the Ouse, Hunts., and the Idle, Notts. 6 Geo. I cc. 27, 28, 29, 30. The other bill may have been the Wisbech Embanking bill or that for supplying London with water from the upper reaches of the Thames.

[7] Willan, p. 158.

'not the least tribute to the foresight of the promoters is that the navigation was completed in the prescribed time'.[1] To say this is to ignore subsequent developments. One suspects that the local gentry had been too much for the promoters and, as Seymour Cholmondeley had hinted, had succeeded in getting the matter 'put into our own friends that they may make the best of it', for nothing whatever came of the act for many years.[2]

Professor Willan seems to assume that the attempts at revising legislation in 1726 and 1727 must have been promoted by the commissioners appointed under the 1721 act,[3] but there is no reference to these bills in the commissioners' minutes, and their history does not suggest that this is the case. Rather, a rival group of undertakers, supported by some of the commissioners, tried to oust the existing undertakers who were not making the slightest attempt to start the navigation. They tried first by parliamentary means to force the issue, but twice failed. Then a compromise was reached, the old undertakers resigned in their favour, and the river was made navigable under the act of 1721. That this was finally done shows clearly that the claims of the petitioners in 1726 and 1727 that a new act was essential were simply untrue. The moving spirits behind these petitions were Thomas Patten of Warrington, Thomas Eyre of Stockport, and John Dickenson of Manchester; as representative of the 'new commercial interests' which had supposedly already triumphed as any three men could well be. Dickenson was a linen-draper and seems to have been a sleeping partner in the venture, his interests being presumably purely financial.[4] Eyre was the largest salt proprietor at Middlewich.[5] Patten was a tobacco merchant of considerable standing at Warrington, where his family seat ultimately became the Town Hall.[6] He (or his father), had been instrumental in making the Mersey navigable to that town. He leased a rock salt pit at Northwich and engaged in shipping on the river when it was opened.[7]

[1] Hughes, pp. 263–4.   [2] Willan, p. 158.   [3] *Ibid.*, pp. 26, 187 n. 2.
[4] *Ibid.*, pp. 43, 50, 83.   [5] Hughes, p. 390.   [6] *V.C.H. Lancs.*, iii, 321.
[7] Willan, pp. 43–4. Hughes, pp. 254, 262, 396.

The details of the story as unrolled in the commissioners' accounts, the *Journals* of both Houses, and the Lords committee book give strength to the supposition that a rival group was at work.[1] The act of 1721 had appointed three undertakers, John Egerton, John Amson and Richard Vernon, who were to employ a subscription of £9,000 to carry out the work. The undertakers were themselves subscribers to the tune of £2,500 and the other subscribers included Langham Booth and Sir George Warburton. These five men were together responsible for half the total subscription.[2] A body of commissioners, composed of landed gentry, were to supervise the proceedings of the undertakers, as was usual in such enterprises.

At the outset, Richard Vernon claimed more than £2,000 'for his bill of charges in procuring the Act'.[3] The unopposed act of 1721 cannot possibly have cost so much, so that Vernon must have been claiming for the abortive bill of 1720 and perhaps for the earlier bills also. Not surprisingly, the commissioners refused to allow this claim, and the fact that nothing was done was later blamed on Vernon's unreasonableness, but the other two undertakers simply refused to work with Vernon, one going so far as to say that 'He would not be concerned with Mr Vernon in this, or any other, affair',[4] and one is inclined to conclude that in so doing they were performing the function for which they had been appointed.

In October 1724, Thomas Patten of Warrington was in Cornwall when he heard from Mr Legh that the statutory annual meeting of the commissioners at Northwich had once again adjourned without taking any positive action. Patten immediately went to London and spent three weeks there consulting Mr Dawson about raising money. He then returned to Cheshire, having obtained from the clerks of the Customs an account of the export of salt for several years past, and a form

---

[1] In the following pages, unless another reference is given, the events of 1724–7 are reconstructed from the Commissioners' accounts passed in 1730, as set out in the River Weaver Book, 1721–52, pp. 17–29, preserved at the Cheshire County Record Office. These are not discussed at any length by Willan (p. 28). I am most grateful to the County Archivist for supplying me with a xerox copy of the pages.   [2] Willan, p. 23.   [3] *Ibid.*, p. 25.   [4] *CJ* xx, 639.

of petition which he then employed William Middlehurst to carry round the county for signature. He employed Edward Vaudrey to tackle the awkward Richard Vernon; Vaudrey was a lawyer and probably also a family friend of the Vernons, since Vernon's widow, Jane, later married Thomas Vaudrey. Patten spent two months in London in the spring of 1725 on the business, but has left no other trace of his activities at that time, and the petition, if it were ever printed, has not survived.

About Michaelmas, 1725, Patten went into partnership with Thomas Eyre of Stockport and with them was associated John Dickenson. Dickenson spent three days at Chester in the autumn and sent two messengers to Warrington, Patten sent two messengers to Stockport and had expenses of £2 0s 9d in going to sundry gentlemen's houses to get a petition signed. In January and February 1726 Eyre was active in getting the petition signed at Northwich and 'on this side the county'; he twice had to spend several days at Chester where he did some treating at 'Mrs Kenney's and other places'. At the beginning of March, Patten and Dickenson went to London with a petition for a new bill. There Patten paid £12 to a Mr Warrell and £20 (of a total bill of £36 10s) to a Mr Robinson 'for soliciting the affair' and five guineas to each of two counsel for 'perusing the Bill'. He had the bill printed at a cost of ten guineas and he paid 'Mr Hamblin's bill the Clerk in Parliament', £15 6s 2d.[1] Dickenson apparently did some lobbying since he tipped the Cheesemongers' porter half a guinea and also gave five shillings each to Hamlyn's and Legh's clerks.

The petition, presented on 10 March 1726 on behalf of the gentlemen, freeholders and inhabitants of the county of Chester claimed simply that the 1721 act had proved ineffectual and begged leave for a new one to improve the navigation of the Weaver to Northwich and of the Dane from Northwich to Wheelock Bridge. The petition was committed

---

[1] The legitimate fees up to the stage of order of leave are a good deal less than this, but the cost of committee fees on the petition would vary from case to case and cannot be guessed. The next year the fees paid by George Legh up to the same stage amount to £8 14s 10d, so one may suppose that in 1726 Hamlyn's bill included something for his own trouble.

to all the members of the adjoining counties and on 25 March Charles Cholmondeley reported in favour of the bill, saying the committee had examined Richard Legh, Ralph Leicester and Joseph Warrell who had all put the blame on Vernon.[1] Cholmondeley, Lord Malpas, John Crewe, Lord Barrymore and Mr Brereton were ordered to bring in a bill but nothing further was done, and the promoters returned home at the end of April, not waiting for the end of the session.

In May 1726 Vernon died, and if he had really been the stumbling block there should have been no further difficulty, but his death did not 'make possible a new approach';[2] matters went on just as before. In October 1726 Eyre visited Lord Malpas, Charles Cholmondeley's whig kinsman, member for East Looe, and the petitioning round began again. In December and January Eyre and Patten were very active, sending messengers about the county and riding to meetings at Chester, Macclesfield, Middlewich and Northwich. Some articles of agreement drawn by Mr Vaudrey were ingrossed. Then Patten went to London where Dickenson had already paid a first instalment of £40 to George Legh[3] who was to act as agent for the 1727 bill. Eyre continued in the country, lobbying the cheese factors.

George Legh's account for the 1727 bill is as complete as an agent's account can well be, and his proceedings were evidently far more sophisticated than Patten's muddled effort of the previous year. Even before he received his first instalment of cash, Legh had prepared the petition and the bill and sent copies of them into the country and to Lord Malpas and the other Cheshire gentlemen in town. The petition was in very similar terms to that of the previous year but its prayer was different, for it was for the navigation of the Weaver only, and again only to Northwich. Cholmondeley was again chairman of the committee on the petition which examined Thomas Legh, Henry Wright and William Middlehurst who gave evidence almost exactly the same as that given

[1] *CJ* xx, 608, 631, 639. [2] Willan, p. 26.
[3] George Legh, son and heir of John Legh of West Chester, gent., admitted Trinity College, Cambridge, April 1712, aged 17. Admitted Lincoln's Inn, 1711, Middle Temple 24 May 1717, called 31 May 1717 (Venn).

by Richard Legh the previous year. Cholmondeley and Malpas were ordered to bring in the bill which they did on 9 March.[1]

Cholmondeley's position as knight of the shire made it inevitable that he should chair the committee and then bring in this bill even though he had always been opposed to the project on public grounds,[2] and this particular bill was so much against his private interest that he had to petition against it, for, he said, he was the proprietor of a salt works which would be ruined if the navigation came only to Northwich, not to Winsford, as had been provided by the 1721 act.[3]

When the opposition appeared in force, George Legh paid 10s each for copies of the petitions against the bill. The petitioners, besides Cholmondeley, included Thomas Vaudrey, as heir to Richard Vernon's interests; Cholmondeley's fellow knight of the shire John Crewe, associated with Christopher Appleby of the Middle Temple; the traders of Manchester; the Mayor and Burgesses of Liverpool; and Charles Duckinfield and associates, including John Daniel of Daresbury putting themselves forward as rival undertakers and promoters. To meet this opposition Legh drew, and paid the parliamentary expenses of, a petition which he got signed by the cheesemongers of London, whom Dickenson had cultivated the previous year, and he drew and had printed a 'Case' to be distributed to members. Legh paid a retainer to Ward who had acted as counsel thus far, briefed leading counsel to appear at the committee,[4] and also briefed John Strange to appear

[1] *CJ* xx, 744, 770–1, 794.

[2] In 1709 Langham Booth thought he could not refuse to present a petition 'sign'd by the gentlemen of the county though in my own opinion I am against it' (Willan, p. 146). Peter Shakerley in 1711 thought a petition would have little chance of success if the knights of the shire refused to present it (Willan, p. 148). The Weaver amending bill of 1760 was being piloted by Lord Strange, knight of the shire for Lancashire, but it was still thought essential that at least one of the Cheshire county members should give their countenance to it (Willan, p. 180). See also above, p. 102.

[3] *CJ* xx, 815. The subsequent proceedings are *CJ* xx, 804, 806, 810, 814, 815, 832, 836.

[4] The committee consisted of fifty-seven named members and all those for the adjoining counties. Legh paid 6s 8d for an order to add more members to the committee but there is no such order in the *Journal*. Legh prepared only twenty copies of the bill for the use of the committee.

specifically against the petitions of Crewe and Vaudrey. During the committee hearings, several compromises were reached. John Dickenson on behalf of the new promoters signed an agreement with Lord Malpas and the Cheshire gentlemen, promising to reduce the tolls after twenty-five years; and a clause was drawn to include the navigation of the River Dane.[1] Patten visited Crewe's lawyer, Appleby, at his house at Kew and an agreement was reached which Legh drew and had settled by counsel. So much can be learned from the accounts, but a comparison of the bill as originally printed[2] with the ingrossed bill at the House of Lords is needed to show what this agreement was: Crewe received a binding promise to investigate his claim for compensation within a reasonable time. Cholmondeley received the same assurance. Vaudrey was also placated: the printed bill originally provided only that the commissioners should assess Vernon's expenses in passing the earlier acts and pay 'a reasonable sum of Money' to his heirs but the ingrossed bill[3] provided for a payment of £525 in compensation and in consideration also of Vaudrey's handing over various maps and plans of the navigation which had belonged to Vernon.

As a result of these agreements, neither Cholmondeley, Crewe, nor Vaudrey opposed the bill in the Lords, leaving Strange free to change sides and appear in the Lords as counsel against the bill.[4] The bill got to the Lords on 17 April and the whole process had to be gone through again. Legh drew two more petitions in favour of the bill (only one of which was presented) and Eyre spent a frantic two weeks riding round the county to get them signed. Legh prepared a new 'Case', briefed Serjeant Darnhall and Randle Wilbraham as counsel, and paid two witnesses to attend the Lords committee (though they, in fact, were never called upon). The 'Case'[5]

---

[1] These changes are incorporated in skins 16 and 33–4 of the ingrossed bill.
[2] BM 357. b. 10(31).   [3] Skin 30.
[4] The Lords committee books show that there were specialist practitioners at the Parliamentary Bar at this time, as there had been from the sixteenth century (Clifford, ii, 871). Sir John Strange, later Master of the Rolls, was one whose name occurs very frequently; in 1742, he retired temporarily from all his appointments including his 'practice at the House of Lords' (*D.N.B.*). Nicholas Fazakerley and Paul Jodrell Jr. were other specialists.   [5] BM 357. b. 9(76).

took credit for the compromises arrived at while the bill was in the Commons, answering the demand of the Liverpool merchants that the navigation should extend to Winsford by the claim that it would be 'absurd' to 'expend so great a sum to be an advantage to two Proprietors only' [Crewe and Cholmondeley] who 'are satisfied with the Provision made them in the Act'. The 'Case' also claimed that Eyre and Patten were acting under an agreement made on 22 January (which could be that drawn by Vaudrey, which was mentioned in the agent's accounts), whereby Egerton and Amson had already agreed to surrender the undertaking to them, so that the Bill was 'in the nature of an amicable Bill in Chancery, filed by Consent of the Parties interested'; the Liverpool merchants had no right to object to it, especially since the bill 'is in substance the very same' as the act of 1721. This last statement is certainly untrue, and the former are at least doubtful. Although some of the opposition had by this time been bought off, Cholmondeley and Crewe, both county members and commissioners, had originally opposed the bill. Also John Daniel and Charles Duckinfield, in their 'Case'[1] claimed that *they* had reached agreement with Egerton and Amson and had actually given security to carry out the undertaking. Unfortunately the Lords committee did not get around to investigating these conflicting claims.

The Lords committee book shows that the opposition there concentrated on the Liverpool petition, which was promoted by the present and former members for the borough, Thomas Brereton and Sir Thomas Johnson. They brought forward their dock engineer, Thomas Steers, an expert in navigations,[2] to prove that this navigation could be made at much less cost than that proposed by Eyre and Patten. Evidence was given at length on the subject, and on the value and effect of different tonnage rates, on 20 and 21 April. Next day (a Saturday), Legh's petition was presented to the House and referred to the committee, but Legh seems to have overreached himself, or perhaps Eyre had not taken sufficient care in obtaining signatures. At the next hearing, on the 25th, Strange was

[1] BM 357. b. 9(72).   [2] Willan, pp. 18, 56.

willing to rest his case on the proofs about cost already brought out, but he remarked that Legh's new petition was supposedly from all the salt proprietors in the Wyches, and yet 'there was not one Proprietor of Rock Salt had sign'd it, and but five Proprietors of the White Salt'. Mr Clarridge, a salt proprietor of Northwich,[1] who had been giving evidence about tonnage rates, was asked about this and confirmed Strange's allegation. The committee adjourned the bill for a month, and so of course it was lost. Later that year John Daniel, later Sheriff of the county and one of the commissioners, was appointed undertaker,[2] so it appears that the Daniel–Duckinfield connection was victorious this time.

The loss of all this expenditure of time and money still did not deter the Eyre–Patten group. In October 1727 Dickenson, and in October 1728 both Dickenson and Eyre, went to Northwich when the commissioners held their annual meeting. On the latter occasion the undertakers resigned and the commissioners appointed in their stead Philip Egerton, Roger Wilbraham and Henry Wright. We have seen that Wright, at least, was a member of the Eyre–Patten connection, but nothing more happened as a result of this change and the reason behind it is completely obscure. The following year, however, some agreement was reached, for a local solicitor, Joseph Hall, drew formal articles providing for the appointment of new undertakers and Eyre spent time in November 'going about to get the agreement signed'. It must have been formally signed and executed, even though not set out in the commissioners' minutes,[3] for not only did Eyre, Patten and Dickenson, at last, commence work as undertakers the following spring, but by January 1732 had actually – almost incredibly – made the Weaver navigable, all the way to Winsford, under the act of 1721.[4]

The agreement evidently included some reimbursement to the new undertakers for their expenses in 1726 and 1727 for Henry Wright, for the one part, and Charles Cholmondeley for the other, sat down at Hulms Chappell with Mr Patten

---

1 Hughes, p. 390.   2 Willan, p. 28.
3 *Ibid.*, p. 29.   4 *Ibid.*, p. 31.

and Mr Eyre on 6 November 1730 to tax the bills. Patten and Dickenson had charged their own time at a guinea a day and Eyre his at two guineas; this was abated in each case to half a guinea a day and they were allowed their out-of-pocket expenses. George Legh had received part payment of his account, but there was some £160 outstanding including his own charge of £50

For my trouble during ye Continuance of this Affair, wch was abt 10 weeks for my frequent Attendances on Lds & Members both at Westmr & their houses & others concerned in ye Bill & also upon Council & my attendances at ye several Committees & other Occasions at both Houses of Parliament & writing Letters & other trouble having charged nothing therefore before.

To this he modestly added

If this last Article shod be thought too much I desire only to be allowed what shall be thought reasonable by every pson, but if I was to charge as Usually is charged on such occasions, vizt. £2. 2s for every attendance on the Comittees & 13s. 4d. other Attendances at Westmr it wod amount to trible this summe.

The assessors made no comment on this but added to the total a payment of twenty guineas to Mr Randle Wilbraham 'for drawing the Bill etc. in 1727' and sent the whole statement off to Wilbraham for his opinion. Wilbraham had been employed as junior counsel in the Lords in 1727; he was a well-known barrister, a kinsman of the Leghs of Lyme and later member for their pocket borough of Newton.[1] He therefore returned the charming reply that the 'allowances considering the nature of the transaction seem to be reasonable in all but one article wch is the allowance to Council for drawing the Bill etc. in 1727 wch may be greatly moderated & will neither be any disappointment nor obligation, to, Sir, Your very humble servant, Ran. Wilbraham' with the postscript 'My humble Service attends the Commissioners & Undertakers'.

There is no doubt that Legh, like Wilbraham, had kept his charges down in order to assist his connections in the county. The other accounts we have do, as Legh says, show 'attendances

---

[1] *The House of Commons, 1754–90.* Harper drew the change of name bill when Wilbraham's son took the name of Bootle [No. 517].

charged by agents mounting up inexorably at 13s 4d a time. Legh charged, apart from his fee, only £49 2s 10d altogether for drafting and out-of-pocket expenses. Promoters would normally face a higher charge than this for legal advice on a local bill. Nevertheless, the Weaver bill of 1727 cost altogether £386 3s 10d for parliamentary expenses alone, including Legh's fee and expenses but excluding all the expenses incurred in the country and in travelling to and fro. This may probably be taken as the minimum for an opposed local bill, whether it passed or not – the Weaver promoters had already incurred all the parliamentary expenses when the bill failed.

The breakdown of the costs shows that while the basic fees of both Houses for a double bill amounted to only £82, incidental costs came to as much again. To the Commons fee of £28 was added more than £40, in large part for committee fees; the remainder amassed gradually, 6s 8d for an order of reference here, 10s for a Journal entry there. The Lords fee of £54 was similarly swollen by nearly £20. Ingrossing, always an expensive business, cost £27 10s, and printing, including the printing of 'cases', nearly £28. The largest single item in the breakdown, however, is more than £70 in fees to counsel and their clerks, for preliminary advice and for attendances, at five or ten guineas a time, on the committees of both Houses. To this category we must add payments totalling £19 11s 4d to Zachary Hamlyn, the unofficial clerk of the Journals. While the bill itself was settled by counsel, the petition for it, and even the speaker's breviate, were 'settled' by Hamlyn, at 13s 4d and two guineas respectively. Moreover there was 'Pd Mr Hamlin for his trouble in that affair in attending the Comittees making proper blanks in the Bill to the House of Comons & for searching for several papers relating to former Acts, his Demands of £16 16 0.' There is a somewhat sour note about the wording of this entry, which comes right at the end of Legh's otherwise strictly chronological account, after the Lords proceedings. It suggests that Legh was not experienced in agency and was somewhat taken aback by Hamlyn's 'demands'. The official fee for a search in the records, payable moreover to the clerk, not to a subordinate, was 6*s* 8*d*; but of course we do not really know how much work Hamlyn did for his money.

Thus for the 1727 Weaver bill the promoters employed a barrister–agent in London, who received assistance from a Commons clerk,[1] but the promoters themselves did the necessary organising and petition signing in the country. A different method was used for the Weaver amending act of 1760, when John Stafford of Macclesfield was appointed 'solicitor in the country for managing such business relating to the obtaining such Act as may be necessary to be done in the country'.[2] A draft of the bill had been prepared by a Manchester counsel,[3] for discussion by the promoters, and his feelings were not to be hurt,[4] but the final bill for presentation in the House was to be redrawn by Mr Yeates 'solicitor in parliament',[5] with whom Stafford was to correspond. In the event Yeates, a Commons committee clerk, fell ill at the crucial time; so Stafford went to London and did most of the work under the guidance of the Earl of Derby's son who was himself piloting the bill through the Commons. Stafford seems to have enjoyed the bustle of his unaccustomed role in London, including convivial meetings with the members named to prepare and bring in the bill,[6] and although he once protested, 'I will as soon be tied to a stake and baited like a bear as engage in any publick litigated concern for the future',[7] this was a temporary exasperation, caused by one of the members for Liverpool having been rude to him and 'the different stations fortune has placed us in makes it necessary for me, in such a business as this, to stifle my resentment'.[8] Stafford was a man of some means – he was later a trustee of the Weaver Navigation and subscribed £500 to the loan of 1761.[9] His fees for the 1760 bill came to nearly £600 but unfortunately we have no breakdown of the details.[10] No doubt he was the type of professional man who was later employed as agent

[1] It is impossible to avoid calling Hamlyn a Commons clerk although in fact he held no official position, see above, pp. 39–40.   [2] Willan, p. 64.
[3] *Ibid.*, pp. 61–2. His name was also, very confusingly, 'Yates'.
[4] *Ibid.*, p. 173.   [5] *Ibid.*, p. 64. On Yeates, see above, pp. 45–7.
[6] Willan, p. 188.   [7] *Ibid.*, p. 190.   [8] *Ibid.*, p. 193.   [9] *Ibid.*, p. 80.
[10] Information most kindly supplied by the Cheshire County Record Office.

in the country for local bills, to give the necessary notices and obtain required consents. Yeates' illness gave Stafford a more prominent part in these proceedings than he would otherwise have had. The intention had been to handle this bill in the classical manner as described in the *Liverpool Tractate*, the county member taking active charge, with the assistance of a country solicitor; however, it was still considered necessary to employ a Commons clerk as agent.

Whether there were attorneys in London who specialised as agents for local bills is a question which must remain unsettled. The evidence of Strahan's printing accounts suggests that it was for local bills that the clerks most usually acted as agents. Nearly two-thirds of all the bills Strahan printed for Rosier and White between 1762 and 1776 are of this nature,[1] but this still accounts for only a small proportion of the bills of these sorts during these years. We do not know whether the clerks were usually associated in these cases with a London agent, as Hamlyn was with Legh, or with a country solicitor, as Yeates was with Stafford, or whether local members handled the bills themselves with the assistance only of a clerk–agent.

What is clear is that, as such local bills became increasingly numerous, Commons procedure on them was a time-consuming matter for the local members concerned.[2] The Weaver act of 1760 was really thrashed out at the stage of the committee on the petition, and although it was hoped to have the bill ready in a week after leave was given on the committee's report,[3] negotiations with the opposition delayed the first reading for a further three weeks and even then the second reading was postponed so that 'the fees of the House may be saved'[4] if it still proved impossible to reconcile the parties. It was feared the committee might require the consents of the creditors of the navigation, although Yeates, still advising the parties on technical matters, 'thinks he can guard against

[1] See above, pp. 47–9.
[2] Dr Thomas cites Sir Roger Newdigate's diary for the diligence with which he promoted the Oxford canal bill of 1769 and remarks that Lord Folkestone's diary for March and April 1774 contains no reference at all to the American debates, but is entirely taken up with two private bills he was sponsoring.
[3] Willan, p. 178.   [4] *Ibid.*, p. 190.

that objection'.[1] Although in the end only one petition was presented at the committee stage, and was easily disposed of, the bill 'being very long and there being many amendments' (introduced by the promoters to ratify compromises agreed upon during its passage), two select committee sessions were needed to go through it.[2]

Such a troublesome piece of legislation as this, multiplied by thirty or more local bills a year in the 1760s and with the numbers steadily increasing, must have led in the end to a complete breakdown of the parliamentary timetable. It is no wonder that committees on opposed bills were becoming disorderly[3] and those on unopposed measures being reduced to formality. Fortunately most bills were not so controversial as those for the Weaver, much less the Bridgewater canal bills; however, even that for the Sankey navigation, which passed very easily, was mentioned in the Commons on ten separate days instead of the basic six. But important interests were affected by these measures, who all quite rightly demanded to be heard and who deserved a proper hearing however much time was taken up.

It is clear that notice of these bills was normally given locally, although there was no order that this must be done. As early as 1678 a bill for the church of St Martin in the Fields was recommitted because 'there was no summons sent forth to the parties concerned'.[4] The opponents of the River Wey bill in 1759 got it thrown out because 'no public notice, either by Advertisement or otherwise was given of the intention to petition Parliament ... as was usual in Matters of this kind'.[5]

The merchants of Liverpool, objecting to the Weaver bill of 1760, were able to make their voices heard so that the bill was to be amended in their favour or lost entirely, despite the fact that the Earl of Derby's son, the chief promoter, was also, according to the ordinary practice, chairman both of the committee on the petition and of the committee on the bill.[6] The story of the Weaver shows clearly that the influence of the local members was not necessarily baleful. A member present-

---

[1] Willan, p. 187. [2] *Ibid.*, p. 195. [3] *Liverpool Tractate*, p. 57.
[4] Clifford, ii, 763. *CJ* ix, 490. [5] *CJ* xxviii, 501. [6] Willan, pp. 64–5.

ing a bill might not agree with it at all and yet even as chairman be unable to prevent its passing. The local gentry were not necessarily a body of like-minded men intent on preserving vested interests.

In the mid-eighteenth century it was still quite usual for the merits of a scheme to be decided in the House itself at second reading, and for counsel to be heard at that time, not only for major proposals like the Bridgewater canal, but also in much smaller affairs such as that of the Tetbury advowson [No. 191] when both counsel and agents for the parties were heard at the bar of the House. But this was a very time-consuming business and had to be abandoned as pressure of private bills increased.[1] In the 1750s and 1760s counsel were much more often ordered to be heard before the committee than at the bar of the House, but at this time it began to be usual to order the stages of opposed private bills, especially the report stage, so that they could not in theory be smuggled through a thin House from a possibly packed committee. Even so it was not easy to compel a good attendance. In 1752 there were forty-two members present when the committee report on the Scarborough harbour bill was taken into consideration, but some of the supporters drifted away. Seven opponents clung on and forced another division which showed only thirty-four members in the chamber. Since it was not four o'clock the speaker waited till he had a House and the opponents then had the satisfaction of reversing the committee's decision.[2]

It has just so happened that our examples in this chapter have all been of river bills. In fact, up to the 1760s turnpike road bills far outnumbered those for river navigations. The general highways bills (which were extremely controversial and the few that passed were subject to immediate demands for repeal) were concerned with the preservation of road surfaces, not with lines of roads or administration.[3] Attempts were made to investigate the results of some turnpike acts and to supervise the commissioners' accounts by means of select committees.[4]

[1] *Private Bill Procedure*, i, 56–7. Spencer, *Municipal Origins*, p. 75.
[2] *CJ* xxvi, 498.   [3] Jackman, *Transportation*, pp. 218–27.
[4] 1752, *CJ* xxvi, 490–3. 1763, *CJ* xxix, 646–64.

Although these did not lead to any immediate practical results they must have had some effect in preventing abuses and teaching lessons which might be incorporated in future measures. Commissioners appointed by the important road and bridge acts required for a rapidly expanding capital city were compelled to lay their proceedings before parliament annually.[1] In 1773, when sufficient experience had been gained, general legislation provided standard clauses for highway and turnpike bills,[2] regulating such things as their width and hedging, providing for the qualifications of trustees, and enabling justices of the peace to supervise proceedings. Separate acts remained necessary to apply these measures to particular roads.

The canal boom proper and the railway boom which finally led to the complete revision of local bill procedure in the nineteenth century, fall outside our period, but in their early stages they were handled in just the same way as road or river bills and were subject to the same deficiencies. The other major group of local bills – those for municipalities – have a long history, but nothing distinctive about their procedure except that they were almost invariably hotly contested. There is nothing like a proposal for local rating for bringing petitioners up to Westminster in droves. So much so that the committee on the petition seemed quite astonished to find the people of Halifax unanimous in desiring a fresh water supply, being agreed on where to find it, and willing to foot the bill.[3] It is these town improvement bills which, in the mid-nineteenth century,[4] became most subject to the charging of multiple fees, for a fee was charged for each separate rate to be levied – for police, paving, lighting and so on.[5] It was because of this development that the fee structure was

[1] Many of these are available at the House of Lords Record Office. See the head 'City of London' in the new *Guide to the Records of Parliament*.
[2] 13 Geo. III cc. 78, 84.   [3] *CJ* xxix, 53–4.
[4] Apparently not earlier. The table of 1834 shows that during the previous three years, while the town improvement bills were the most expensive of the different types of bill, the costliest of these came only to £321 9s 10d (HC (350) 1834, xi, *321–4*).
[5] Third report of committee on private bills (HC (705) 1847, qus. 697, 1174). Agents reported that they had been charged sixteen and eighteen fees.

completely reformed in 1847, providing for fees in all cases to be based on a sliding scale depending on the capital cost of the works involved.[1]

Parliamentary procedures may have been cumbersome and expensive but one cannot consider them unnecessary in the absence of any other method of reconciling opposing local interests. One cannot avoid a certain sense of despair as one sees a bill for the repair of the same small stretch of road coming up for consideration session after session; almost every turnpike act seems to have been in continual need of extension or amendment. Yet this dismal fact is in itself the justification of the procedure. One need not become lyrical about the experimental potentialities of private bill procedure,[2] to appreciate that if the making of a few miles of road could not be carried out satisfactorily under a local act without the need for amendment, general legislation was likely to be even less satisfactory. Administrative machinery for the investigation of technical questions in public enquiry was what was needed, not blanket legislative powers. Even under modern procedures it is still a lengthy, expensive and frustrating process to settle the line of a new road.

[1] *CJ* cii, 524. [2] Compare Holdsworth, xi, 351.

9

PROMULGATION OF THE STATUTES

The King's Printer's patent gave him the right to print all acts of parliament, but he had discretion as to the exercise of his prerogative and, since the Treasury was his largest customer, he came under Treasury supervision. A clerk at the House of Lords prepared bills for the Royal Assent,[1] dividing them into the categories of public and private. Public acts received the assent in the form 'le roi le veult' and private in the form 'soit fait comme il est desiré'. At the House of Lords, the original acts, ingrossed on parchment rolls, were numbered and preserved in the order in which they had received the assent, sometimes on several separate occasions during a session, public and private being therefore mixed up together. The division into public and private as we know it today was made by the King's Printer when he came to make up his sessional set of acts. He arranged the public and the private acts in two separately numbered series, printing the texts of the former, but only a list of the titles of the latter.

He printed the text of all the truly public general acts, such as the supply and mutiny acts and all matters of state; these acts were of their own nature public and did not contain a clause declaring them to be so. But from at least the late seventeenth century, it became usual to insert such a clause into privately promoted bills, especially the local acts for roads, rivers, town improvements and so on. These acts received the public form of assent and as a result the sets of public acts, which were officially distributed at public expense to a large number of recipients, became greatly swollen and proportionately more expensive. The Treasury reacted by striking a

---

[1] In the nineteenth century this was the task of the clerk of inrolments, but this office was not officially established until 1820 (HLRO Memorandum No. 22).

number of names from the official list of recipients,[1] but this expedient did not get any one very far, since it did not reduce the quantity of printing, and in November 1703 the King's Printer was examined by the Treasury Board and told he must moderate his bills.[2] The clerk of the House of Commons and the clerk assistant of the Lords were also summoned to this meeting, so evidently something was to be done in parliament to make retrenchment possible. To associate the subsequent developments with this meeting can only be conjecture, but it is a fact that the following session, the printing of private bills by the parties begins, by an order from the Lords only. The next year both Houses made standing orders that such bills must be printed in future, and two years later the King's Printer ceased to include in his official set many of the local acts, notwithstanding that they had the public clause and had received the Royal Assent as public acts. It looks as though this was an experiment which did not quite come off. The printing of bills was obviously desirable in itself, if the increasing number of bills was to be properly considered in parliament. But a printed bill was no substitute for a printed copy of the act until it became usual to reprint the bill with amendments. Perhaps it was intended to carry the experiment further, in which case it was probably blocked by the King's Printer standing upon his patent rights. In the event, the King's Printer took it upon himself to reclassify the acts, so as to achieve the desired economy. He began to number and list as 'private' those local acts that he was not going to print, notwithstanding that they had the 'public' clause and had received the public assent.

It is from this point (1708) that there arises the great confusion between the numbering of public and private acts in the

[1] *Cal. T.B.*, xv, 16, 174. This was in October 1699; by the end of the next century several of the deprived parties had crept back on to the list – the secretaries of state and the Master of the Rolls, for instance; the Chancellor of the Exchequer and the Lord Chief Baron were having their sets bought for them by the Usher of the Exchequer Court; but the Lord Privy Seal had not regained his privilege. Compare the list of distribution in the 1796 Report of the Committee on the Promulgation of the Statutes, First Series, xiv, 127–8.

[2] *Cal.T.B.*, xviii, 83. The point was somewhat academic because the Printer was scarcely being paid at all. See his petition, *Cal.T.P. 1702–7*, p. 139 no. 69 and many later pleas for the payment of arrears.

Statutes at Large as compared with the *Statutes of the Realm*. The latter followed the parliament roll in Chancery and therefore included as public all the acts that had received the public form of assent. The *Statutes at Large* followed the King's Printer in treating most, but not all, of the local acts as private. That a few of the local acts continue to be printed in the general collection suggests that their printing was paid for by the parties, just as, in the sixteenth century, parties might, if they wished, have their private acts enrolled on payment of a fee.

This situation came to an end in 1720 when the House of Lords ordered that acts with the public clause must all be printed.[1] This order would not by itself have been effectual, unless the Treasury relented, or the parties accepted the necessity to pay the King's Printer as one more item in the cost of obtaining a local act. Whatever the reason, from this date to 1752 the King's Printer did include in his set all the local acts having the public clause, as well as the truly private acts; and he gave the titles of the private acts in his tables, simply following the order in which the royal assent 'soit fait' was given in the Lords.

In 1753 however, the King's Printer reverted to a practice similar to that which had obtained before 1720. He dropped some of the local acts from his officially printed set, but instead of classifying them as private (as before 1720) he retained the correct public classification, numbering the acts he did not print as public, in series following those that were printed. These local acts he printed separately, not in the official collection, in impressions of 200 only and none of them received free distribution, at government expense, to the public offices.[2] The hand of the Treasury is clearly at work again. However, although these local acts are normally described as 'road acts' and the majority do relate to turnpike roads, in fact a few road acts were still printed in the main collection, and

[1] *LJ* xxi, 347.
[2] Or so it was said in 1796, but in 1781 the King's Printer delivered eight sets of road acts to the House of Lords and three sets to the Commons, for which the Treasury paid £1 13s a set (PRO T. 38/695).

many of the so-called 'road acts' relate to other things than roads.[1]

Following this reorganisation comes a new development to make the matter even more confusing: one begins to find acts with the public clause receiving the private assent and being classified as private acts. That these are not simply mistakes may be inferred from the fact that a common sense consideration of the titles will often discover them: if a title looks odd amongst the private acts then quite likely an examination of the original will show that it has the public clause – a poor rates act, a major fen drainage scheme, an act to close a public road, for instance.[2] The most striking examples are the Duke of Bridgewater's canal acts. All four of these, passed over a period of eight years, have the public clause and yet notwithstanding the importance of the subject, each of them received the private assent, is classified as a private act and is not printed by the King's Printer.[3] The first one of these might have been a mistake, since they are believed to be the very earliest canal acts, and having the name of a peer prominently displayed, might be assumed from the title to be estate acts; but the Duke would hardly have permitted the error to happen three times more; he must have wished for, or at least have been satisfied with, the private assent. All other canal bills became public acts and are often in fact included in the printed set, amongst the general public acts.[4]

The King's Printer can have had no concern with this development; the discrepancies occurred in the House of Lords when

---

[1] For instance in 1764, the following are included amongst the so-called 'road acts':
   4 Geo. III c. 50   Mercers Company
               cc. 55, 56, 57, 59, 60, 89, 90, 91   Poor rates of various towns
               c. 72   Dover Harbour
               cc. 75, 93   Wigan and Knaresborough fresh water
[2] 7 Geo. III pr. c. 111; 6 Geo. III pr. c. 93; 4 Geo. III pr. c. 74.
[3] They are 32 Geo. II pr. c. 2, 33 Geo. II pr. c. 2, 2 Geo. III pr. c. 11, and 6 Geo. III pr. c. 17.
[4] From 1759 the parliament roll ceases to contain even the titles of private acts, which had previously been given there. It may be significant that this coincides with the first example I have found of a private act containing the public clause, though of course I do not pretend to have examined all the acts. By this time too, it has become usual to reprint bills as amended, so parties might have a correct, though unofficial, printed text at little more than the obligatory cost of the bill printing.

the bills were arranged for the Royal Assent. It is clear that the printer never saw the private acts and could not have known which clauses they contained; he simply took the list of titles of acts that had received the assent 'soit fait' and printed it as it stood, as his list of private acts. Therefore the King's Printer could not have known that the evidence he gave to the 1796 committee on temporary laws, to the effect that he printed either generally or specially all the acts containing the public clause, was false. Unfortunately that committee report has been accepted as a correct statement of the method of promulgation of the statutes before 1798.[1] The report states that the King's Printer's 'yearly collections ... contain all the Acts of a public nature, or which are made so by special clause, except Road Acts; viz. Acts for Churches, Bridges, Navigations, Drainage and sometimes Inclosures'.[2] We have already seen that, apart from the question of private acts with the public clause, the classification of 'road acts' is far from precise, and altogether the generally accepted view of the position before 1798 (when a complete alteration took place) is considerably oversimplified. To summarise:

Before 1753, private acts receiving the assent 'soit fait' never contain a public clause; after that date some do have it.

The King's Printer never printed in his official collection the text of any act that received the assent 'soit fait'.

The King's Printer included in his official collection all the truly public acts, but of acts with the public clause which received the public assent:

[1] The confusion may even have been deliberate for Charles Abbot and the speaker had agreed that 'the less was said to expose the deformed and shapeless condition of the present mode of giving publicity to our laws, the more discreet it would be'. (*The Diary and Correspondence of Charles Abbot, Lord Colchester*, edited by his son. (3 vols. London, 1861), i, 72, hereafter cited as *Abbot Diary*.)

[2] Report of the committee on temporary laws, First Series, xiv, 35. The table printed in the report on promulgation of the statutes, First Series, xiv, 122, shows that 'Inclosures' above means only those few (usually involving large drainage works) which were printed amongst the general public acts. The table says there were only two such in each of the sessions 1785, 1787 and 1788; these can readily be identified as 25 Geo. III cc. 14, 92, 27 Geo. III cc. 53, 66, and 28 Geo. III cc. 14, 71. In this last year, 28 Geo. III, four ordinary inclosure acts have the public clause; they are private caps. 11, 35, 47 and 49 and were, of course, not printed at all.

between 1708 and 1719 he printed only a few and classified the rest as private acts

between 1720 and 1752 he printed them all

between 1753 and 1797 he printed some and classified the
rest as 'road acts'

Thus from 1753 to 1797 there are, broadly speaking,[1] five
different kinds of acts:

1 Truly public acts.
2 Acts with the public clause, receiving the public assent,
printed with the public acts in class 1.
3 Acts with the public clause, receiving the public assent,
classified as public acts but printed in a separate group as
'road acts'.
4 Acts with the public clause, receiving the private assent,
classified as private acts, listed with class 5 and not printed.
5 Truly private acts.

That the House of Commons, at least, thought they meant
something by the public clause, is shown by three occasions
on which it was inserted into bills[2] which by all appearance
would not seem to need it. To add the public clause would
seem only to cast doubt on the truly public character of the
act if it were challenged in court. Conversely, in 1791, the
public clause was struck out of two inclosure bills.[3]

---

[1] There are always exceptions. The clerks worked under great pressure at the end
of a session and uniformity is scarcely to be expected. An act of 1781 concerning a
new road in the centre of Halifax does not contain the 'public' clause, but it
received the public assent, 'le roi le veult'; nevertheless, the King's Printer
classified it as a private act and did not print it. (21 Geo. III pr. c. 27.)

[2] (a) An act to allow further time for the enrolment of solicitors, 37 Geo. III c. 93.
Although this was no doubt promoted by the professional bodies, the bill was
introduced on motion and the attorney and solicitor general were in charge of
it; it went to committee of the whole house (*CJ* lii, 642, 654, 660).

(b) Gilbert's Poor Act, 22 Geo. III c. 83 had the public clause and in the
amending act 41 Geo. III c. 9 the clause was added on third reading (*CJ* lv, 886).
This bill also was introduced on motion and went through committee of the
whole house.

(c) Fox's India Bill of 1783 had the public clause added on third reading
(*CJ* xxxix, 824, 831).

[3] 31 Geo. III pr. cc. 35, 69. The clauses were struck out on third reading (*CJ* xlvi,
404, 658), and both received the private assent. Most of the major fen drainage
bills, such as those for the Bedford Level, had usually become public acts and were
included in the King's Printer's public set. The practice of putting a public
clause into ordinary inclosure bills, affecting only a limited area, seems not to

In practice, none of this mattered very much. The confusion by now seems scandalous and the whole procedure virtually meaningless, but in fact, no one but the historian was deceived by it. If one wished for a copy of one's private act, for the muniment room, a King's Printer's copy, though black-letter, was not a specially good-looking document: many printed bills, embellished with wood-cuts and other devices, and sometimes with very impressive title pages, were much prettier. If one was serious about the family records, one obtained, not a print, but a certified manuscript copy on parchment, from the Parliament Office, with a box purpose made in which to keep it, adorned with all the skills of the bookbinder's art.

If one had the misfortune to run into litigation, a certified copy from the Parliament Office, in more sober dress, was what had to be obtained. No one looked at the Parliament Roll in Chancery.[1] Even if one's act had originally been printed by the King's Printer, unless it had appeared in the bound set of the public statutes, the original copies had probably been lost, or mutilated, and new ones would have to be obtained.[2]

---

have developed until quite late. The earliest I know of is the Lanchester Act of 1773 which is further discussed below. In some sample years which have been examined in detail:

1768   19 inclosure acts, none having the public clause.

1779   71 inclosure acts. Only the Lanchester amending Act, 19 Geo. III pr. c. 55 has the public clause.

1788   34 inclosure acts, four having the public clause, 28 Geo. III pr. caps. 11, 35, 47, 49.

[1] It appears from the lists in the *Statutes of the Realm* that at least up to the end of the reign of Anne enrollment was a real process and local acts with the public clause were, as they ought to have been, enrolled, even though not printed by the King's Printer. By the end of the eighteenth century, the roll was being made from the King's Printer's set and could not contain anything that was not printed. (Report on Ingrossing Bills, HC (552) 1823, iv, *69* p. 8.) I do not know when the change took place: in 1781 the King's Printer was regularly supplying two sets of public acts to the House of Lords 'for ingrossers use' (PRO T. 38/695). Similarly by 1834, and again, probably very much earlier, the manuscript 'house copy' of a private bill was made from the printed copy (HC (540) 1834, qus. 399, 400). And by at least 1809, the ingrossed bill was made, not from the manuscript 'house copy' but from a corrected copy of the print (*Clerical Organization*, p. 230).

[2] It was said that people usually took two manuscript copies as a precaution, and still often had to come back for more (*LJ* xli, 460–1). If an act was printed by the King's Printer, he felt bound to keep it in print, that is, to reprint it if required, no matter how many years later. He charged a moderate sum to private parties and made no charge to the public, though he wryly remarked that when a single

The courts, from the very earliest times, ignored the parliamentary classification into 'public' and 'private' acts. They made their distinction between 'general' and 'special' acts on the merits of each particular case, relying heavily on decisions made by Coke in the early seventeenth century. 'Special' acts included those concerning 'only a particular species or thing': not only those relating to 'any particular Place or Town', or even to 'one or divers particular counties'; but 'acts relating to the Bishops only', and even 'Acts for Toleration of Dissenters'.[1] It is obvious that these definitions include not only all local and private acts, however classified, but also many acts which the layman would regard as truly public in all their forms.

The courts were cognisant of the private acts that contained the public clause, and treated them, like all other acts, on their merits. In 1790 the solicitor general argued that the Lanchester inclosure act, 13 Geo. III pr. c. 67,

was to be considered as a public act, only for the purpose of being judicially taken notice of by the Judges, without being specially pleaded; and for no other purpose whatsoever. That this kind of acts, though declared for the special purpose mentioned in them, to be publick acts, are never kept in the parliament rolls, are never printed among the statutes, and do not receive the royal assent in the same words by which publick acts receive it 'le roi le veult'; but in the words by which private acts receive the royal assent 'soit fait comme il est desiré'; that they were in fact to be considered as parliamentary conveyances, and not as publick statutes, which concern all the King's subjects.[2]

The Lord Chief Baron ignored this plea, and gave judgement against the solicitor general, on the general meaning of the disputed enacting clause, just as he would have done had it

---

copy of a public act was wanted in after years, this was usually for the purpose of repealing it, so that he could have no sale for the reprint (Report on the King's Printer's Patent, HC (713) 1831–2, p. 29). It seems that, in the nineteenth century at least, the King's Printer would print any earlier private act, if it was wanted, even though he had not printed it originally: for example, the Duke of Shrewsbury's Act, 6 Geo. I pr. c. 29, was printed in official form in 1856.

[1] Report on promulgation of the statutes, First Series, xiv, 122.
[2] H. Gwillim, *A Collection of Acts and Records of Parliament with Reports of cases argued and Determined in the Courts of Law and Equity Respecting Tithes* (4 vols. London, 1801), iv, 1390.

been a public act: but he relied, for precedent, upon a decision concerning an estate act, where the public clause was not in question at all.[1]

Thus the public clause was virtually meaningless so far as the courts were concerned. Even after the reorganisation of 1815 had resolved the eighteenth century confusion about the promulgation of the statutes, the courts continued to apply their old distinctions, if anything even more restrictively. Often the most they would allow was that a printed copy might be relied on without proof of its having been examined with the record. It was still necessary for a private act to be specially pleaded, that is, set out at length and correctly in the pleading, only those portions so set out to be relied upon. Even local acts declared public might be so regarded only in respect of the method of pleading, and still be held (like private acts) to bind only the parties consenting to them, the benefits they conferred on promoters being strictly construed. Many of the leading cases are concerned with nineteenth-century railway acts.[2]

It appears that the committees on the promulgation of the statutes and the Houses in following their recommendations, had no very clear idea of what they were trying to achieve in respect of private acts. The whole movement for reform, which resulted in several major changes from 1798 onwards, began on the initiative of Charles Abbot. As a very new member, seeking to win (and not yet knowing he must not wear) his spurs,[3] he decided on this method of furthering his parliamentary ambitions.[4] Before he attended his first Speaker's Dinner, he was running about London seeking information on

---

[1] Cruise, *Digest*, v, paras. 48, 43, 45.   [2] Holdsworth, xi, 296–8.

[3] He entered the House in October 1795 and made his maiden speech on 3 December. On 18 March he was told he was 'disorderly' to wear his spurs 'as none but *county* members were entitled to that privilege'. He would not believe old Popham, who told him so, until the criticism was confirmed by the solicitor general. (*Abbot Diary*, i, 45–6.)

[4] 'An occupation coinciding with my former habits and pursuits, and tending to those which I am most desirous of cultivating in future, as connected with my Parliamentary and professional views' (*Abbot Diary*, i, 189). This entry is dated 1 Oct. 1799 and relates to the Record Commission, on which see R. B. Pugh, 'Charles Abbot and the Public Records: The First Phase', *Bulletin Inst. Hist. Res.*, xxxix (1966), 69–85. That it represents Abbot's attitude at an earlier date is confirmed by his summary of 1796 in his manuscript journal, not included in the printed *Diary* (P.R.O. 30/9/31 unfoliated).

the promulgation of the statutes.[1] Abbot drew up this information in the form of a report and, through a friend and older
member, brought it to the attention of speaker Addington who
said he would discuss it with Pitt.[2] Not hearing anything more
for some days, Abbot began to attend the committee on Sinclair's
general inclosure bill and was there able to bring himself to
Pitt's notice.[3]

On 11 April, the speaker gave his blessing to the plan for a
committee on temporary laws. He dictated to Abbot the list
of the committee he should name and said he wished the report
to be tabled within two or three weeks, so that it might be
printed for consideration against the next session. The committee met four times, the second meeting being held at the
British Museum, where Abbot had carefully arranged a little
exhibition of manuscripts.[4] It went through the evidence
Abbot had collected and examined the King's Printer and the
clerk assistant of the Lords, but it does not appear that any
material alterations were made to the report, which had been
approved by the attorney and solicitor general 'with a few
corrections in pencil' before the committee met at all.[5] The
statement in the report concerning the history of the King's
Printer's activity in promulgating the statutes is in essence that
which Abbot entered in his diary following his visits to Strahan
in February.

Before he left London for the summer, Abbot again visited
the King's Printer and the Parliament Office to gather material
for his next report, and as soon as the new session began he
warned the speaker 'that I should soon trouble him with
papers'.[6] By the end of October they had had several conversa-
tions, not only concerning the new method of promulgation,
which was the immediate object, but also about Abbot's great
design for an official publication of all the statutes (which
finally resulted in the publication of the *Statutes of the Realm*).
When Abbot said that another committee would be needed to

---

[1] *Abbot Diary*, i, 32–6. Entries for 16, 18 and 23 February 1796. The dinner was on
the 20th and the future speaker made very careful observations as to how everything was done.   [2] *Ibid.*, 39–43.   [3] *Ibid.*, 48–9.
[4] *Abbot Diary*, i, 52–3 and P.R.O. 30/9/31 f. 74.
[5] *Abbot Diary*, i, 53–6.   [6] *Ibid.*, 60, 67.

prepare for this, the speaker replied 'That you know very well you must do yourself; you must do the previous business of the previous committee.'[1] For the present enterprise, Abbot had already done all that was necessary. He and the speaker went through 'my proposed draught of Report ... word by word' and settled the wording of the motion and the membership of the committee. The committee met three times in November and on 5 December 1796 agreed to the report, which was presented the same day.[2]

The conversion of the committee's report into practical effect took a good deal longer. Apart from technical problems, as to whether proceedings should be by bill, resolution or address, other matters such as the French landing at Fishguard and the bank suspension of cash payments demanded more urgent attention. Abbot became immersed in the work of his finance committee.[3] Nevertheless, resolutions embodying the committee's proposals were passed by the Commons in March,[4] but further consideration of them was postponed; it was not until May that they were communicated to the Lords, and though the Lords agreed to them in June, so many difficulties were encountered that in the end the matter was put off to the next session.[5]

The main recommendations of the committee had been that all local acts should be removed into a separate class; that the thus very much reduced number of truly public general acts should be circulated free to a very much wider circle (3,550 copies) than had hitherto received them; and that 200 copies of the local acts should have an official distribution (in addition to any that the King's Printer might continue to produce for private sale), the recipients to include all the clerks of the peace. It was not over these important recommendations that difficulties arose. Proposals for numbering the clauses of bills were dropped without being put to the House,[6] but the House did adopt the committee's suggestion that all promoters of private bills should be required to pay for the printing of copies of their acts by the King's Printer. The clerks opposed these

---

[1] *Abbot Diary*, i, 72. [2] *Ibid.*, 72–6. [3] *Ibid.*, 83–8, 92–3. [4] *CJ* lii, 412–13.
[5] *Abbot Diary*, 94, 99, 104, 107–16. [6] *Ibid.*, 92.

proposals, Hatsell objecting to any printing of private acts, and the clerk assistant of the Lords 'raising difficulties throughout'.[1] Abbot believed that Cowper went so far as deliberately to make no entry of the Lords resolutions in the minutes and to fail to send the message to the Commons that was resolved on, but Lord Auckland accepted the clerk's explanation that the omission was due to pressure of business and the difficulty of drafting an appropriate minute.[2]

In the next session the Commons resolutions were renewed on 17 November, but on 22 December the speaker asked Abbot 'to move a resolution respecting the Private Acts, so as to make it optional in the parties to pay for the printing and have their Acts made public',[3] and this was duly done before the Lords committee, which had been abandoned the previous summer, met to make final arrangements for the compensation to the clerks in the Parliament Office.[4] The alteration was made because it was feared that to add an additional compulsory charge to the House fees might be a deterrent to the inclosure movement, and also because Abbot, at least, thought that the Lords proposals for compensation to their clerks (which had been shown to him in the summer) were much too generous.[5]

With this one major alteration, the committee's proposals took effect for the acts of the session 1797–8, 38 Geo. III. The result is, if anything, even more chaotic than the situation before the reform. Not only inclosure acts, but ordinary private

---

[1] *Abbot Diary*, i, 92, 107. [2] *Ibid.*, i, 107–8 and P.R.O. 30/9/32 f. 92.
[3] *Abbot Diary*, i, 120, 124. [4] Com. Bks. 5 July, 30 December 1797.
[5] Draft letter to the speaker, 1 October 1797, bound into the MS journal, P.R.O. 30/9/32 f. 131 and summary of the year 1797, *ibid.*, f. 163. The Lords committee book, 5 July 1797, contains summaries of the clerks' claims which show that office copies of less than half the private acts passed had ever been required by the parties. If all the acts were required to be printed, the clerks would take a copy fee on each one, thus gaining a considerable increase in income. The Lords also proposed to allow some additional small fees, to compensate for the loss of sale of sets of 'Acts' (see above, p. 108). It is no wonder that Abbot found the King's Printer (in contrast to the clerks) affable and obliging in discussing the proposed reforms, for one result of them, if the printing had been made compulsory, would certainly have been the transfer to Strahan's printing house of most of the printing of private bills, which otherwise was shared amongst several printers; this quite apart from the completely new source of profit arising from the printing of private acts.

estate acts are given a clause declaring them to be public acts,[1] receive the assent as public acts, and are printed with the local acts in the new collection of 'Local & Personal Acts', while exactly similar acts, without the clause, continue to receive the private form of assent and remain unprinted. In 1801 the committee on the promulgation of the statutes following the union with Ireland, increased the number of copies to be printed and circulated to take account of that event, and repeated the order for the printing of private acts in slightly different words.[2]

Some difficulties of which we have no knowledge must have occurred as a result of these orders, for in 1803, in the midst of a first-rate political crisis, the orders were vacated and it was declared

That so much of the Resolutions of the Lords and Commons, of Session 1801, as related to the printing and distribution of Private Acts of Parliament, shall be construed to extend only to such Acts of Parliament in which a clause shall be inserted, declaring that such Act shall be printed by the Printer to the King's Most Excellent Majesty, and may be given in evidence in all courts of Justice, and before all Judges and Justices, who shall take judicial notice thereof in like manner as if the same had been declared to be a Public Act.[3]

The reader may be relieved to hear that George Bramwell, the foremost authority on private acts of his day, thought that this resolution 'is not quite clearly expressed'.[4] He thought the last phrase 'who shall take judicial notice ...' 'rather ambiguous'. 'But it is presumed that the meaning was, not that the act should be judicially noticed *without being specially pleaded*, but that printed copies should be received in evidence, *without proof of such copies having been examined with the record.*' Bramwell was comforted by the fact that the clause actually

---

[1] For example 39 Geo. III loc. 7, 57 are inclosure acts, loc. 56, 66, 67, 68, 79 and 80 are estate acts, the rest are the sort of local acts that would previously have been 'road acts'. The wording chosen for the 'public' clause continues to vary from act to act. Though local acts, as they have always done, usually have the words 'this Act shall be deemed, adjudged and taken to be a public act', there are many variants even in this group; and an estate act might have a clause 'that this Act be, and the same is hereby declared to be a Publick Act' (39 Geo. III loc. 56).   [2] First Series, xiv, 149. *CJ* lvi, 370.   [3] *CJ* lviii, 273, 281.
[4] *The Manner of Proceeding on Bills in the House of Commons* (London, 1823), p. 12.

adopted for insertion into the acts read, 'that this act shall be printed ... [by the King's printers] ... and that a copy thereof so printed by any of them, shall be admitted as evidence by all judges, justices and others'. Bramwell does not appear to have noticed that the confusion he was criticising had already obtained for five years and was now about to be cleared up. The clause just quoted, which became known as the 'evidence' clause, was inserted into those estate and inclosure acts which would have been private acts before the alteration of 1798. Local acts, on the contrary, had the 'public' clause, 'that the Act shall be deemed and taken to be a Public Act and shall be judicially taken notice of ... without being specially pleaded'.[1] Acts with the 'evidence' clause received the assent 'soit fait' and those with the 'public' clause received the public assent, but both were numbered and printed together as 'Local & Personal (to be judicially noticed)'. All private acts without either clause received the assent 'soit fait' and were not printed, but listed as 'Local & Personal not printed'. Thus, so far as the King's Printer is concerned, there ceased to be a category of 'private acts' at all from 1803 to 1814.

From its inception in 1798, the greater part of the 'Local & Personal' printed set consisted of local acts of the sort that would previously have been 'road acts'. Some private estate acts were included, but most of these remained unprinted. The proportion of inclosure acts that was printed gradually increased, but many remained unprinted.[2] In 1815 there was another rearrangement, which holds good to 1850. The private acts with the 'evidence' clause, officially printed, were taken out

[1] *Statutes of the Realm*, i, p. xxxv n. 5.

[2]

		Printed		Not printed	
		Total	Inclosure	Total	Inclosure
1799	39 Geo. III	83	2	120	64
1802	42 Geo. III	119	19	120	80
1803	43 Geo. III	147	33	120	76
1813	53 Geo. III	216	52	79	61

There are still some discrepancies, which are presumably simply errors; e.g. 53 Geo. III pr. c. 24 has the 'evidence' clause, but it is in the King's Printer's 'not printed' category.

of the category 'Local and Personal' and restored to the category of Private Acts, which were numbered in one series, the first part of which, for each session, consisted of the printed acts and the second of those not printed.

The King's Printer thus once more has a table of private acts and, for instance in 1815, numbers 1–72 are printed, numbers 73–112 are not. I have not traced any order for this rearrangement. George Bramwell claimed that it was done at his suggestion and that thus 'the apparent inaccuracy of continuing to place, among the public acts, ... such private acts as are printed by the King's printers, notwithstanding the omission of the public clause, is avoided – and the ancient boundaries between public and private acts are preserved'.[1]

[1] Bramwell, *The Manner of Proceeding on Bills*, p. 13.

10

CONCLUSION

To five of the men who have been mentioned in this story we owe some of the most important and extensive collections for the parliamentary history of the sixteenth and eighteenth centuries now in the British Museum, and they were typical of the age that founded that institution. Nicholas Hardinge, Francis Hargrave, Robert Harper, Philip Webb and James West, moving in the triangle Bloomsbury – Chancery Lane – Westminster, must have known one another, although we know almost nothing about their relationships. Four were contemporaries, Hargrave much younger, so the connection goes on into the second generation. Webb, who did not become a barrister until late in life, was called at Lincoln's Inn on the same day as Robert Harper junior. Webb, West, Harper's son Samuel and Hardinge's son George were all fellows of the Royal Society. Hargrave acknowledged Samuel Harper's help with the book he intended as the first volume of a definitive edition of Hale's writings. Hardinge and West made purchases at Le Neve's sale in 1731, before either held any official position. All five were collectors according to their means; with West it was a passion and he was the only one wealthy enough to indulge his taste to the full. They have come together in this book, not because of their literary and antiquarian interests but because they were all concerned with the task of getting legislation through parliament. All five were trained to the law and practised for at least some part of their careers; all but Hardinge belonged to Lincoln's Inn; all but Harper held Treasury posts at some time.

Robert Harper built up an old-fashioned conveyancing practice into an efficient machine for private bill legislation; unlike the others, his deposit in the Museum is the record of his working life, not of his hobby. Hardinge[1] developed a

---

[1] Nicholas Hardinge (1699–1758), son of vicar of Kingston, Surrey. Eton. Fellow of King's College, Cambridge 1722–37. Middle Temple 1721, called 1725. Clerk

solicitor's 'parliamentary business' at least in respect of record-keeping and publication into a House of Commons organisation more appropriate to the developing place of parliament in the community. With West,[1] as joint secretary to the Treasury, he assisted in putting the Treasury's business through the House and may have been partly responsible for the innovations which resulted in the beginning of the office of parliamentary counsel, the post later held by Francis Hargrave.[2] Philip Webb,[3] as the lord chancellor's assistant and as Treasury solicitor, was also responsible for Treasury business in parliament.

These men were not in the first rank of political life and cannot be blamed for what may be regarded as their seniors' failure to do more than tinker with the increasing complexity of legislative processes. However, while the old structure of

---

of the Commons 1732–48. M.P. 1748–58. Joint Secretary to the Treasury 1752–8. His papers are the least significant of the five. There is no information about how his few private papers came into the Lansdowne collection. He died intestate. He had inherited the manor of Kingston from his father's cousin and the MSS include some collections on the history of the district (BM Lansdowne MSS 225, 226) and some legal tracts and common-place books (Lans. 281, 566, 569, 604, 619, 620, 634, 635, 866, 1151). Much more important is the calendar of House of Commons papers compiled under his aegis as clerk (Lans. 553) and the precedent books which probably belong to the same set (Lans. 507, 544–52).

[1] James West (1703–72). Balliol. Inner Temple 1721, called 1728. Lincoln's Inn 1738. M.P. 1741–72. Joint secretary to Treasury 1746–56 and 1757–62. West was instrumental in obtaining the Harleian collection for the nation. The sale of his own books and antiquities lasted more than twenty-four days, but his MSS were bought privately by Shelburne. The most important section is the Burghley papers, now Lans. 1–122. The story that Shelburne learned his trade as chancellor of the exchequer by studying the papers he bought from West (Norris, *Shelburne*, p. 100), is not true. Only a small section of West's correspondence with the antiquary Thomas Hearne (Lans. 778) went to Shelburne. The greater part of West's personal and political correspondence remained with his family, although some are now Add. MSS 34,727–47.

[2] Francis Hargrave (?1741–1821) son of Christopher Hargrave of Chancery Lane. Lincoln's Inn 1760, called 1771. Parliamentary counsel to the Treasury 1781–9. A distinguished legal editor. The Hargrave MSS contain some useful copies of seventeenth-century parliamentary materials and his books many of the rarest eighteenth-century tracts, often with his own annotations.

[3] Philip Carteret Webb (1700–70), son of Daniel Webb, of Devizes. Middle Temple 1727. Lincoln's Inn 1741, called 1754. M.P. 1754–68. Secretary of Bankrupts in Chancery, 1746–66. Treasury solicitor 1756–65. He collected thirty volumes of Rolls of Parliament which were used for the official edition. At his death, his MSS on parchment were sold by auction, but his paper MSS were bought privately by Shelburne, the most important group being the Julius Caesar MSS, now BM Lansdowne MSS 123–74.

legislation was maintained and indeed, in some senses, developed to a size and complexity never known before, parliamentary processes altered imperceptibly to cope with the mass. Procedures did change, slowly and without any avowed reforming aim, the process beginning long before the date (1774) generally accepted for the very beginning of reform, itself a date well within the eighteenth century.

In parliament, opposed and unopposed bills were distinguished, procedure for the latter being greatly simplified and safeguards being introduced for the former by the ordering of stages and the development of detailed provisions for securing the consent of the parties affected. The printing of bills was unknown at the beginning of the century, by the end of it, without any orders on the subject, reprinting at each stage had become a routine. Conveyancers as a body have been blamed for the poor quality and inordinate length of statutes. However, the House of Commons led the way in the development of common form clauses, a process later carried perhaps to extremes, by the Lord Chairman of committees, whose office was in existence long before it was officially recognised in the nineteenth century. Government drafting and the management of government legislation in parliament were organised on a formal basis by the appointment of the Treasury counsel and agent in 1769, regularising an informal arrangement which had existed for at least a decade at that date.

More attempts at general reforming legislation were made than the century is usually given credit for. But faced with the increasing complexity of political and economic life, a piecemeal approach was preferred. There was no general agreement on the theoretical necessity for reform; little possibility that the bureaucratic structures involved could, practically, be established, much less accepted. Eighteenth-century parliamentarians clung to the old ways, preferring the waste of time involved in protecting their own interests and those of their constituents to delivering themselves up to unknown bureaucrats.

It is striking that the most bitter contemporary criticism of drafting in general and private bill legislation in particular should have come from two lord chancellors. If one wishes to

Conclusion

find a scapegoat, the guardian of the laws of England is surely a good candidate for the position. However, it is perhaps not to be expected that a functionary who personally drew £10 from the House of Lords fees on every private bill should be in the vanguard of a reforming movement, no matter how violently he might express himself in the heat of debate. From the time, in about the 1770s, when pressure of business began to make some reform very desirable, the speakers of the House of Commons were not administrators of reforming temperament. No eighteenth-century clerk of the parliaments performed any but purely formal functions, and though the last of them, George Rose, was a most able man of many talents, it never occurred to him to do more than draw the fees of the clerkship. In the Commons, Hatsell thoroughly enjoyed his semi-sinecure, attending to the minutiae of the patronage involved with an enthusiasm worthy of a better cause, and attending the House for the sake of improving his income and his acquaintance among the mighty. The difference between the modest economy of the *Method of Proceedings* and the muddled anti-quarianism of the massive four volumes of Hatsell's *Precedents* points the contrast between what was becoming necessary and the situation which was actually allowed to develop from the absence of any policy.

The enormous increase of business arising from the Napoleonic wars and the union with Ireland, coupled with the evergrowing mass of private bills attending the industrial revolution and the inclosure movement, threw strains upon the legislative process which made some changes inescapable. Charles Abbot devoted himself energetically to making a name by reforming zeal and, at least in the early days of their acquaintance, had very little patience with Hatsell, who resisted one of his proposed reforms, 'as an innovation merely, and upon the general principle that he would resist all changes, great or small, upon the single reason of their being changes'.[1] The load he had to bear after becoming speaker made Abbot increasingly aware of the need for new regulations.

The process was hastened (as so often in the history of

[1] *Abbot Diary*, i, 76.

parliamentary reform) by the occurrence of one flagrant case indicating that the system was on the verge of breakdown. From about 1779, Hardinge Stracey had received an additional allowance of twenty guineas a year for the examination of ingrossments of public bills. If Stracey ever performed this function he soon ceased to do so: the examination of public ingrossments was done by an unofficial clerk. In 1808, this clerk, working under impossible pressures, was conned into altering the text of an ingrossed bill.[1] From 1779 John Rosier had been given an additional allowance 'in consideration of his attending to the private bills brought into the House of Commons and taking care that nothing passes therein which may be prejudicial to the interest of the Crown and the public'.[2] Rosier considered, from the point of view of the interest of the crown, those private bills that were referred to him by the Treasury, and this process developed into a routine under his successor; but no-one scrutinised private bills in the interest of the public. It was scarcely possible that anyone should do so in view of the huge quantity of such proposals coming before the House. It was this situation which led to the establishment of the Private Bill Office, but the problem of conflict of public and private interest in this sphere was not really solved until the chairman of ways and means and the speaker's counsel were given the supervision of private bills in the mid-nineteenth century.[3]

The establishment of the Private Bill Office, however, clarified the situation in several ways. On 15 June 1809 speaker Abbot 'Went to Perceval to settle the notice of limiting time for receiving private petitions next session to the first fourteen days, and also to require all persons soliciting Bills to name a Parliamentary Agent amongst some of the Clerks of the House who may be responsible for the due conduct of business. To both which he agreed.'[4] The diligent Abbot lost no time in

---

[1] *Clerical Organization*, pp. 231–4.   [2] *Clerical Organization*, p. 170.
[3] *Private Bill Procedure*, i, 94–102. The Lord Chairman's supervision seems to have been confined to form rather than substance. The Lord Chairman's counsel, from 1804, was Edward Stracey, Hardinge Stracey's nephew, despite Abbot's vehement protests that it was quite improper for a parliamentary agent to act in such a capacity (*Clerical Organization*, pp. 156–7).   [4] *Abbot Diary*, ii, 197.

sending notice of what was intended to the solicitors' professional body, in slightly different words: 'Also that some one of the
Clerks attending the House should be employed by the Parties
having business before the House as a Parliamentary Agent or
Solicitor; who may be ready to answer any question and give
any explanations which may be required in the course of the
business depending.'[1] The Society of Gentlemen Practisers
received this notice with alarm. They called a special meeting
of the society which appointed a select committee to draw a
representation against it which they sent to the speaker,
chancellor of the exchequer, the law officers and a select
group of members of the profession in parliament.

Speaker Abbot was not much impressed by 'this voluminous
piece of Eloquence ... it never having been in the contem-
plation of anybody to create a *monopoly* of Parliamentary Agency
& Solicitorship in the Clerks of the House of Commons';
but something had to be done in view of 'the increasing multiplicity of Private Bills, coming not only from respectable and
known persons' like the Law Society 'but from all corners of
the United Kingdom'.[2] The clerks themselves were not at first
happy about the new regulations 'which they fear will be
prejudicial to them'.[3] The Law Society obtained a promise
that the speaker would meet their representatives before anything further was done and persuaded the attorney general to
intercede on their behalf. He obtained the assurance

that the duty which is intended to be imposed on the Clerks of the
House is merely that which at present lies upon no one to perform,
that it will be no more than what is deemed necessary for the security
of those whom the Bills may affect, that it will not exclude the usual
Parliamentary Agents from any part of their employment, that they
may name what clerk they please for this particular duty, and that
the fees of such Clerk will be regulated.[4]

Thus it came about that the Private Bill Office was established. Its establishment settled once for all the difference

[1] *Records of the Society*, p. 214.
[2] Abbot to Perceval, 4 January 1810. I am most grateful to Mr D. C. L. Holland
for providing me with a copy of this letter from his Spencer Perceval papers.
[3] PRO Abbot's MS Journal, 20 January 1810.
[4] *Records of the Society*, pp. 221–2.

between public and private bills and enabled the state of progress of the latter at any one time to be seen at a glance. It made clear the position of the clerks: those in the new office were from the first prohibited from agency, and later all were compelled to choose between clerkships and private work. The clerks' fears about the new regulations proved to be justified, for they gave official status to the outdoor agents and by simplifying their work reduced the amount of agency obtained by those clerks who did not belong to the leading firms of agents; it was no longer necessary for an outdoor agent to fee a clerk to find out what was going on in the House.[1]

Although the reforms of the nineteenth century have been called the 'attainment of a complete code' of standing orders, the process was attended with many difficulties, false starts and subsequent revisions, and even so left untouched, in 1942, the fossilised remains of many of the very earliest orders.[2] In many cases the progress of reform justified the more cautious approach of the eighteenth century. An elaborate machinery for appeal against the alleged abuses of private bill committees was completely ineffectual.[3] Outside the House, the Preliminary Enquiries Act of 1846 was a total failure.[4] 'It is not so easy a matter as some gentlemen suppose to constitute a tribunal out of doors which will deal satisfactorily with these matters.'[5] Now that we are familiar with tribunals out of doors we should be in a better position to sympathise with the eighteenth-century attitude. Nor has their development eliminated the need for private bills to enable local authorities to maintain grass verges. Complaints of cost and of bad drafting are also still with us. As I write, in April 1970, *The Times* on two successive days carries a complaint of the cost of briefing counsel and witnesses for an enquiry into the Greater London Development Plan, and an angry correspondence on the proposition 'that lawyer MP.'s are as capable of drafting legislation as the professional draftsman'.

[1] HC (540) 1834, qus. 530, 587.   [2] *Private Bill Procedure.*
[3] *Private Bill Procedure*, ii, 202.   [4] *Ibid.*, i, 115–16.   [5] Holdsworth, xi, 349–50.

APPENDIX I

BILLS DRAWN BY ROBERT HARPER

The nature of Robert Harper's collections and the indexes to them have been described briefly in the text.[1] The only section of Harper's professional papers now extant, with the exception of a little of his 'great precedent book' is that covered by the index at Lincoln's Inn which is entitled 'Index to Acts of Parliament'. When these volumes were acquired by the Museum they appear to have been catalogued at first as they stood, under references beginning 356 to 358. Each volume was usually in the order: printed private bills; printed public bills and other parliamentary papers; a section in manuscript containing copies or drafts for the measures with which Harper had been personally concerned. At some later date in the nineteenth century, the printed private bills were removed from these volumes and used to make up the set of so-called 'Private Acts' under press-mark BS Ref. 2. Almost all the private bills were removed in this manner so that copies remain under references 356 to 358 only if Harper had two copies, or if (rarely) the Museum possessed a clean copy from another source (except those in the King's Library, under references 212 to 215, which were then, as they are still, sacrosanct). But the original Museum references, beginning 356 to 358, can still be seen pencilled on the private bills now bound under BS Ref. 2 and these have been of assistance in reconstructing the volumes. Most of the printed papers are catalogued, by their individual titles, under the head 'England–Parliament' in the *General Catalogue of Printed Books*. Harper's manuscript sections appear never to have been catalogued at all.

Volume 1 had already been altered from its original form before reaching the Museum, by the insertion in it, under item references lettered A, B, etc., some papers which originally formed part of 'the great precedent book, No. 1'. Nor is it now possible to reconstruct volumes 2 to 4 completely, but from volume 5, 1728, onwards, the collection is almost complete. From that date to 1756 the printed private bills are usually to be found under the appropriate year in

---

[1] Above pp. 4-8.

the set of 'Private Acts' and the remainder of the volume, as Harper himself possessed it, remains under the equivalent reference in the volumes titled 'Bills', 356 to 358.

Harper collected all the printed private bills, not only those with which he was himself concerned, and numbered them through, for the purposes of his indexes, usually following the order of the statute book. In almost every session some bills are excluded since certain classes of bills were not required to be printed and Harper usually kept manuscript copies only of those he had drawn himself. Harper's item numbers, written in ink, can usually still be seen on the papers, with his initials RH in the corner of his own bills. Harper's item numbers for each volume continue in order, after the private bills, through the public bills, cases and other parliamentary papers in the equivalent volume under references 356 to 358. Finally, in these volumes, follow Harper's manuscript items, which he sometimes numbered and sometimes paginated; in either case they have usually been assigned item numbers in the Museum's pressmarks.

From 1757 (Harper's volume 34) the additional printed papers, other than private bills, begin to become less common, and in that year Harper changed his practice of numbering each volume through from 1, but instead used the chapter numbers of the private acts as his own item numbers, so that there are gaps in his numeration where private bills were not printed. From 1760 (vol. 37) Harper took the King's Printer's printed table of Private Acts and used it as his index. From the following year to the end of Harper's career, the volumes under reference 356 to 358 no longer exist as such, having been removed bodily to the set of 'Private Acts'. Harper's additional material, now consisting of only one or two public papers and a few MS petitions, are bound at the end of the 'Private Acts' for each year.

Harper's list of 'Acts Drawn' gives no details except the nature of the bill and the regnal year. This list is reproduced below as the basis for an index to Harper's surviving papers in the British Museum. Since Harper's list is not quite complete, bills with which he was apparently connected, because of the survival of MS material amongst his papers, have been interspersed at the places where they appear in Harper's volume order, even if they are not on the list.

The columns of the list below show:

1. The number assigned to each item by Harper in his list of 'Acts drawn'. Interspersed items are not numbered.

2. The title under which the bill occurs in the *General Indexes to the Journals of the House of Lords*, since this supplies the most

convenient reference to the parliamentary history of each measure. Most of these are personal names. I have added the word [inclosure] to place names for bills of that nature (though the *Journal* does not always give the modern spelling of place names). If the entry in the *General Index* differs markedly from the title used by Harper, his title is given in square brackets. The latter method is also used for bills which did not reach the Lords; the parliamentary history of such bills is indicated in footnotes.

3. The chapter number of each bill enacted: c. indicates public and pr. c. private acts.

4. The column headed R.H. gives Harper's original reference by volume and item number. By means of these references, Harper's indexes at Lincoln's Inn and his cross-references on the papers in the Museum, may still be used. In the earlier years, when several of Harper's copies of bills are missing, the item numbers have been supplied, if they occur there, from the indexes at Lincoln's Inn. In the middle years, some few of the copies do not carry Harper's numbers and may not have belonged to him; in these cases the item number is omitted.

5. The column headed Bill gives the present location of Harper's own copy, or copies, of each bill. These are printed unless otherwise stated. The British Museum reference BS Ref. 2 indicates the bound set of so-called 'Private Acts' in the State Paper Room; items with this reference will be found under the appropriate regnal year unless another year is given – a few are misbound. Copies of bills other than those belonging to Harper are not noted.

6. The column headed MS gives the location (British Museum pressmark) and nature of Harper's manuscript material, if any, relating to each item. This usually takes the form of the draft petition for the bill (P) and/or the draft judges' report (JR); the nature of other MS material is indicated in footnotes.

Outline list of Robert Harper's volumes
with equivalent British Museum pressmarks

1	1701–23		357. b. 1	26	1749	22 Geo. II	357. d. 4
2	1715–27 cannot be		357. b. 2	27	1750	23 Geo. II	357. d. 5
3	reconstructed. Items		357. b. 3	28	1751	24 Geo. II	357. d. 6
4	occur under these		357. b. 4	29	1752	25 Geo. II	357. d. 9
	pressmarks		357. b. 9	30	1753	26 Geo. II	357. d. 10
			356. m. 3	31	1754	27 Geo. II	357. d. 11
5	1728	1 Geo. II	356. m. 4	32	1755	28 Geo. II	357. d. 12
6	1729	2 Geo. II ⎫		33	1756	29 Geo. II	358. b. 1
7	1730	3 Geo. II ⎬ 357. b. 11		34	1757	30 Geo. II	358. b. 2
8	1731	4 Geo. II	356. m. 2	35	1758	31 Geo. II	358. b. 3
9	1732	5 Geo. II	357. b. 12	36	1759	32 Geo. II	357. c. 13
10	1733	6 Geo. II	356. m. 5	37	1760	33 Geo. II	358. b. 5
11	1734	7 Geo. II ⎫					
12	1735	8 Geo. II ⎬ 357. c. 2					
13	1736	9 Geo. II	356. m. 6				
14	1737	10 Geo. II	357. c. 4				
15	1738	11 Geo. II	357. c. 6				
16	1739	12 Geo. II	357. c. 7				
17	1740	13 Geo. II	357. c. 8				
18	1741	14 Geo. II	357. c. 9				
19	1742	15 Geo. II	357. c. 10				
20	1743	16 Geo. II	357. c. 12				
21	1744	17 Geo. II	358. b. 4				
22	1745	18 Geo. II	357. c. 14				
23	1746	19 Geo. II	357. d. 1				
24	1747	20 Geo. II	357. d. 2				
25	1748	21 Geo. II	357. d. 3				

From this point there are no separate volumes with these pressmarks. The contents of the original volumes are now bound in the set of 'Private Acts' BS Ref. 2, under the appropriate regnal year.

38	1761	1 Geo. III	358. b. 6
39	1762	2 Geo. III	358. b. 7
40	1763	3 Geo. III	358. b. 8
41	1764	4 Geo. III	358. b. 9
42	1765	5 Geo. III	358. b. 11
43	1766	6 Geo. III	358. c. 2
44	1767	7 Geo. III	358. c. 4

The other volumes in the series 356 to 358, which do not appear to have belonged to Harper, are as follows:

1696–1750	356. m. 1	1732	357. c. 1
1747	357. b. 5	1736	357. c. 3
1719 and 1724	357. b. 6	1745	357. c. 5
1725	357. b. 7	1742 and 1745	357. c. 11
1726	357. b. 8	1751	357. d. 7 and 8
1727	357. b. 10		

BILLS DRAWN BY ROBERT HARPER

		R.H.	Bill	MS
	1717	3 Geo. I	Vol. 1	
1	Rutland, John, Duke of	pr. c. 6	16	BS Ref. 2	357. b. 1(24)ᵍ
					357. b. 1(26) P
					357. b. 1(27)ᵇ
	1718	4 Geo. I			
2	Harborough, Bennet, Lord	pr. c. 13	18	BS Ref. 2	357. b. 1(30) PJR
3	Kent, Henry, Duke of [Lord Harrold]	pr. c. 9	22	BS Ref. 2	
			38	BS Ref. 2	
	1720	6 Geo. I			
4	Hales, Sir John	pr. c. 12	—	missing	357. b. 1(43) P
	1721	7 Geo. I			
5	Rochford, Frederick, Earl of [Lord Rivers]	pr. c. 11	28	BS Ref. 2	357. b. 1(52)ᶜ
6	Addison, John	—	29A	BS Ref. 2 MS copy	357. b. 1(55) JR
	1722	8 Geo. I	Vol. 3		
7	Milbanke, Sir Ralph	pr. c. 7	7	missing	
—	Addison, John	—	8	357. b. 4(8)	357. b. 1(53) P
					357. b. 1(54) JR
	1723	9 Geo. I			
8	Kingston, Evelyn, Duke of [Croxden]	pr. c. 12	9	missing	ᵈ
9	Dawes, Darcy	pr. c. 1	21	BS Ref. 2 5 Anne	ᵉ
10	Clifton, Sir Gervas	pr. c. 20	—	missing	
	1725	11 Geo. I			
11	Kent, Henry, Duke of	pr. c. 31	50	missing	
12	Puleston, Thomas	pr. c. 10	51	BS Ref. 2	
13	Barrymore, James, Earl [Brignall]	pr. c. 16	53	missing	ᶠ

ᵃ Articles of agreement.

ᵇ 357. b. 1(27) is the judges' report. The breviate and accounts are bound following this item, unnumbered.

ᶜ The note on difficulties which arose before the judges is bound following the bill in BS Ref. 2. 357. b. 1(52) is the judges' report.

ᵈ Account of committee fees bound, unnumbered, following 357. b. 1(27).

ᵉ The petition, judges' report, and a note on trusteeship are bound following the bill in BS Ref. 2 for 5 Anne. Harper numbered these items also as Vol. 1, nos. 23B and 24.

ᶠ Petition and judges' report bound in BS Ref. 2 preceding 11 Geo. I pr. c. 41. The note on the change of judges is bound following 356. m. 3(17), unnumbered.

		R.H.		Bill	MS
	1725 cont.	11 Geo. I	Vol. 2		
14	Bolton, Charles, Duke of	pr. c. 15	21	BS Ref. 2	356. m. 3(35) P
			22	BS Ref. 2	356. m. 3(36) JR
			Vol. 3		
15	Blackett, Sir Edward	pr. c. 20	56	missing	
16	Clifton, Sir Gervas	pr. c. 19	57	missing	
	1726	12 Geo. I	Vol. 4		
17	Fangfosse cum Spittle [inclosure]	pr. c. 5	8	missing	
18	Waldegrave, James, Lord	pr. c. 20	20	missing	
19	Grosvenor, Dame Mary	pr. c. 23	23	missing	
	1727	13 Geo. I			
20	Goulston, Francis	pr. c. 19	47	missing	357. b. 9(98) P
					357. b. 9(99) JR
21	Conyers, Sir Baldwyn [Stoughton Rectory]	pr. c. 20	48	missing	357. b. 9(100) P
					357. b. 9(101) JR
22	Rand, Thomas	pr. c. 22	50	missing	357. b. 9(97) JR
23	Canterbury, Diocese of	pr. c. 27	56	BS Ref. 2	*a*
24	Lowndes, Charles	pr. c. 36	67	missing	357. b. 9(96) JR
			68	BS Ref. 2	
25	[Copper & Brass]	—*b*	85	357. b. 9(86)	
	1728	1 Geo. II	Vol. 5		
26	Bentinck, Lord George	pr. c. 5	2	BS Ref. 2	356. m. 4(33) P
					356. m. 4(34) JR
27	Davie, Sir William	pr. c. 6	3	BS Ref. 2	356. m. 4(31) P
					356. m. 4(32) JR
28	Bromley, William	pr. c. 7	4	BS Ref. 2	
29	Brown, Thomas	pr. c. 11	8	BS Ref. 2	356. m. 4(35) JR
30	Wittewronge, Sir John	pr. c. 19	14	356. m. 4(14)	*c*
			15	BS Ref. 2	
31	Overton Longville [inclosure]	pr. c. 26	22	BS Ref. 2	*d*
32	Sheldon, Francis	pr. c. 27	23	BS Ref. 2	356. m. 4(36) JR
	1729	2 Geo. II	Vol. 6		
33	Grey, Lady Mary [Stean]	pr. c. 7	3	BS Ref. 2	357. b. 11(42) P

a A MS draft clause is bound following the bill in BS Ref. 2.

b *CJ* xx, 798, 807. Dropped after second reading.

c The MS material is bound in 356. m. 4 as follows: (37) petition for the bill; (39) petition to the King; (40)(41) consents; (43) accounts; draft King's consent and two more pages of accounts, unnumbered, bound at the end of section 356. m. 4.

d Petition written on the bill in BS Ref. 2.

			R.H.	Bill	MS
	1729 cont.	2 Geo. II	Vol. 6		
34	Grandison, John, Earl of	pr. c. 8	4	BS Ref. 2	
35	Molyneux, Richard Viscount	pr. c. 9	5	BS Ref. 2	357. b. 11(43) JR
36	Chaytor, Henry	pr. c. 10	6	BS Ref. 2	357. b. 11(44) JR
37	York, Archbishop of [Brasserton]	pr. c. 20	16	BS Ref. 2	357. b. 11(45) P
38	Thurnscoe [inclosure]	pr. c. 27	24	BS Ref. 2	*a*
—	Goddard, Margaret	—	40	357. b. 11(40) MS copy	357. b. 11(41) JR
	1730	3 Geo. II	Vol. 7		
39	[Flecknoe inclosure]	—*b*	9	357. b. 11(55)	
40	[Dunchurch inclosure]	—*c*	10	357. b. 11(56)	357. b. 11(81) P
41	Calvert, Felix	—	11	357. b. 11(57)	357. b. 11(82) P
42	Horninghold [inclosure]	pr. c. 7	18	BS Ref. 2	357. b. 11(83) JR 357. b. 11(84) P
43	Morpeth, Henry, Viscount [Hickling]	pr. c. 14	24	BS Ref. 2	357. b. 11(85) P 357. b. 11(86) JR
44	Satisfatt. Roger	pr. c. 19	—	BS Ref. 2*d*	
45	Jervoise, Thomas	pr. c. 20	30 31	357. b. 11(76) BS Ref. 2	357. b. 11(87) JR
	1730	3 Geo. II	Vol. 8		
46	Kennet, River of	c. 35	23	356. m. 2(49)	
	1731	4 Geo. II			
47	Tachbrooke, Bishop's [inclosure]	pr. c. 3	34	BS Ref. 2	
48	Nuneaton and Attleborough [inclosure]	pr. c. 9	36	BS Ref. 2	356. m. 2(105)*e*
49	Biscathorpe [inclosure]	pr. c. 17	43	BS Ref. 2	
50	Slaughter [inclosure]	pr. c. 18	44 45	356. m. 2(50) BS Ref. 2	

a The petition for the bill is written inside the docket of pr. c. 26 which has been detached from that bill and is now bound as 357. b. 11(24). The petition for the Archbishop's commission, with Harper's note, and the power of attorney to Charles Palmer and Robert Harper are 357. b. 11(46) and (47).

b *CJ* xxi, 507, 541 dropped in committee.

c *CJ* xxi, 490 petition and leave, but no bill introduced.

d This is probably not Harper's copy. It should be his item number 29.

e Letter of attorney.

		R.H.	Bill	MS
	1731 cont.	4 Geo. II	Vol. 8		
51	Player, Thomas	pr. c. 26	55	356. m. 2(57)	356. m. 2(105)[a]
			56	BS Ref. 2	356. m. 2(106) JR
52	Westby, Robert	pr. c. 29	60	BS Ref. 2	356. m. 2(107) JR
53	Queeneborough [inclosure]	—	65	356. m. 2(71)	
54	[London Brokers]	—[b]	71	356. m. 2(77)	
	1732	5 Geo. II			
—	Haijman, Nicholas	pr. c. 34	102	356. m. 2(108) [c] MS copy	
			Vol. 9		
55	Drake, Sir Francis Henry	pr. c. 7	4	BS Ref. 2	357. b. 12(70) P 357. b. 12(71) JR
56	Hyde Park Conduit	pr. c. 8	5	BS Ref. 2	
57	Paddington Church-yard	pr. c. 10	7	357. b. 12(7)	
—	Stanhope, Sir William	pr. c. 12	9	BS Ref. 2	357. b. 12(77) JR
58	Lambe, John	pr. c. 16	13	BS Ref. 2	357. b. 12(72) P 357. b. 12(73) JR
59	Abbott, Robert	pr. c. 20	17	357. b. 12 (17)	
60	Francis, John	pr. c. 25	22	BS Ref. 2	
61	Mill, Barbara	pr. c. 26	23	BS Ref. 2	357. b. 12(76) JR
62	Gace, Joseph	pr. c. 27	24	BS Ref. 2	357. b. 12(74) P 357. b. 12(75) JR
63	Puriton [Momes Leaze inclosure]	pr. c. 31	28	BS Ref. 2	
64	Lombe, Sir Thomas [silk engine]	c. 8	31	357. b. 12(31)	
65	Tiverton [rebuild]	c. 14	32	357. b. 12(32)	
66	Pilots [Trinity House]	c. 20	36	357. b. 12(36)	
67	Derwentwater, Earl of	c. 23	43	357. b. 12(43)	
68	Charitable Corpora-tion [commissioners]	c. 31	49	357. b. 12(49)	[d]
69	Charitable Corpora-tion [directors]	c. 32	50	357. b. 12(50)	
70	Yorkshire [cloth]	—	62	357. b. 12(61)	
			63	357. b. 12(62)	

[a] Petition, written on the verso of the Nuneaton letter of attorney.

[b] *CJ* xxi, 663, 718 negative to committal.

[c] The last page of the draft, the petition, and the memorandum on passing a natural-isation bill are misbound at the end of section 356. m. 3.

[d] MS rough notes written upon a 'Case' 357. b. 12(53).

		R.H.		Bill	MS
	1733	6 Geo. II	Vol. 10		
71	America, Sugar colonies in	c. 13	17	356. m. 5(17)	
72	Barston [inclosure]	pr. c. 3	24	BS Ref. 2	
73	Sheldon, Francis	pr. c. 4	25	BS Ref. 2	356. m. 5(67) P
74	Chipping Warden [inclosure]	pr. c. 6	26	BS Ref. 2	356. m. 5(69) P
75	Buckland Newton [inclosure]	pr. c. 7	27	BS Ref. 2	
76	Aston Magna [inclosure]	pr. c. 8	28	BS Ref. 2	
77	Abergavenny, William, Lord	pr. c. 10	30	BS Ref. 2	356. m. 5(70) JR
78	Tynte, Sir John	pr. c. 19	39	BS Ref. 2	356. m. 5(65) P 356. m. 5(66) JR
79	Drax, Thomas Erle	pr. c. 20	40	BS Ref. 2	356. m. 5(68) P
80	Cowper, William, Earl	pr. c. 26	46	BS Ref. 2	
81	Roberts, David	pr. c. 33	54	BS Ref. 2	
82	Brandon, William	pr. c. 34	55	BS Ref. 2	
83	Harvest, George	pr. c. 35	56	BS Ref. 2	
	1734	7 Geo. II	Vol. 11		
84	Wollesthorpe [inclosure]	pr. c. 2	7	BS Ref. 2	
85	Strode, William	pr. c. 5	9	BS Ref. 2	
86	Horner, Thomas Strangeways [Hopsford, Duchess of Hamilton]	pr. c. 10	16	BS Ref. 2	
87	Craven, William, Lord [Pesthouse Field]	pr. c. 11	17	BS Ref. 2	
88	Boone, Charles [Houses in Blechingley]	pr. c. 12	19	BS Ref. 2	*a*
89	Boone, Charles [Evelyn]	pr. c. 13	20	BS Ref. 2	
90	Lightwood Forest [inclosure]	pr. c. 14	21	BS Ref. 2	
91	Cleybrooke [inclosure]	pr. c. 15	22	BS Ref. 2	*b*
92	Smith, Thomas [Morland]	pr. c. 16	24	BS Ref. 2	
93	Culliford, John	pr. c. 17	25	BS Ref. 2	
94	Coventry, William, Earl of	—	30A	357. c. 2(31)	
95	Calverley, Walter	pr. c. 4	44	BS Ref. 2 MS copy	

a A printed 'case', numbered 357. c. 2(18) is bound following 357. c. 2(37).
b Copy of the *London Gazette* bound following the 'case' relating to [No. 88].

		R.H.	Bill	MS
	1735	8 Geo. II Vol. 12		
96	Rutland, John, Duke of	pr. c. 2	1	BS Ref. 2 MS copy	357. c. 2(77) P
97	Peterborough, Charles, Earl of	pr. c. 4	3	BS Ref. 2	
98	Dyke, Edward	pr. c. 8	7	BS Ref. 2	357. c. 2(78) P 357. c. 2(79) JR
99	Appleton, Henry	pr. c. 9	8	BS Ref. 2	
100	Forester, William	pr. c. 11	10	BS Ref. 2	357. c. 2(75) P 357. c. 2(81) JR
101	Edgar, Robert	pr. c. 12	11	BS Ref. 2	357. c. 2(82) JR
102	Hunningham [inclosure]	pr. c. 14	13	BS Ref. 2	
103	Shoreditch Church	c. 27	17	357. c. 2(65)	
104	Sheffield Church	—	19	357. c. 2(67)	
105	Tunstall, Cuthbert	—	22	357. c. 2(70) MS copy	
—	[Tayler, Nicholas]	—[a]	—		357. c. 2(72) P
—	[Copyright of books]	—[b]	—		357. c. 2(80) P
	1736	9 Geo. II Vol. 13		
106	Cowper, William, Earl	pr. c. 5	1	BS Ref. 2	
107	Pembroke, Henry, Earl of	pr. c. 7	3	BS Ref. 2	
108	Cavendish, Lord Charles	pr. c. 8	4	BS Ref. 2	357. c. 2(76) P[c] 356. m. 6(48) JR
109	Astley, Sir John	pr. c. 9	5	BS Ref. 2	356. m. 6(50) P 356. m. 6(53) JR
110	Gee, William	pr. c. 15	11	BS Ref. 2	356. m. 6(56) P 356. m. 6(57) JR
111	Banks, Joseph	pr. c. 16	12	BS Ref. 2	356. m. 6(54) P 356. m. 6(55) JR
112	Alderminster [inclosure]	pr. c. 17	13	BS Ref. 2	
113	Gilbert, John	pr. c. 27	17	BS Ref. 2	356. m. 6(49) P
114	Cooke, John	pr. c. 32	21	BS Ref. 2	356. m. 6(51) P
115	Pitt, Samuel	pr. c. 33	22	BS Ref. 2	357. c. 2(71) P[c] 356. m. 6(52) P
116	Vaux, Thomas	pr. c. 34	23	BS Ref. 2	357. c. 2(87) JR
117	Stafford, West [inclosure]	pr. c. 35	24	BS Ref. 2	

[a] No petition offered in either House. The petition is the original, signed by the parties.
[b] Introduced in the Commons and lost in the Lords. Harper's copy of the bill is missing, but his papers include a draft of the Commons committee report and a printed case, 357. c. 2(73) and (74), as well as the petition. The petition and report differ slightly from those printed *CJ* xxii, 400, 411–12.
[c] These two petitions [Nos. 108 and 115] may be those presented the previous year, 1735, on which the judges did not report.

		R.H.		Bill	MS
	1736 cont.	9 Geo. II	Vol. 13		
118	Smith, George	pr. c. 25	26	BS Ref. 2 MS copy	356. m. 6(46) P
119	[Registering ships]	—a	27	356. m. 6(27)	
120	[Assize of bread]	—b	30	356. m. 6(30)	
121	[Lighting London streets]	c. 20	31	356. m. 6(31)	357. c. 2(84)c
122	Stallingborough [inclosure]	—d	35	356. m. 6(35)	
122	Harrison, John [Newport]	pr. c. 1	60	356. m. 6(60) MS copy	
—	Shales, John	pr. c. 24	—	—	356. m. 6(47) P
—	Stamford, Harry, Earl	pr. c. 6	—	BS Ref. 2e	356. m. 6(58) P
					356. m. 6(59) JR
—	Ashenden [inclosure]	—	—		357. c. 2(89) Pf
	1737	10 Geo. II	Vol. 14		
123	Maynard, Sir John [Gunnersbury]	pr. c. 4	4	BS Ref. 2	356. m. 6(64) P
					356. m. 6(65) P
124	Kellow, Thomas	pr. c. 10	9	BS Ref. 2	357. c. 2(48) JR
125	Pitt, Thomas [Swallowfield]	pr. c. 12	11	BS Ref. 2	356. m. 6(61) P
					356. m. 6(62) JR
126	Rockingham, Lewis, Earl of [Furnese]	pr. c. 15	13	BS Ref. 2	357. c. 4(49) P
					357. c. 4(50) JR
127	Dudley, Sir William	pr. c. 16	14	BS Ref. 2	357. c. 2(86) P
128	Graham, Sir Reginald	pr. c. 17	15	BS Ref. 2	356. m. 6(66) P
					356. m. 6(67) JR
129	Woolnoth, St Mary	pr. c. 19	17	BS Ref. 2	357. c. 2(47) JR
130	Trench, Frederick	pr. c. 23	21	BS Ref. 2	357. c. 2(90) P
131	Cary, George	pr. c. 24	22	BS Ref. 2	357. c. 2(85) P
					357. b. 1(18)g
132	Stallingborough [inclosure]	pr. c. 28	26	BS Ref. 2	
133	Abthorp Chapel	c. 21	27	357. c. 4(24)	
134	Westminster Bridge	c. 16	30	357. c. 4(27)	
135	London [paving]	c. 22	37	357. c. 4(34)	

[a] Introduced in the Commons, but dropped after committee report *CJ* xxii, 643, 696.

[b] Introduced in the Commons, but dropped in committee *CJ* xxii, 626, 679.

[c] The MS material consists of calculations concerning the number of houses in London and 'Heads of a report about the lights' which is not the same as the committee report, *CJ* xxii, 583–4, but is on similar lines.

[d] The petition was committed and reported on in the Commons, *CJ* xxii, 568, 596, but no bill was introduced. See [No. 132].

[e] This copy of the bill may not be Harper's.

[f] Petition of Viscount Cobham. A bill to this effect passed 11 Geo. II pr. c. 20 but is not on Harper's list that year. No such petition was presented earlier.

[g] Cary's previous petition, for leave to proceed out of time, is bound as a precedent in Harper's volume 1, under this reference.

		R.H.		Bill	MS
	1738	11 Geo. II	Vol. 15		
136	Devonshire, William, Duke of	pr. c. 2	1	BS Ref. 2	357. c. 6(50) P
					357. c. 6(51) JR
137	Bedford, John, Duke of	pr. c. 3	2	BS Ref. 2	357. c. 6(52) JR
138	Molyneux, Richard, Viscount	pr. c. 5	4	BS Ref. 2	356. m. 6(63) JR
139	Jervoise, Thomas [Stratford Toney]	pr. c. 8	8	BS Ref. 2	357. c. 6(53) P
					357. c. 6(54) JR
					357. c. 6(55)*a*
140	Coles, Barnaby	pr. c. 10	10	BS Ref. 2	
141	Studholme, William	pr. c. 12	12	BS Ref. 2	
142	Packer, Robert	pr. c. 13	14	BS Ref. 2	
143	Byde, Thomas Plummer	pr. c. 14	15	BS Ref. 2	357. c. 6(58) P
144	Clerk, Dorothea	pr. c. 16	17	BS Ref. 2	
				357. c. 6(18)	
145	Speen Mead [inclosure]	pr. c. 21	22	BS Ref. 2	
146	Binbrooke [inclosure]	pr. c. 22	23	BS Ref. 2	357. c. 4(51) P
			24	BS Ref. 2	
			25	BS Ref. 2	
147	Banks, Joseph	—*b*	26	357. c. 6(28)	357. c. 6(56) P
					357. c. 6(57) JR
148	Westminster Bridge	c. 25	33	357. c. 6(39)	
149	Liverpool Dock	c. 32	38	357. c. 6(44)	
			39	357. c. 6(45)	
	1739	12 Geo. II	Vol. 16		
150	Inchiquin, William, Earl of	pr. c. 21	1	BS Ref. 2	
151	Langdale, Jordan	pr. c. 27	7	BS Ref. 2	
152	Lear, Sir John	pr. c. 28	8	BS Ref. 2	
153	Fownes, Thomas	pr. c. 29	9	BS Ref. 2	
154	Pailton [inclosure]	pr. c. 30	10	BS Ref. 2	
155	Sayer, Richard [W. Townsend]	pr. c. 4	16	BS Ref. 2	
156	Sherwin, John	pr. c. 6	18	BS Ref. 2	357. c. 7(57) P
157	Mackenzie, Sir James [Royston, Lord]	pr. c. 7	19	BS Ref. 2	357. c. 7(56) P
158	Brooksbank, Stamp	pr. c. 8	20	BS Ref. 2	
159	Worth, John	pr. c. 9	21	BS Ref. 2	
160	Hunmanby [inclosure]	pr. c. 10	22	BS Ref. 2	

a Party's consent.
b Committed in House of Lords for 18 March, but according to the committee book no committees met that day.

Appendix I

		R.H.		Bill	MS
	1739 cont.	12 Geo. II	Vol. 16		
161	Newcastle, Thomas Holles, Duke of [Stapylton]	pr. c. 17	24	BS Ref. 2	357. c. 7(58) P 357. c. 7(59) JR
162	Cowper, William, Earl	pr. c. 20	27	BS Ref. 2	357. c. 7(54) P 357. c. 7(55) JR
163	Westminster Bridge	c. 33	35	357. c. 7(36)	
164	Woolwich Church	c. 9	40	357. c. 7(42)	
165	[Ribble Bridge]	—ᵃ	42	357. c. 7(44)	
166	[General Register]	—ᵇ	46	357. c. 7(48)	
			47	357. c. 7(49)	
	1740	13 Geo. II	Vol. 17		
167	Craven, Fulwar, Lord	pr. c. 2	2	BS Ref. 2	
168	Bircham, Great [inclosure]	pr. c. 3	3	BS Ref. 2	357. c. 8(52) P
169	Conyers, Maurice	pr. c. 11	8	BS Ref. 2	357. c. 8(54) P
170	Gore, William	pr. c. 13	10	BS Ref. 2	357. c. 8(53)ᶜ
171	Inwen, Thomas	pr. c. 14	11	BS Ref. 2	
172	Talbot, Henry	pr. c. 15	12	BS Ref. 2	357. c. 8(55) P
173	Stivichall [inclosure]	pr. c. 18	15	BS Ref. 2	
174	Gunnerton [inclosure]	pr. c. 19	16	BS Ref. 2 357. c. 8(17)	
175	Whitehaven harbour	c. 14	21	357. c. 8(23)	
176	Colchester, river [Wivenhoe channel]	c. 30	22	357. c. 8(24)	
177	Sheffield Church	c. 12	23	357. c. 8(25) 357. c. 8(26)	
—	Staines Bridge	c. 25	24	357. c. 8(27) 357. c. 8(28)	357. c. 8(51) P 357. c. 8(56)ᵈ
178	[Registering seamen]	—ᵉ	33	357. c. 8(38)	
—	Collieries	c. 21	38	357. c. 8(43)	ᶠ
—	[Wool, Yorkshire]	—	45	—	357. c. 8(50) Pᵍ

ᵃ *CJ* xxiii, 298, 329 dropped at second reading.
ᵇ Introduced in the Commons, *CJ* xxiii, 315. Considered in Committee of the Whole House in the Lords when the Chancery Clerks were heard by Counsel, see their 'Case' 357. c. 7(50). Finally the matter was dropped and the judges were ordered to prepare a new bill for the next session (*LJ* xxv, 398, 408, 416). The following year the bill was introduced in the Lords (see copies 357. c. 8(34) and (35)) and after long debate, sent to the Commons, where it was lost in committee of the whole (*CJ* xxiii, 518, 524).
ᶜ Agreement signed 23 February 1739.
ᵈ Under this reference and immediately preceding it, unnumbered, are MSS concerning the bridge including extracts of acts and patents going back to the reign of Elizabeth.
ᵉ Introduced in the Commons, but negatived on the motion to commit (*CJ* xxiii, 390, 447, 468). There is a copy of the bill in the Abbot Collection, B. 4.
ᶠ The bill is not marked 'R.H.' but with it are two MS pages of draft, the docket addressed to a colliery owner, 'Nath. Richardson at the George Inn, High Holborn'. 357. c. 8(44) and (45) are printed 'Cases' on the same subject.
ᵍ Leave was given *CJ* xxiii, 481, but no bill introduced.

		R.H.		Bill	MS
	1741	14 Geo. II	Vol. 18		
179	Scawen, Robert	pr. c. 6	5	BS Ref. 2	
180	Lewis, Thomas	pr. c. 7	6	BS Ref. 2	357. c. 9(58) JR
181	Hudleston, William	pr. c. 8	7	BS Ref. 2	
182	Western, Thomas	pr. c. 10	9	BS Ref. 2	357. c. 9(57) P
183	Sherston [inclosure]	pr. c. 13	12	BS Ref. 2	
184	Brincklow [inclosure]	pr. c. 14	13	BS Ref. 2	
185	Edmunds, Thomas	pr. c. 18	14	BS Ref. 2	357. c. 9(49) P
					357. c. 9(50) JR
186	Cowper, William, Earl	pr. c. 27	17	BS Ref. 2	357. c. 9(51) P
					357. c. 9(52) JR
187	Garnock, George, Viscount	pr. c. 29	19	357. c. 9(22) BS Ref. 2	
188	Clopton, Sir Hugh	pr. c. 30	20	BS Ref. 2	357. c. 9(53) P
					357. c. 9(54) JR
					357. c. 9(55)[a]
189	Pemberton, Francis	pr. c. 31	21	BS Ref. 2	357. c. 9(47) P
					357. c. 9(48) JR
190	Knutsford, Chapelry	c. 5	23	357. c. 9(27)	
191	Tetbury, Church of	—	32	357. c. 9(36)	
192	Porter, Joseph [silk licence]	c. 4	33	357. c. 9(37)	
193	Coggs, John	c. 30	34	357. c. 9(38)	
194	Seamen [registering]	c. 38	35	357. c. 9(39)	
195	Market Street Chapel	c. 26	38	357. c. 9(42)	
196	[Encouragement of privateers]	—	—		357. c. 9(56)[b]
	1742	15 Geo. II	Vol. 19		
197	Godolphin, Francis, Earl of [inclosure]	pr. c. 3	1	BS Ref. 2[c]	357. c. 10(49) P
					357. c. 10(50) JR
—	Montfort, Henry, Lord	pr. c. 5	4	BS Ref. 2	357. c. 10(51) P
					357. c. 10(52) JR
198	Biggs, John [Pigott]	pr. c. 8		BS Ref. 2[d]	
199	Yorke, Philip	pr. c. 13	7	BS Ref. 2	
200	Horne, John	pr. c. 23	15	BS Ref. 2	
201	Carlisle, Henry, Earl of	pr. c. 24	16	BS Ref. 2	357. c. 10(53) P
					357. c. 10(54) JR
202	Brooke, Sir Job	pr. c. 28	—	BS Ref. 2[d]	357. c. 10(55) P
					357. c. 10(56) JR
203	Walcot, John	pr. c. 31	22	BS Ref. 2	357. c. 10(60) P
204	Harvey, Michael	pr. c. 34	—	BS Ref. 2[d]	

[a] Sir H. Clopton's revocation.
[b] MS draft bill. No such bill was offered this year.
[c] Copy of Dean of Ely's consent endorsed on the bill.
[d] The copies of these three bills in BS Ref. 2 are probably not Harper's.

		R.H.	Bill	MS
	1742 cont.	15 Geo. II Vol. 19		
205	Bentley, John	pr. c. 35	26	BS Ref. 2	
206	Lucas, Robert	pr. c. 37	28	BS Ref. 2	357. c. 10(57) P 357. c. 10(58) JR
207	Sutton, Beds. [Burgoyne, Sir R.]	pr. c. 40	34	BS Ref. 2	
208	Aston Cantlow [inclosure]	pr. c. 42	32	BS Ref. 2	
209	Walsingham, James	pr. c. 43	33	BS Ref. 2	357. c. 10(61) JR
210	Rolt, Edward Bayntun	pr. c. 44	34	BS Ref. 2	
211	[Amending Poor Act]	— a	38	357. c. 10(39)	
212	Fenchurch Street Church [St Catherine Colman]	c. 12	41	357. c. 10(42)	
213	Stowerbridge Church	—b	44	357. c. 10(45) 357. c. 10(46)	
214	[River Trent]	—c	45	357. c. 10(47)	
—	Hopkins, John	pr. c. 45	—	—	357. c. 10(59) P
	1743	16 Geo. II Vol. 20		
215	Kingston, Evelyn, Duke of [Stanton exchange]	pr. c. 2	1	BS Ref. 2	357. c. 12(77) JRd
216	Petre, Robert Edward, Lord	pr. c. 4	3	BS Ref. 2	357. c. 12(75) JR
217	Nuneaton [tithes]	pr. c. 6	4	BS Ref. 2	357. c. 12(81) JR
218	Holder, Charles	pr. c. 7	5	BS Ref. 2	357. c. 12(73) P
219	Chadwicke, Evelyn [Wheeler, West Leake]	pr. c. 8	6	357. c. 12(45)e	
220	Fitzherbert, Thomas	pr. c. 10	9	BS Ref. 2	357. c. 12(72) JR
221	Gape, Thomas	pr. c. 12	11	BS Ref. 2	357. c. 12(80) P

[a] Introduced in the Commons but dropped after first reading (*CJ* xxiv, 246, 268). The bill was ordered to be printed by the House, copy in the Abbot Collection, B. 12.

[b] Introduced in the Commons and lost when the report stage was put off for two months (*CJ* xxiv, 95, 217).

[c] Introduced in the Commons, but dropped after first reading (*CJ* xxiv, 112, 163). A printed 'case' and a map of the navigation are bound, unnumbered, at the end of volume 357. c. 10.

[d] Under reference 357. c. 12(82) are five papers with Harper's item numbers 42A to 45A dating from 1730–3. These were originally folded together and endorsed 'Copy of the Instruments for Uniting and Consolidating the two medieties of Cotgrave Church into one Rectory'; they include the Duke of Kingston's petition to the Archbishop of York and the Archbishop's agreement. These papers are followed by 'Wise William Pierrepont's reasons against a public register', 357. c. 12(83).

[e] MS amendments to this bill are endorsed on the copy of pr. c. 7 in BS Ref. 2.

		R.H.		Bill	MS
	1743 cont.	16 Geo. II	Vol. 20		
222	Aston Tirrold [inclosure]	pr. c. 15	14	BS Ref. 2	
223	Earley Common [inclosure]	pr. c. 17	16	BS Ref. 2	
224	Cooke, James (jr) [Ravensworth]	pr. c. 30	24	BS Ref. 2	357. c. 12(76) JR
225	Savage, Thomas	pr. c. 31	25	357. c. 12(64)	357. c. 12(78) P
			26	BS Ref. 2	357. c. 12(79) JR
226	Delahay, Thomas	—	32	357. c. 12(71)[a]	357. c. 12(74) P
	1744	17 Geo. II[b]	Vol. 21		
227	Schutz, Augustus	pr. c. 3	2	BS Ref. 2	
228	Westonbirt [inclosure]	pr. c. 5	4	BS Ref. 2	
229	Abergavenny, William, Lord	pr. c. 13	—	BS Ref. 2	358. b. 4(56) P
230	Bassledon Heath [inclosure]	pr. c. 15	7	BS Ref. 2 358. b. 4(7)	
231	Flecknoe Common [inclosure]	pr. c. 16	8	BS Ref. 2	
232	Langton [inclosure]	pr. c. 17	9	BS Ref. 2	
233	Clarke, Godfrey [Roehampton, Bagenall]	pr. c. 19	11	BS Ref. 2	358. b. 4(48) JR 358. b. 4(49) JR
234	Bowater, Edward	pr. c. 20	12	BS Ref. 2	358. b. 4(50) PJR
235	Powys, Edward	pr. c. 21	13	BS Ref. 2	
236	Buccleuch, Francis, Duke of [Lord Dalkeith]	pr. c. 23	—	BS Ref. 2	
237	Plimouth, Other Lewis, Earl of	pr. c. 23 [24]	15	BS Ref. 2	358. b. 4(54) P 358. b. 4(63) P[c]
238	Sutton, Sir Robert	pr. c. 25 [26]	17	BS Ref. 2	358. b. 4(53) JR
239	Thornhagh, John	pr. c. 27 [28]	19	BS Ref. 2[d]	358. b. 4(61) P
240	Cliffe, Richard	pr. c. 28 [29]	20	BS Ref. 2	
241	Downes, George	pr. c. 30 [31]	22	BS Ref. 2	
242	Cullum, John	pr. c. 31 [32]	23	BS Ref. 2	358. b. 4(57) P
243	Fownes, Thomas	pr. c. 33 [34]	25	BS Ref. 2	358. b. 4(60) JR

[a] Harper's comments on the bill are endorsed on this printed copy.
[b] There are two chapter numbers 23 in the printed table of private acts. I give the chapter numbers in use at the British Museum in square brackets when they differ from those of the printed table.
[c] Marked 'The last petition'.   [d] Two copies.

		R.H.		Bill	MS
	1744 cont.	**17 Geo. II Vol. 21**			
244	Hawker, Peter	pr. c. 34 [35]	26	BS Ref. 2	358. b. 4(59) P
245	Stoneham, North [inclosure]	pr. c. 35 [36]	—	BS Ref. 2	
246	Rippon [inclosure]	pr. c. 36 [37]	28	BS Ref. 2	358. b. 4(55) P[a]
247	[Aire & Calder rivers]	—	39	358. b. 4(44)	358. b. 4(45)[b]
—	[Gloucester clothiers]	—	—	—	358. b. 4(52)[c]
—	[Wark, Northumberland inclosure]	—	—	—	358. b. 4(58)[d]
—	[Snaith inclosure]	—	—	—	358. b. 4(64)[e]
	1745	**18 Geo. II Vol. 22**			
—	York Buildings Co. [Lord Widdrington]	c. 37	—	ƒ	
248	Peachy, Sir John	pr. c. 6	1	BS Ref. 2	
249	Penton, Dorothy	pr. c. 7	—	BS Ref. 2	357. c. 14(37) P
250	Petersfield [Churcher's charity]	pr. c. 10	4	BS Ref. 2	357. c. 14(44) P
251	Myddleton, Sir William	pr. c. 15	7	BS Ref. 2	357. c. 14(50) P
252	Sutton, Sir Robert	pr. c. 17	9	BS Ref. 2	357. c. 14(38) P 357. c. 14(40) JR
253	Robinson, William	pr. c. 18	10	BS Ref. 2	357. c. 14(47) P
254	Gould, Edward	pr. c. 23	17	BS Ref. 2	357. c. 14(42) JR
255	Keck, Anthony	pr. c. 20	14	BS Ref. 2	357. c. 14(41) JR
256	Wright, Robert	pr. c. 24	18	BS Ref. 2	
257	Hobbes, Rodolph	pr. c. 25	19	357. c. 14(20)	
258	Luscombe, Richard	pr. c. 26	20	BS Ref. 2	
259	Faxton [inclosure]	pr. c. 27	—	BS Ref. 2	
260	Navy [courts martial]	c. 35	24	357. c. 14(27)	
261	Surgeons of London	c. 15	28	357. c. 14(31) 357. c. 14(32)	357. c. 14(43) P
262	Hanbury, William [R. Bateman]	—	41	357. c. 14(46) MS copy	357. c. 14(45) JR
—	Fane, Charles, Viscount	—	—	—	357. c. 14(48) P[g]
—	Owen, Humphrey	—	—	—	357. c. 14(49) P

[a] Petition and articles of agreement.
[b] 'Mr Milne's observations.' 358. b. 4(46) and (47) are the petition and committee report as printed *CJ* xxix, 520–1, 577–8. The bill dropped after first reading (*ibid.*, p. 644).
[c] Petition for opening Levant trade, not presented.
[d] Petition, not presented. [e] Articles of agreement, see [No. 391].
ƒ This item occurs, unnumbered, in Harper's list of 'Acts drawn', but there is no sign of any papers on the subject in the collection.
[g] No petition offered this year. See [No. 330].

		R.H.	Bill	MS
	1746	19 Geo. II	Vol. 23	
263	Vincent, Francis	pr. c. 1	1	BS Ref. 2	357. d. 1(41) P
				357. d. 1(42) JR
264	Alie, Richard	pr. c. 3	2	BS Ref. 2	
				MS copy	
265	Grimston, William, Viscount	pr. c. 6	3	BS Ref. 2	
266	Rippon [inclosure]	pr. c. 9	6	BS Ref. 2	357. c. 1(1)[a]
					357. d. 1(43)
267	Kelfield [inclosure]	pr. c. 10	7	BS Ref. 2	
268	Rolt, Edward Bayntun	pr. c. 11	8	BS Ref. 2	357. d. 1(50) P
					357. d. 1(51) JR
269	Leeds, Thomas, Duke of	pr. c. 12	9	BS Ref. 2	
270	Plimouth, Other Lewis, Earl of	pr. c. 17	13	BS Ref. 2	357. d. 1(45) JR
271	Lechmere, Richard	pr. c. 20	15	BS Ref. 2	357. d. 1(39) P
					357. d. 1(40) JR
272	Manners, John	pr. c. 21	16	BS Ref. 2	357. d. 1(47) P
					357. d. 1(48) JR
273	Sill, Joseph	pr. c. 22	17	BS Ref. 2	357. d. 1(38) JR
274	Daniel, Sir William Duckinfield	pr. c. 28	18	BS Ref. 2	
				MS copy	
275	Bennet, Thomas	pr. c. 29	19	357. d. 1(20)	357. d. 1(49) JR
			20	BS Ref. 2	
276	Pitt, Lora [Dorchester Road]	c. 24	24	357. d. 1(25)	357. d. 1(44) P
			25	357. d. 1(26)	
—	Orme, Garton	—	—	—	357. d. 1(46) P
	1747	20 Geo. II	Vol. 24		
277	Stamford, Harry, Earl of	pr. c. 2	1	BS Ref. 2	
278	Leicester, Thomas, Earl of	pr. c. 3	2	BS Ref. 2	357. d. 2(44) P
					357. d. 2(45) JR
279	Byron, William, Lord	pr. c. 4	3	BS Ref. 2	357. d. 2(64) P
280	Parkyns, Sir Thomas	pr. c. 5	4	BS Ref. 2	357. d. 2(65) P
281	Smith, Lillie	pr. c. 7	6	BS Ref. 2	
282	Dring, Edmund	pr. c. 8	7	BS Ref. 2	357. d. 2(63) P
283	Sutton Marsh [Lascelles Metcalf]	pr. c. 9	8	BS Ref. 2	357. d. 2(41) P[b]

[a] Draft inclosure award. Gregory Rhodes (father-in-law of Robert Harper junior) was one of the commissioners named in the act.

[b] 357. d. 2(42) and (43) are a petition to the Duchy of Lancaster for permission to proceed with the bill, and a report on the circumstances from the Attorney General of the Duchy to the Chancellor.

Appendix I

		R.H.		Bill	MS
	1747 cont.	20 Geo. II	Vol. 24		
284	Kynaston, Thomas	pr. c. 10	9	BS Ref. 2	357. d. 2(67) P
285	Burton, Simon	pr. c. 11	10	BS Ref. 2	
286	Leicester, Joceline, Earl of	pr. c. 12	11	BS Ref. 2	357. d. 2(58) P 357. d. 2(59) JR
287	Oakeley, Richard	pr. c. 13	12	BS Ref. 2	
288	Talbot, Henry	pr. c. 14	13	BS Ref. 2	357. d. 2(51) P
289	Moore, William	pr. c. 15	14	BS Ref. 2	357. d. 2(68)[a]
290	Colmore, Anne	pr. c. 16	15	BS Ref. 2	357. d. 2(49) P
291	Sambrooke, Mary	pr. c. 17	16	BS Ref. 2	357. d. 2(50) JR 357. d. 2(60) P 357. d. 2(61) JR
292	Mitchell, William	pr. c. 18	17	BS Ref. 2	
293	Garrard, Thomas	pr. c. 19	18	BS Ref. 2	357. d. 2(46) P 357. d. 2(47) P 357. d. 2(48) JR
294	Kemeys, Jane	pr. c. 22	21	BS Ref. 2	357. d. 2(52) P 357. d. 2(53) JR
295	Northumberland, Mary, Duchess of [Miss Parsons, Frogmore]	pr. c. 24	23	BS Ref. 2	357. d. 2(66) P
296	Gwillym, Robert	pr. c. 25	24	BS Ref. 2	
297	Drew, Robert	pr. c. 26	25	BS Ref. 2	357. d. 2(54) P 357. d. 2(55) JR
298	Kelfield [inclosure]	pr. c. 29	28	BS Ref. 2	
299	[Iver Common inclosure]	—[b]	29	357. d. 2(30)	357. d. 2(62) P
300	Orme, Garton	—[c]	30	357. d. 2(31)	357. d. 2(56) P 357. d. 2(57) JR
301	Wednesfield Church	c. 27	31	357. d. 2(32)	
302	St Andrews University	c. 32	37	357. d. 2(38)	
	1748	21 Geo. II	Vol. 25		
303	Lanesborough, George, Viscount	pr. c. 6	4	BS Ref. 2	
304	Walter, Abel	pr. c. 9	6	BS Ref. 2	[d]
305	Carthew, Thomas	pr. c. 13	11	BS Ref. 2	
306	Fleetwood, Henry	pr. c. 14	12	BS Ref. 2	
307	Dawson, Roper	pr. c. 16	14	BS Ref. 2	357. d. 3(45) JR

[a] Power of attorney to Robert and Samuel Harper to give consents before the committee.
[b] The petition is as printed *CJ* xxv, 194–5; it was committed to a select committee (*ibid.*, p. 256), which did not report.
[c] Passed the Lords, but the Commons committee did not report (*CJ* xxv, 359).
[d] Draft petition for the King's consent to this bill is written upon the printed bill [No. 227] 17 Geo. II pr. c. 3 in BS Ref. 2.

		R.H.		Bill	MS
	1748 cont.	21 Geo. II	Vol. 25		
308	Fox, James	pr. c. 17	15	BS Ref. 2	357. d. 3(48) P
309	Chafin, George	pr. c. 18	16	BS Ref. 2	357. d. 3(44) P
310	Naish, Hugh [Creed]	pr. c. 20	18	BS Ref. 2	357. d. 3(51) P
					357. d. 3(52) JR
311	Keck, Anthony	pr. c. 21	19	BS Ref. 2	357. d. 3(49) P
					357. d. 3(50) JR
312	Rugby School	pr. c. 23	21	BS Ref. 2	357. d. 3(53) P
313	Williams, Richard	pr. c. 24	22	BS Ref. 2	357. d. 3(46) P
					357. d. 3(47) JR
314	Faceby [inclosure]	pr. c. 25	23	BS Ref. 2	
315	Holton [inclosure]	pr. c. 27	25	357. d. 3(25)	
			26	BS Ref. 2	
316	Navy [courts martial]	c. 11	29	357. d. 3 (29)	
317	Liverpool Church	c. 24	32	357. d. 3(32)	
318	Scotland [treason]	c. 19	33	357. d. 3(33)	
319	Scotland [disarming]	c. 34	34A	357. d. 3(35)	
	1749	22 Geo. II	Vol. 26		
320	Woodhey, East [inclosure]	pr. c. 1	1	BS Ref. 2	
321	Betlow [rates]	pr. c. 6	2	BS Ref. 2	
322	Broughton [titles]	pr. c. 9	5	357. d. 4(5)	
323	Luther, Richard	pr. c. 10	6	BS Ref. 2	
324	Rogers, John	pr. c. 11	7	BS Ref. 2	357. d. 4(51) P
325	Kimpson, Thomas [Harrison]	pr. c. 13	8	BS Ref. 2 MS copy	357. d. 4(62) P
326	Rash, Samuel	pr. c. 15	9	BS Ref. 2	
327	Burnett, Dr Gilbert	pr. c. 21	12	BS Ref. 2	357. d. 4(58) P
					357. d. 4(59) JR
328	Teynham, Henry, Lord	pr. c. 23	14	BS Ref. 2	357. d. 4(56) P
					357. d. 4(57) JR
329	Vane, William, Viscount	pr. c. 24	15	BS Ref. 2	357. d. 4(63) JR
330	Fane, Charles, Viscount	pr. c. 25	16	BS Ref. 2	357. d. 4(64) P
331	Williams, Sir John	pr. c. 27	18	BS Ref. 2	357. d. 4(54) P
					357. d. 4(55) JR
332	Levinz, William	pr. c. 28	19	BS Ref. 2	357. d. 4(50) P
333	Lockwood, John	pr. c. 31	22	BS Ref. 2	357. d. 4(52) P
334	Lytton, William Robinson [Lawrence Williams]	pr. c. 34	25	BS Ref. 2	
335	Gwyn, Francis	pr. c. 35	26	BS Ref. 2	357. d. 4(53) JR
336	Lymington, Catherine	pr. c. 43	28	BS Ref. 2	357. d. 4(65) P
					357. d. 4(66) JR
337	Mansfield, Paul	pr. c. 45	29	BS Ref. 2	357. d. 4(60) JR
338	Blundson, Broad [inclosure]	pr. c. 46	33	BS Ref. 2	

		R.H.	Bill	MS
	1749 cont.	22 Geo. II Vol. 26		
339	Weymouth Harbour	c. 22	35	357. d. 4(35)
340	Whittlesey Fen	c. 19	36	357. d. 4(36)
—	[River Ouse]	—	47	357. d. 4(47)[a]
—	[Ellenfoot Harbour]	—	—	357. d. 4(61)[b]
	1750	23 Geo. II Vol. 27		MS[c]
341	Bradford, Thomas, Earl of	pr. c. 6	1	BS Ref. 2
342	Pembroke and Montgomery, Earl of	pr. c. 13	4	BS Ref. 2 · 357. d. 5(p. 25) JR
343	Northumberland, Hugh, Earl of	pr. c. 14	5	BS Ref. 2 MS copy · 357. d. 5(p. 41) P
344	Lake, Dame Mary [Thurrock Marsh]	pr. c. 16	7	BS Ref. 2 · 357. d. 5(p. 39) P
345	Trevor, John	pr. c. 17	—	BS Ref. 2 · 357. d. 5(36) P / 357. d. 5(37) JR
346	Barker, Hugh (jr)	pr. c. 19	10	BS Ref. 2 · 357. d. 5(p. 36)P
347	Lanoe, Charles	pr. c. 20	11	BS Ref. 2 · 357. d. 5(35) P
348	Hylton, John	pr. c. 21	12	BS Ref. 2
349	Walters, Henry	pr. c. 22	13	BS Ref. 2 · 357. d. 5(p. 29) P
350	Shepheard, Samuel	pr. c. 23	14	BS Ref. 2 · 357. d. 5(34) P
351	Dolman, Robert	pr. c. 26	17	BS Ref. 2 · 357. d. 5(17)
352	Sergison, Thomas	pr. c. 28	19	BS Ref. 2
353	Orme, Garton	pr. c. 30	21	BS Ref. 2
354	Heyford, Nether [inclosure]	pr. c. 31	22	BS Ref. 2
355	Culcheth [inclosure]	pr. c. 32	23	BS Ref. 2
356	Gloucester, City of	c. 15	26	357. d. 5(27)
357	Loyne, alias Lune, River of [Lancaster Quay]	c. 12	27	357. d. 5(28)
—]	Bulstrode, Edward	—	—	— · 357. d. 5(p. 20) P
—	Myddelton, Richard	—	—	— · 357. d. 5(p. 33) P
—	Bulkeley, James, Viscount	—	—	— · 357. d. 5(p. 42) P

[a] Printed bill, much amended. 357. d. 4(48) is a 'case' on the same subject. The bill was dropped in committee (*CJ* xxv, 733, 786, 837, 849, 858, 861, 866).

[b] Petition to the Commons as printed *CJ* xxv, 709. Leave given (*ibid.*, p. 719), but no bill introduced. See [No. 478].

[c] In this volume, British Museum item numbers have not been assigned to the MS material beyond item (37), so I give instead Harper's MS pagination. The manuscript section concludes with a note of the 'Method of sending a Letter or Packet express by the Post' between Doncaster and London, 357. d. 5(p. 47).

		R.H.		Bill	MS
	1751	24 Geo. II	Vol. 28		
358	Courtenay, George	pr. c. 42	1	BS Ref. 2	
359	Courtenay, Kellond	pr. c. 41	2	BS Ref. 2	
360	Newland, William	pr. c. 39	4	BS Ref. 2	357. d. 6(50) JR
361	Blois, Ralph	pr. c. 37	6	BS Ref. 2	357. d. 6(56) P
362	Dalkeith, Francis, Earl of	pr. c. 35	8	BS Ref. 2	
363	Powis, Henry Arthur, Earl of	pr. c. 33	10	BS Ref. 2	357. d. 6(44) P
364	Hutton Bushell [inclosure]	pr. c. 27	12	BS Ref. 2	357. d. 6(47) P
365	Besford Common [inclosure]	pr. c. 26	13	BS Ref. 2	357. d. 6(45) P
366	Dunsby [inclosure]	pr. c. 25	14	BS Ref. 2	357. d. 6(54) P
367	Farthingstone [inclosure]	pr. c. 24	15	357. d. 6(16)	
368	Moyle, Thomas	pr. c. 20	19	BS Ref. 2	357. d. 6(55) P
369	Bulstrode, Edward	pr. c. 18	21	BS Ref. 2	357. d. 6(51) JR
370	Ellerker, Eaton Mainwairing	pr. c. 17	22	BS Ref. 2	
371	Pleydell, Edmund	pr. c. 15	24	BS Ref. 2	357. d. 6(43) P
372	Jekyll, John	pr. c. 14	25	BS Ref. 2	357. d. 6(42) P
373	Egmont, John, Earl of	pr. c. 11	28	BS Ref. 2	357. d. 6(53) JR
374	Cowper, William, Earl	pr. c. 10	29	BS Ref. 2	357. d. 6(52) P
375	Hulse, Edward	pr. c. 6	32	BS Ref. 2	
—	Ancaster, Peregrine, Duke of	—	33	357. d. 6(34)	357. d. 6(46) P
376	Bulkeley, James Viscount	—	34	357. d. 6(35)	
377	Carlisle [Road]	c. 25	38	357. d. 6(39)	
—	Leyborne, William	pr. c. 29	—	357. d. 6(49) MS copy	357. d. 6(48) P
	1752	25 Geo. II	Vol. 29		
378	Devonshire, William, Duke of	pr. c. 2	2	BS Ref. 2	
379	Powis, William, Marquis of	pr. c. 4	5	BS Ref. 2	
380	Heathcote, Sir Thomas	pr. c. 8	8	BS Ref. 2	
381	Bland, Sir John	pr. c. 9	9	BS Ref. 2	357. d. 9(47) JR
382	Blantyre, William, Lord	pr. c. 5	10	BS Ref. 2	*a*
383	Wyndham, William	pr. c. 12	12	BS Ref. 2	

a 'Consent of Lady Dowager Blantyre ... in ye Scots form' and extract of judges' report are 357. d. 5(pp. 45, 46).

		R.H.	Bill		MS
	1752 cont.	25 Geo. II	Vol. 29		
384	Barnesley, William	pr. c. 15	16	BS Ref. 2	
385	Wicker, John	pr. c. 16	17	BS Ref. 2	357. d. 9(49) P
386	Preston, John	pr. c. 17	18	BS Ref. 2	357. d. 9(48) P
					357. d. 9(51) JR
387	Lascelles, Daniel	pr. c. 19	19	BS Ref. 2	
			20	BS Ref. 2	
388	Hunter, Thomas Orby	pr. c. 21	22	BS Ref. 2	
389	Ombersley [manor]	pr. c. 22	23	BS Ref. 2	357. d. 9(50) P
390	Narborough [inclosure]	pr. c. 23	24	BS Ref. 2	
391	Snaith [inclosure]	pr. c. 26	25	357. d. 9(24)	[a]
392	Drayton [inclosure]	pr. c. 25	27	357. d. 9(26)	[b]
393	Wytham on the Hill	pr. c. 27	29	357. d. 9(28)	
	Infield [inclosure]		30	BS Ref. 2	
394	Pusey [tithes]	—	31	357. d. 9(30)[c]	
395	Donegall, Arthur, Earl of	—	32	357. d. 9(31)	
—	Chandler, Richard	pr. c. 28	—	BS Ref. 2 MS copy	
	1753	26 Geo. II	Vol. 30		
396	Pusey, John Allen	pr. c. 9	1	BS Ref. 2	
397	Scudamore, Frances Fitzroy	pr. c. 34	4	BS Ref. 2	
398	Inge, Theodore William	pr. c. 12	6	BS Ref. 2	357. d. 10(48) P
399	Chadwicke, Evelyn	pr. c. 22	7	BS Ref. 2	
400	Rawstorn, William [Bassledon to sell to Lord Fane]	pr. c. 38	10	BS Ref. 2	357. d. 10(49) P
401	Brain, Benjamin	pr. c. 36	12	BS Ref. 2	357. d. 10(47) P
402	Ashburnham, John, Earl of	pr. c. 32	13	BS Ref. 2	
403	Croft, Stephen [Stillington prebend]	pr. c. 25	14	BS Ref. 2	357. d. 10(53) P
404	Pitt, George	pr. c. 24	15	BS Ref. 2	
405	Jekyll, Ann	pr. c. 19	18	BS Ref. 2	357. d. 10(51) P
406	Small, John Foyle	pr. c. 11	19	BS Ref. 2	357. d. 10(52) P
407	Gilbert, Alice	pr. c. 10	20	BS Ref. 2	
408	Meynell, Littleton Pointz	pr. c. 42	21	BS Ref. 2	357. d. 9(52) JR
409	Felton Common [inclosure]	pr. c. 46	23	BS Ref. 2	

[a] MS articles of agreement, see above, 1744, following [No. 248].
[b] MS amendments to this bill are noted on 25 Geo. II pr. c. 24 in BS Ref. 2.
[c] Harper's notes on this bill occur on p. 3 of this printed copy.

		R.H.		Bill	MS
	1753 cont.	26 Geo. II	Vol. 30		
410	Hexham [inclosure]	pr. c. 29	24	BS Ref. 2	
411	Leathley [inclosure]	pr. c. 28	25	BS Ref. 2	
412	Eastley Martin, alias Botherup [inclosure]	pr. c. 27	30	BS Ref. 2	
413	Wich, Sir Cyril	pr. c. 33	31	BS Ref. 2	357. d. 10(50) P
414	[Broad Wheels]	c. 30	38	357. d. 10(38)	
	1754	27 Geo. II	Vol. 31		
415	Kemp, William	pr. c. 6	2	BS Ref. 2	357. d. 11(32) JR
416	Kitchin, Elizabeth	pr. c. 7	3	BS Ref. 2	
417	Simonburn [inclosure]	pr. c. 8	4	BS Ref. 2	
418	Shildon [inclosure]	pr. c. 10	6	BS Ref. 2	
419	Normanton [inclosure]	pr. c. 11	7	BS Ref. 2	357. d. 11(33) P
420	Somerset, Charles, Duke of [Sale of Lindsey House]	pr. c. 18	10	BS Ref. 2	357. d. 11(34) P
421	Powis, Henry Arthur, Earl of [Sale of Hendon]	pr. c. 19	11	BS Ref. 2	
422	Powis, Henry Arthur, Earl of [fee-farm in Ireland]	pr. c. 20	12	BS Ref. 2	
423	Clinton, Hugh, Earl	pr. c. 21	13	BS Ref. 2	
424	Bulkeley, Thomas James, Viscount	pr. c. 22	14	BS Ref. 2	357. d. 11(39) P 357. d. 11(40) JR
425	Pitt, George	pr. c. 24	15	BS Ref. 2	357. d. 11(37) P 357. d. 11(38) JR
426	Scudamore, Charles	pr. c. 23	16	BS Ref. 2	357. d. 11(36) P
427	Colebrooke, Robert	pr. c. 25	17	BS Ref. 2	357. d. 11(41) P 357. d. 11(42) JR
428	Speke, Anne	pr. c. 26	18	BS Ref. 2	
429	Pryce, John Powell	pr. c. 29	21	BS Ref. 2	357. d. 11(43) JR
430	Barker, Hugh	pr. c. 33	25	BS Ref. 2	
431	Daly, Charles	pr. c. 34	26	BS Ref. 2	
432	Noguier, Mary	pr. c. 38	30	BS Ref. 2	357. d. 11(35) P
	1755	28 Geo. II	Vol. 32		
433	Crowle, Richard	pr. c. 41	4	BS Ref. 2	357. d. 12(61) P
434	Christ's Hospital	pr. c. 7	5	BS Ref. 2	
435	Hampden, John	pr. c. 14	6	BS Ref. 2	357. d. 12(53) P
436	Mason, Thomas	pr. c. 16	7	BS Ref. 2	357. d. 12(57) P
437	Leheup, Peter	pr. c. 13	8	BS Ref. 2	
438	Morice, Sir William [St Aubyn]	pr. c. 8	9	BS Ref. 2	357. d. 12(52) P
439	Chester, Archdeaconry [Mortuaries in Cheshire]	c. 6	10	357. d. 12(10)	

		R.H.		Bill	MS
	1755 cont.	28 Geo. II	Vol. 32		
440	St John, Ellis [St Mary Hall]	pr. c. 6	11	BS Ref. 2	357. d. 12(62) P
441	Ibbetson, Sir Henry	pr. c. 10	12	BS Ref. 2	357. d. 12(58) P
442	Northleigh, Stephen	pr. c. 12	13	BS Ref. 2	
442A	Sankey Brook	c. 8	—	—	357. d. 12(66)*a*
443	Chudleigh, Sir George	pr. c. 11	14	BS Ref. 2	
444	Blewitt, Edmond	pr. c. 18	16	BS Ref. 2	357. d. 12(59) P
445	Middleton, Francis, Lord [Exchange of lands in Leake]	pr. c. 43	17	BS Ref. 2	357. d. 12(54) P
446	Walter, Edward	pr. c. 45	18	BS Ref. 2	357. d. 12(51) P
447	Spelman, Edward	pr. c. 17	20	BS Ref. 2	357. d. 12(60) P
448	Myton [Stapylton]	pr. c. 42	21	BS Ref. 2	357. d. 12(70) P
449	Colt, Sir John Dutton	pr. c. 44	22	BS Ref. 2	
450	Berkeley, Augustus, Earl of	pr. c. 4	24	BS Ref. 2	357. d. 12(69) P
451	Caldecot, Gilbert	pr. c. 48	25	BS Ref. 2	357. d. 12(56) P
452	Northumberland, Mary, Duchess of [Lambard to sell to Lady Jane Coke]	pr. c. 5	26	BS Ref. 2	357. d. 12(55) P
453	Breaston Cow Pasture [inclosure]	pr. c. 51	28	BS Ref. 2	357. d. 12(63) P
—	Calverley [inclosure]	pr. c. 29	29	BS Ref. 2	357. d. 12(72)*b*
454	Marsk [inclosure]	pr. c. 30	35	BS Ref. 2	
455	Nunburnholme [inclosure]	pr. c. 27	37	BS Ref. 2	
456	Osmotherley [inclosure]	pr. c. 50	38	BS Ref. 2	
457	Slingsby [inclosure]	pr. c. 25	41	BS Ref. 2	
458	[Bentham Moor inclosure]	—*c*	42	357. d. 12(42)	
459	Moreau, David	—	45	357. d. 12(46)	
—	Morgan, Richard	pr. c. 49	46 46B	357. d. 12(48) BS Ref. 2	357. d. 12(64)*d*
—	Broadhead, Theodore Henry	pr. c. 34	47	357. d. 12(49) MS copy	
—	[Leeds Watch]	—	—	—	357. d. 12(65)*e*

a Petition for the bill and a petition in favour of it, as printed *CJ* xxvii, 53, 55. Also a second petition in favour which is printed in abbreviated form (*ibid.*, p. 56).

b A petition against the bill and a draft arbitration agreement.

c Dropped after first reading in the Commons (*CJ* xxvii, 98, 181).

d Petition. Copies of summonses for witnesses to attend in this divorce case are bound as precedents in Harper's volume 1, 357. b. 1(9) and (10).

e Petition to the House of Commons. No such petition was offered this year.

Appendix I

		R.H.		Bill	MS
	1756	29 Geo. II	Vol. 33		
460	Hanmer, Esther	pr. c. 5	3	BS Ref. 2	358. b. 1(68) P
461	Radway Field [inclosure]	pr. c. 7	5	BS Ref. 2	
462	Vere of Hanworth, Vere, Lord	pr. c. 18	11	BS Ref. 2	358. b. 1(66) P
463	Lane, Ralph	pr. c. 19	12	BS Ref. 2	358. b. 1(74) P
464	Broadhead, Theodore Henry	pr. c. 23	16	BS Ref. 2	358. b. 1(69) P
465	Roper, Trevor Charles	pr. c. 24	17	BS Ref. 2	358. b. 1(67) P
466	Baugh, Thomas Folliot	pr. c. 25	18	BS Ref. 2	
467	Catherine Hall, Cambridge	pr. c. 26	19	BS Ref. 2	
468	Talbot, John (jr)	pr. c. 28	21	BS Ref. 2	358. b. 1(70) P
469	Francke, Evelyn Charles	pr. c. 31	24	BS Ref. 2	
470	Awbrey, Richard Gough	pr. c. 32	25	BS Ref. 2	
471	Glover, Richard	pr. c. 34	27	BS Ref. 2	
472	Cranston, James, Lord	pr. c. 46	35	BS Ref. 2	
473	Bulkeley, Thomas James, Viscount	pr. c. 47	36	BS Ref. 2	
474	Williams, Sir Hutchins	pr. c. 48	37	BS Ref. 2	358. b. 1(72) P
475	Delaval, Francis Blake	pr. c. 49	38	BS Ref. 2	
476	Mundy, Wrightson	pr. c. 50	39	BS Ref. 2	
477	Egleton, alias Edgeton [inclosure]	pr. c. 52	41	BS Ref. 2	357. d. 12(71) P
478	Ellenfoot Harbour	c. 57	42	358. b. 1(44)	357. d. 4(61) P
479	Irwin, Henry, Viscount	—	45	358. b. 1(46)	358. b. 1(73)[a]
480	Nine, alias Nen, alias Nene, River of	—	48	358. b. 1(47)	
481	Wheelwright, John [Riley]	pr. c. 41	64	358. b. 1(63*) MS copy	358. b. 1(64) P 358. b. 1.(65) P
482	[Wakefield Roads]	—[b]	63	358. b. 1(63)	
—	Heneage, George Fieschi	—	—	—	358. b. 1(71) P
	1757	30 Geo. II	Vol. 34		
483	Burchester, alias Burcester, alias Bissiter Market End [inclosure]	pr. c. 7	7	BS Ref. 2	
484	Richmond and Lenox, Charles, Duke of	pr. c. 10	10	BS Ref. 2	

[a] Judges' report and MS draft bill.
[b] Dropped after first reading (*CJ* xxvii, 572). The print is marked 'R.H. part'.

		R.H.	Bill	MS
	1757 cont.	30 Geo. II	Vol. 34	
485	Sutton Coldfield [Luttrell]	pr. c. 13	13	358. b. 2(57) P
486	Jeffreys, Mary	pr. c. 14	14	BS Ref. 2
487	Stragglethorpe [inclosure]	pr. c. 15	15	BS Ref. 2
488	Piddington [inclosure]	pr. c. 17	17	BS Ref. 2
489	Wingerworth [Tupton inclosure]	pr. c. 18	18	BS Ref. 2
490	Arundell of Wardour, Henry, Lord	pr. c. 23	23	BS Ref. 2
491	Irwin, Henry, Viscount	pr. c. 24	24	BS Ref. 2
492	Chafin, George	pr. c. 27	27	BS Ref. 2
493	Bagster, Thomas	pr. c. 28	28	BS Ref. 2 · 358. b. 2(58) P
494	Matfen, West [inclosure]	pr. c. 34	34	BS Ref. 2
495	Pocklington [inclosure]	pr. c. 38	38	BS Ref. 2
496	Ward, Charles	pr. c. 47	47	BS Ref. 2
497	Molineux, Crispe	pr. c. 48	48	BS Ref. 2
498	Vince, Henry Chivers	pr. c. 50	50	BS Ref. 2 · 358. b. 2(56) P
499	Buchanan, George	pr. c. 57	57	BS Ref. 2 MS copy
500	Steavens, Sir Thomas	—	60	358. b. 2(52)
501	[Guardians of Plymouth poor]	—[a]	61	358. b. 2(53)
—	Lloyd, Simon	—	—	358. b. 2(59) P
—	[Iron imports]	—	—	358. b. 2(60)[b]
—	Ferrers, Mary, Countess of	—	—	358. b. 2(61) P[c]
	1758	31 Geo. II	Vol. 35	
502	Churches [50 new]	pr. c. 2	2	BS Ref. 2 · 358. b. 3(50) P
503	Egmont, John, Earl of	pr. c. 12	12	BS Ref. 2 · 358. b. 3(55) P
504	Verney, Ralph, Earl of	pr. c. 13	13	BS Ref. 2 · 358. b. 3(54) P
505	Bulkeley, Thomas James, Viscount	pr. c. 15	15	BS Ref. 2
506	Kirkleatham [Sir W. Turner's charities]	pr. c. 16	16	BS Ref. 2 · 358. b. 3(49) P
507	Read, William	pr. c. 18	18	BS Ref. 2 · 358. b. 3(51) P

[a] Petition committed in the Commons and leave given but no bill introduced (*CJ* xxvii, 691, 719).

[b] Draft petition to the Commons by iron manufacturers of Birmingham for import of bar iron duty free; no such petition recorded *CJ*.

[c] Wording differs slightly from that printed *LJ* xxix, 98–9.

		R.H.		Bill	MS
	1758 cont.	31 Geo. II	Vol. 35		
508	Tufnell, George Forster	pr. c. 21	21	BS Ref. 2	358. b. 3(53) P
509	Leeds, Town of [Brandling waggon way]	pr. c. 22	22	BS Ref. 2	
510	Ottringham [inclosure]	pr. c. 23	23	BS Ref. 2	
511	Brompton [inclosure]	pr. c. 24	24	BS Ref. 2	
512	Newton Moor [inclosure]	pr. c. 26	26	BS Ref. 2 358. b. 3(24)	
513	Helmdon [inclosure]	pr. c. 33	33	BS Ref. 2	
514	Molyneux, Charles William	—	43	*a*	358. b. 3(52) P
515	Calder, River of	c. 72	45	358. b. 3(40)	357. b. 1(11)
—	Collins, Robert	—	*b*	—	
	1759	32 Geo. II	Vol. 36		
516	Bentley [inclosure]	pr. c. 4	4	BS Ref. 2	357. c. 13(67) P
517	Bootle, Richard [Wilbraham]	pr. c. 12	12	BS Ref. 2 MS copy	
518	Kingston, Evelyn, Duke of	pr. c. 21	21	BS Ref. 2	357. c. 13(61) P 357. c. 13(68) JR
519	Powis, Henry Arthur, Earl of	pr. c. 25	25	BS Ref. 2*c*	357. c. 13(58) P
520	Onslow, Thomas, Lord	pr. c. 26	26	BS Ref. 2	357. c. 13(62) P 357. c. 13(63) JR
521	Phipps, Constantine [Duchess of Bucks.]	pr. c. 27	27	BS Ref. 2	
522	Blackett, Sir Edward	pr. c. 30	30	BS Ref. 2	357. c. 13(66) P
523	Bouverie, Hon. Edward	pr. c. 31	31	BS Ref. 2	
—	Widdrington, Catherine	pr. c. 32	32	BS Ref. 2	357. c. 13(69)*d*
524	Molyneux, Charles William	pr. c. 33	33	357. c. 13(28)	
525	Rolle, Denys	pr. c. 35	35	BS Ref. 2	357. c. 13(64) P 357. c. 13(65) JR
526	Barry, James	pr. c. 36	36	BS Ref. 2	

a The bill is misbound, BS Ref. 2, as 32 Geo. II, pr. c. 33.

b Bound as a precedent in Harper's volume 1, his number 5A, and indexed as 'petition by an agent for leave to present a petition out of time'. The petition was read in the Lords (*LJ* xxix, 255), and leave given, but no bill introduced.

c Two versions.

d Draft agreement concerning inclosure of lands at Bewcastle, part of the estate in question; another agreement is written on the printed copy of the bill.

		R.H.	Bill		MS
	1759 cont.	32 Geo. II	Vol. 36		
527	Warburton, William	pr. c. 38	38	BS Ref. 2	357. c. 13(59) P
528	Buckley, Thomas	pr. c. 39	39	BS Ref. 2	357. c. 13(60) P
529	Plunkett, Arthur	pr. c. 40	40	BS Ref. 2	
530	Harmston [inclosure]	pr. c. 45	45	BS Ref. 2	
531	Cotham, East [inclosure]	pr. c. 48	48	BS Ref. 2	
532	Westminster [coals]	c. 27	—	—*a*	
533	Molton, South [road]	c. 45	—	—*b*	
534	Wakefield [road]	c. 48	—	—*b*	
535	Wear, River of	c. 64	—	—*b*	
536	Wear, River of [Sunderland Harbour]	c. 65	—	—*b*	
	1760	33 Geo. II	Vol. 37		
537	Goodflesh, Mark	pr. c. 14	14	BS Ref. 2	
538	Lethieullier, Smart	pr. c. 29	29	BS Ref. 2	
539	Freeman, John	pr. c. 30	30	BS Ref. 2	
540	Coopey, John	pr. c. 31	31	BS Ref. 2	
541	Walton [inclosure]	pr. c. 44	44	BS Ref. 2	
542	Coddington [inclosure]	pr. c. 46	46	BS Ref. 2	
543	Abergavenny, Town of [Bedgeworth tithes & Jesus College]	pr. c. 52	52	BS Ref. 2	
544	Bertie, Lord Robert [Chislehurst charities]	pr. c. 56	56	BS Ref. 2	358. b. 5(62) P 357. b. 1(16) JR
545	Spencer, John	pr. c. 57	57	BS Ref. 2	
546	Fetherston, Sir Matthew	pr. c. 58	58	BS Ref. 2	358. b. 5(60) P
547	Fagge, John Meres	pr. c. 60	60	BS Ref. 2	
548	Raymond, Hugh	pr. c. 63	63	BS Ref. 2	
549	Strode, William	pr. c. 64	64	BS Ref. 2	358. b. 5(61) P
550	Thomas, James	pr. c. 65	65	BS Ref. 2	
551	Wall, Anna Maria	pr. c. 67	67	BS Ref. 2	
552	Leeds Bridge	c. 54	—	—	358. b. 5(63) P
553	[St Aubyn & Plymouth fort]*c*	—	—	—	—

a Introduced from the expiring laws committee and ordered to be printed (*CJ* xxviii, 486, 493). Harper's copy has not survived, but there is a copy in the Abbot Collection, B. 110.

b These four local bills are on Harper's list, but no material relating to them is to be found amongst his papers. In fact no printed copies of the bills cc. 45, 64 and 65 are known at all. There are two copies of c. 48 in the British Museum under references 212. k. 7(3) and (44) but these did not belong to Harper.

c No papers have survived. The petition was committed and the report referred to committee of supply (*CJ* xxviii, 881).

Appendix I

		R.H.		Bill	MS	
	1761	1 Geo. III	Vol. 37		MS[a]	
554	Clarke, Bartholomew	pr. c. 41	41	BS Ref. 2		
555	Thornton, William	pr. c. 13	13	BS Ref. 2	p. 27	P
556	Lemon, William	pr. c. 16	16	BS Ref. 2		
557	Tudway, Charles	pr. c. 17	17	BS Ref. 2		
558	Pool Common [inclosure]	pr. c. 36	36	BS Ref. 2[b]		
559	Burton Pidsea [inclosure]	pr. c. 37	37	BS Ref. 2		
560	Bolingbroke, Frederick, Viscount	pr. c. 40	40	BS Ref. 2	p. 11	P
561	Dodwell, Sir William	pr. c. 43	43	BS Ref. 2		
562	Willis, Brown	pr. c. 45	45	BS Ref. 2	p. 22	P
563	Morse, John	pr. c. 46	46	BS Ref. 2	p. 1	P
564	Tancred, Christopher	—	48	BS Ref. 2		
565	Croydon Church	c. 38	—	—	—	
—	Carew, Sir Nicholas Hackett	—	—	—	p. 17	P
	1762	2 Geo. III	Vol. 38		MS[c]	
565	Woods, John	pr. c. 12	12	BS Ref. 2	p. 10	P
566	Wyndham, Sir William	pr. c. 13	13	BS Ref. 2		
567	Tancred, Christopher	pr. c. 15	15	BS Ref. 2		
568	Williams, Lady Frances Hanbury	pr. c. 17	17	BS Ref. 2 MS copy		
569	Whissondine [inclosure]	pr. c. 30	30	BS Ref. 2		
570	Bolingbroke, Frederick, Viscount	pr. c. 32	32	BS Ref. 2		
571	Sproatley [inclosure]	pr. c. 44	44	BS Ref. 2		
572	Skipsea [inclosure]	pr. c. 45	45	BS Ref. 2		
573	Towcester [inclosure]	pr. c. 46	46	BS Ref. 2		
574	Rotherham [inclosure]	pr. c. 47	47	BS Ref. 2	p. 14	P
575	Beaufort, Charles Noel, Duke of	pr. c. 49	49	BS Ref. 2		
576	Winterton, Edward, Lord	pr. c. 52	52	BS Ref. 2[d]		
577	Carew, Sir Nicholas Hacket	pr. c. 53	53	BS Ref. 2	see 1761, p. 17	

[a] There is no separate volume for this year. The MS material is bound at the end of BS Ref. 2, 1 Geo. III. I give Harper's MS pagination.

[b] 2 versions.

[c] No separate volume. I give Harper's MS pagination of the material bound at the end of BS Ref. 2, 2 Geo. III.

[d] Two versions.

		R.H.		Bill		MS	

	1762 cont.		2 Geo. III	Vol. 38			
578	Ram, Humfreys	pr. c. 55	55	BS Ref. 2			
579	Perkins, Matthias	pr. c. 56	56	BS Ref. 2		p. 1	P
580	Ruggles, Thomas	pr. c. 57	57	BS Ref. 2			
581	Dicker, Samuel	pr. c. 61	61	BS Ref. 2		p. 6	P
—	[Earl of Warwick, Cadoxton sea wall]	—	—	—		p. 12	P[a]

	1763		3 Geo. III	Vol. 40		MS[b]	
582	Marfleet [inclosure]	pr. c. 30	30	BS Ref. 2			
583	Dashwood, Samuel	pr. c. 38	38	BS Ref. 2		p. 10	P
584	Rich, Thomas	pr. c. 40	40	BS Ref. 2			
585	Doncaster [turnpike]	—	48	BS Ref. 2			
—	Penryn [turnpike]	c. 52	—	—		p. 1	P
—	Edwardes, William [to sell Holland House]	—	—	—		p. 6	P

	1764		4 Geo. III	Vol. 41			
586	Tuddenham [Badley Moor inclosure]	pr. c. 10	10	BS Ref. 2			
587	Newport, John	pr. c. 24	24	BS Ref. 2			
588	Stoke Albany [inclosure]	pr. c. 41	41	BS Ref. 2			
589	Horton, Thomas	pr. c. 49	49	BS Ref. 2			
590	Bulwer, William Wigget	pr. c. 52	52	BS Ref. 2			
591	Young, William	pr. c. 54	54	BS Ref. 2			
592	Ashburnham, John, Earl of	pr. c. 68	68	BS Ref. 2			
593	Barrymore, James, Earl	pr. c. 70	70	BS Ref. 2			
594	Griffin, Sir John Griffin	pr. c. 78	78	BS Ref. 2 2 versions			

	1765		5 Geo. III	Vol. 42			
595	Wilson, Ann	pr. c. 12	12	BS Ref. 2			
596	Denford [inclosure]	pr. c. 34	34	BS Ref. 2			
597	Tetbury Church	pr. c. 52	52	BS Ref. 2			
598	Dobinson, William	pr. c. 53	53	BS Ref. 2			
599	Vernon, Henry [Shipbrook]	pr. c. 90	90	BS Ref. 2			
600	Phelps, Mary	pr. c. 98	98	BS Ref. 2			
601	Ayscough, Edward	pr. c. 101	101	BS Ref. 2			

[a] Petition to the House of Commons, but no bill introduced (*CJ* xxix, 162).

[b] No separate volume. I give Harper's MS pagination of the material bound at the end of BS Ref. 2, 3 Geo. III.

		R.H.	Bill	MS	
	1765 cont.	5 Geo. III	Vol. 42		
602	Carlisle, Henry, Earl of	pr. c. 109	109	BS Ref. 2	
603	Shelburne, William, Earl of [Clare Hall]	pr. c. 48	48	BS Ref. 2	
			118	BS Ref. 2	
	1766	6 Geo. III	Vol. 43		
604	Aldcroft, Charles	pr. c. 35	35	BS Ref. 2	
605	Chetwode, Sir John	pr. c. 34	34	BS Ref. 2	
606	Ince, Mary	pr. c. 65	65	BS Ref. 2	
607	Lloyd, Thomas	pr. c. 63	63	BS Ref. 2	
608	Midleton, George, Viscount	pr. c. 39	39	BS Ref. 2	
609	Plimouth Dock [Navy Commissioners]	c. 102	94	BS Ref. 2	
610	Powis, Henry Arthur, Earl of	pr. c. 58	58	BS Ref. 2	
611	Parsons, Sarah	pr. c. 62	62	BS Ref. 2	
612	Smith, John Silvester	pr. c. 44	44	BS Ref. 2	
613	Yorkshire [cloth]	c. 23	—	—	*a*
	1767	7 Geo. III	Vol. 44*b*		
—	Gresley, Sir Nigel	pr. c. 56	56	BS Ref. 2	
—	Talbot, John (jr.)	pr. c. 60	60	BS Ref. 2	
—	Hill, Haydock	pr. c. 70	70	BS Ref. 2	
—	Rycroft, Richard	pr. c. 76	76	BS Ref. 2	
—	Osborne, John	pr. c. 82	82	BS Ref. 2	
—	Saunders, Erasmus	pr. c. 98	98	BS Ref. 2	
—	Hoskins, William	pr. c. 102	102	BS Ref. 2	

a There are no papers concerning this act. Two versions of the act on the same subject of the previous year occur in BS Ref. 2 for 5 Geo. III.

b Harper's list concludes with 1766. The items below are marked 'R.H.'.

APPENDIX II

NOTE ON PARLIAMENTARY SOURCES

The promulgation of the statutes is discussed in chapter 9. Throughout the work, I have not adopted the very complicated differentiation by style of numbers used in the printed editions, but have used only arabic numerals, with the abbreviations c. for public acts, pr. c. for private, and loc. for those few references to acts classified as local after 1798. For details of the official numbering see R. W. Perceval, 'Chapter Six, VI, vi, 6 or 6?', *Parliamentary Affairs*, iii (1950), 506–13.

HOUSE OF LORDS

A new *Guide to the Records of Parliament* is to be published by H.M. Stationery Office in 1971 and will cover, comprehensively, the materials available in the House of Lords Record Office (HLRO).

A description of the principal types of private bills and the classes of records relating thereto is available in 'The Private Bill Records of the House of Lords' (HLRO Memorandum No. 16, 1957). This is particularly useful for the nineteenth century, when the surviving papers are much more numerous and more complex than for the eighteenth century.

For the purpose of this work, much use has been made of the committee books, containing the minutes of select committees of the House on private bills and other matters. The eighteenth-century volumes are not numbered, and not all of them are paginated, so the only reference necessary is the date of the meeting of the committee. This is given either in the text, or in footnotes with the abbreviation Com. Bk.

Select committees of enquiry into procedural matters are listed in 'A Guide to the Parliament Office Papers' (HLRO Memorandum No. 18, 1958). The following committee reports, printed in the *Journals of the House of Lords (LJ)* are referred to in the text:

The Parliament Office and state of the Journals. 1717. *LJ* xx, 529–30.

Fees of officers of the House. 1726. *LJ* xxii, 627–9.

Compensation to officers for losses by printing the private statutes. 1797–8. *LJ* xli, 460–1.

Fees payable on private bills. 1827. *LJ* lix, 563–615.

HOUSE OF COMMONS

An account of the compilation and printing of the Commons Journal will shortly be published by Dr David Menhennet, Deputy Librarian of the House of Commons, as *The Journal of the House of Commons* (House of Commons Library Document No. 7, H.M.S.O. 1971). This contains valuable advice on the use of the Journal and the indexes thereto, and includes also the text of the 1742 committee report on the Journal printing.

The list below includes only those reports of select committees which bear upon the procedural points under discussion. I have excluded from it those committees which simply reported resolutions that became standing orders, since these are fully covered by O. C. Williams, *Private Bill Procedure.*

Some eighteenth-century reports are printed in the *Journals of the House of Commons (CJ)*.

Others are printed in *Reports from Committees of the House of Commons, 1715–1801; Forming the Series of Fifteen Volumes of Reports.* Volumes i to iv were published in 1773. These were reprinted, together with eleven more volumes and an index volume, 1803–20. Referred to as First Series.

Nineteenth-century reports are to be found in the bound sessional set of Parliamentary Papers and are referred to in footnotes by the sessional number of the paper, the year, and the printed pagination or question number. The list below gives the number of the volume in the sessional set in which the paper appears, and the MS pagination of the item in the bound volume.

Fees of officers of the House. 1732. Table of fees only printed *CJ* xxi, 807–9. Report printed from a manuscript in HLRO by O. C. Williams, *Clerical Organization*, 305–12.

Printing of the Commons Journals. 1742. *CJ* xxiv, 262–6, reprinted in House of Commons Library Document No. 7 (see above).

Methods to enforce attendance of members. 1744. *CJ* xxiv, 684–5.

Table of fees for private bills. 1751. *CJ* xxvi, 277–8.

Standing orders relating to private bills. 1775. *CJ* xxxv, 443–4.

Appendix II

Precedents of amendments made by the Lords to bills of inclosure. 1780. *CJ* xxxvii, 820–32.

Cultivation of Waste Lands. 1795–6. First Series, ix, 199–215.

Temporary Laws, Expired or Expiring. 1796. First Series, xiv, 34–72.

Promulgation of the Statutes, 1796–7. First Series, xiv, 119–37.

Cultivation of Waste Lands, 1797. First Series, ix, 217–25.

First and Second reports from the committee appointed to inquire into the state of the Public Records. 1800. First Series, xv, 1–667.

Facilitating bills of inclosure. 1800. First Series, ix, 227–38.

Promulgation of the Statutes of the United Kingdom. 1801. First Series, xiv, 138–49.

Expired and Expiring Laws of the United Kingdom. 1802. First Series, xiv, 73–118.

Ninth report from committee on public expenditure (Printing and stationery). HC (373) 1810, ii, 551–90.

The present method of ingrossing bills. HC (552) 1823, iv, 69–100.

Private business of the House. First Report HC (432) 1824, vi, 497–500. Second report HC (468) 1824, vi, 501–6.

Constitution of committees on private bills. HC (457) 1825, v, 103–6.

King's Printer's Patent. HC (713) 1831–2, xviii, 1–366.

Establishment of the House of Commons. HC (648) 1833, xii, 179–464.

Private bill fees. HC (540) 1834, xi, 333–448.

Private business. HC (679) 1837–8, xxiii, 405–80.

Private business. First Report. HC (51) 1839, xiii, 101–4. Second Report. HC (520) 1839, xiii, 105–42.

Laws affecting aliens. HC (307) 1843, v, 145–258.

Private bills. Third report. HC (705) 1847, xii, 357–758.

INDEX

References in italic indicate items in Appendix I; numbers in parentheses are assigned to the unnumbered items, e.g. the last seven items are referred to as *613(1)* to *613(7)*.

Index

Bills—*cont.*

drainage, 132, 145, 147–8, 176 n. 2, 177 n. 3, *340*

estate, 7, 10, 11, 28, 34, 42, 49, 52–3, 55, 85, 94–6, 105–6, 184–5; *see* Chapter 6, and for Harper's bills, App. I *passim*

harbours, 5, 84–5, 169, 175, *149*, *175*, *339*, *340(2)*, *357*, *478*, *536*

inclosure, 7, 11, 48–50, 52–3, 85, 92 n. 3, 93, 95, 98 n. 2, 105, 108, 110–11, 127, 176–7, 179, 181, 183, 185; *see* Chapter 7, and for Harper's bills, items so marked in App. I

name, 7, 11, 12, 52–3, 96, 102, 128 n. 1, 164 n., *95*, *96*, *105*, *113*, *114*,*118*, *122*, *198*, *214(1)*, *264*, *274*, *281*, *282*, *325*, *343*, *370*, *377(1)*, *395(1)*, *459(2)*, *481*, *517*, *540*, *568*

naturalisation, 11, 52–3, 87, 96–7, 102–3; fees on, 31–9; general legislation, 77–83; *54(1)*, *249*, *432*

poor rates, 52, 175 n. 1, *501*, *543*

rivers and canals: *see* Bridgewater, Weaver; 49 n. 2, 85, 105, 150–3, 169–71, 175, *46*, *176*, *214*, *247*, *340(1)*, *357*, *442A*, *480*, *515*, *535*, *536*

roads and bridges, 30, 52–3, 55, 84–5, 102 n. 1, 105, 150, 169, 174–7, 185, *134*, *148*, *163*, *165*, *177(1)*, *276*, *377*, *482*, *509*, *533*, *534*, *552*, *585*, *585(1)*

schools and universities, *302*, *312*, *434*, *467*

town improvements, 49 n. 2, 54, 65, 85, 96, 150, 152, 155 n. 6, 170, 175, *56*, *65*, *121*, *135*, *356*, *459(3)*

Binbroke, Lincs., inclosure, *146*

Birch, Dr Thomas (1705–66), 2

Bircham, Norfolk, inclosure, *168*

Biscathorpe, Lincs., inclosure, *49*

Bisley, Glos., inclosure, 139–40

Blackburn, Lancelot, archbishop of York (d. 1743), 137, *37*, *215*

Blackett, *see* Calverley

Blackett, Sir Edward, 3rd Bt (d. 1756), *15*; 4th Bt (1719–1804), *522*

Blackstone, Sir William (1723–80), 11

Bland, Sir John, 6th Bt (1722–55), *381*

Blantyre, *see* Stuart

Blewitt, Edmond, *444*

Blois, Rev. Ralph, of Yoxford, Suffolk, *361*

Blunsdon, Wilts., inclosure, *338*

Bolingbroke, *see* St John

Bolton, *see* Paulet

Bond, Denis MP (d. 1658), 54

Boone, Charles MP (d. 1735), *88*, *89*

Booth, James (d. 1778), 11, 122, 127

Booth, Langham MP (d. 1724), 154, 157, 160 n. 2

Bootle, Richard Wilbraham MP (1725–96), name, 164 n., *517*

Boston, *see* Irby

Bouverie, Hon. Edward MP (1738–1810), *523*

Bouverie, Jacob Pleydell, styled Vt Folkestone, 2nd Earl Radnor (1750–1828), 167 n. 2

Bowater, Edward (d. 1777), *234*

Bowyer, William (1699–1777), 43

Bozeat, Northants., inclosure, 95

Brabazon, Edward, 4th Earl of Meath (d. 1708), 31

Bradford, *see* Newport

Brain, Benjamin, *401*

Bramwell, George, 84 n. 4, 111, 184–6

Brandon, William, of Portsmouth (d. 1704), 116, *82*

Braye MSS, 18 n. 6, 20 n. 1, 20 n. 3

Bread, assize of, 42 n. 1, 73, *120*

Breaston, Derbyshire, inclosure, *453*

Brent, *see* Coopey

Brereton, later Salusbury, Thomas MP (d. 1756), 159, 162

Bridgewater, *see* Egerton

Bridgewater canal, 48, 64 n. 1, 150–2, 168–9, 175

Brincklow, Warws., inclosure, *184*

Brinckman, *see* Broadhead

British Museum, 2–3, 181, 187; Harper's collections, ix, 5–8, 38, 106–7, App. I; Lansdowne MSS, 23 n. 4, 24, 26, 43 n. 2, 45 n. 6, 187–8; treatises on procedure, 4, 19–21, 63 n. 3

Broadhead, Theodore Henry: name, *459(2)*; *464*

Brodrick, George, 3rd Vt Midleton (1730–65), *608*

Brokers, of London, *54*

Index

Bromley, Henry, 1st Bn Montfort (1705–55), *197(1)*

Bromley, William, of Baginton, speaker HC (1664–1732), 20, 21 n. 3, 63 n. 3

Bromley, William, of Upton, Worcs., *28*

Brompton, Yorks., inclosure, *511*

Brooke, Sir Job, 3rd Bt (d. 1770), *202*

Brooksbank, Stamp MP, *158*

Brougham, Henry, 1st Bn (1778–1868), 37, 56

Broughton, Bucks., *322*

Brown, Thomas, of Manchester, *29*

Browne, John, cler. Parl. (d. 1691), 19 n. 1, 20

Buccleuch, *see* Scott

Buchanan, George, merchant, *499*

Buckland Newton, Dorset, inclosure, 138, *75*

Buckley, formerly Foster, Thomas, of Preston, Lancs., *528*

Bulkeley, James, 6th Vt (1717–52), 115, *357(3)*, *376*; Thomas James, 7th Vt (1752–1822), *424, 473, 505*

Bull, John, clerk HC, 21

Bulstrode, Edward, of Inn. Temp., 112 n., 114, 117, *357(1)*, *369*

Bulwer, William Wiggett, *590*

Burchester, Oxon., inclosure, *483*

Burgoyne, John MP (1723–92), 60

Burke, Edmund MP (1729–97), 98

Burman, John, clerk HC, 41, 74

Burnet(t), Dr Gilbert (d. 1715), *327*

Burrough, Hicks, clerk HC (d. 1733), 42 n. 6, 44

Burton, Dr Simon (d. 1744), *285*

Burton Pidsea, Yorks., inclosure, *559*

Byde, Thomas Plummer MP (d. 1789), *143*

Byron, William, 5th Bn (1722–98), 279

Caldecot, Gilbert, of Beckering, Lincs., *451*

Calverley, Yorks., inclosure, *453(1)*

Calverley, Sir Walter, 2nd Bt MP (1707–77), name, *95*

Calvert, Charles, 5th Bn Baltimore (1699–1751), 78 n. 9

Calvert, Felix, 115, *41*

Cambridge University Library, MSS in, 18 n. 2, 21 n. 3

Campbell, John, styled Lord Glen-

orchy, 3rd Earl of Breadalbane (1696–1782), 113

Canterbury, Diocese of, *23*

Carew, Sir Nicholas Hacket, 2nd Bt (d. 1762), *565(1)*, 577

Carlisle, *see* Howard

Carlisle, road, *377*

Carthew, Thomas (d. 1741), *305*

Cary, George, of Tor Abbey, Devon, 114, *131*

Cary, Gertrude, 39 n. 6

Catherine Hall, Cambridge, *467*

Cavendish, *see* Chandler

Cavendish, Lord Charles (d. 1783), *108*

Cavendish, William, 3rd Duke of Devonshire (1698–1755), *136, 378*

Cecil, James, 49 n. 3

Chadwicke, Evelyn, of Leake, North-ants., *219, 399*

Chafin, George, of Chettle, Dorset, 10, 123 n. 5, *309, 492*

Chandler, Richard, name, *395(1)*

Charitable Corporation, 74, *68, 69*

Chawton, Hants., inclosure, 130 n. 4

Chaytor, Henry, of Croft, Yorks., *36*

Chester, archdeaconry, *439*

Chesterfield, *see* Stanhope

Chetwode, Sir John, 3rd Bt (1732–79), 605

Chichester, Arthur, 4th Earl of Done-gall, (1695–1757), *395*

Chipping Warden, Northants., in-closure, 140, *74*

Cholmondeley, Charles MP (1685–1756), 154, 159–63

Cholmondeley, George, styled Vt Malpas, 3rd Earl Cholmondeley (1703–70), 159–61

Cholmondeley, Seymour (1690–1739), 155–6

Christ's Hospital, *434*

Chudleigh, Sir George, 4th Bt (d. 1738), *443*

Churchill, Sarah, Duchess of Marl-borough, (1660–1744), 118, 120

Clarke, Bartholomew, merchant of London (d. 1746), *554*

Clarke, Godfrey, of Chilcot, Derbysh., *233*

Clarridge, Benjamin, of Northwich, 163

Clementson, John, serjeant at arms, 99 n. 1

Index

Clerk, Dorothea, *144*

Cleybrooke, Leics., inclosure, 130 n. 4, *91*

Cliffe, Richard, of Sutton, Surrey (d. 1740), 123 n. 5, *240*

Clifford, Frederick, *Private Bill Legislation*, viii, 13, 76 n. 5, 84–5, 134, 145 n. 3, 150–1

Clifton, Sir Gervas, 4th Bt (d. 1731), *10, 16*

Clinton, *see* Fortescue

Clopton, Sir Hugh Kt, of Mid. Temp., *188*

Cloth, 57; Glos., *247(1)*; Yorks., 49, 73, 70, *178(3), 613*

Clyde, river, 49 n. 2

Coal: collieries, *178(1)*; measure, *532*

Coddington, Notts., inclosure, *542*

Coggs, John, goldsmith, *193*

Coke, Sir Edward MP (1552–1634), 22, *179*

Coke, Thomas, Earl of Leicester (1697–1759), *278*

Colchester, river at, *176*

Cole, George, clerk HC, 41

Colebrooke, Robert MP (1718–84), *427*

Coles, Barnaby, of Woodfalls, Wilts. (d. 1737), *140*

Collins, Robert, merchant of Bristol, divorce, 12, *515(1)*

Colmore, Anne, *290*

Colt, Sir John Dutton, 2nd Bt (1725–1809), *449*

Coningesby, *see* Williams, Frances

Constable, *see* Tunstall

Constantine, John, 34

Conveyancing, 1, 6–9, 122, 189

Conyers, Sir Baldwyn, 4th Bt (d. 1731), *21*

Conyers, Maurice, of Rusthall, Kent, 112, *169*

Cooke, George MP (d. 1768), 100–1

Cooke, George Wingrove (1814–65), 145 n. 3

Cooke, James jr, of Yarm, Yorks., *224*

Cooke, John, of Fawley Court, Bucks., name, *114*

Cooper, *see* Gilbert

Coopey, Dr. John, of Oxford, name, *540*

Copper, *25*

Copyright, *105(2)*

Cornwall, Charles Wolfram MP (1735–89), 98

Cotham, Yorks., inclosure, *531*

Courtenay, George, *358*

Courtenay, Kellond MP (d. 1748), *359*

Courthope, James, clerk HC, viii, 14 n. 4, 41, 42 n. 1, 100, 104

Coventry, William, 5th Earl of (1688–1751), 115, *94*

Cowper, Henry, clerk HL, 183

Cowper, William, 2nd Earl (1709–64), 10, *80, 106, 162, 186, 374*

Cowper, William, cler. Parl. (d. 1740), 10

Cransto(u)n, James, Lord (d. 1773), *472*

Craven, Fulwar, 4th Bn (d. 1764), *167*

Craven, William, 3rd Bn (1700–39), 87

Creevey, Thomas MP (1768–1838), 58 n. 3

Crewe, John MP (d. 1752), 154, 159–62

Crewe, Sir Thomas MP (1565–1634), 63

Croft, Stephen, *403*

Crowle, Richard MP (1699–1757), *433*

Croydon, Surrey, church, *565*

Culcheth, Lancs., inclosure, *355*

Culliford, John (d. 1728), *93*

Cullum, John, 5th Bt (1699–1774), *242*

Cumberland, William, Duke of (1721–65), 43

Dalkeith, *see* Scott

Daly, Charles, of Callow, Co. Galway, *431*

Daniel, John, of Daresbury, Chesh. (1685–1736), 160, 162, 163

Daniel, Sir William Duckinfield, 3rd Bt (d. 1758), name, *274*

Darn(h)all, Sir John (1672–1735), 161

Dashwood, Samuel, of Well, Lincs., *583*

Davidson, Henry, agent, 49 n. 2

Davie, Sir William, 4th Bt (1662–1707), 27

Dawes, Sir Darcy, 4th Bt (d. 1724), 121, 9

Dawes, Sir William, 3rd Bt, archbishop of York (d. 1724), 121

Dawson, —, raising money, 157

Dawson, Roper, *307*

De Grey, Thomas MP (1717–81), 98

De Grey, Thomas, 2nd Bn Walsingham,

233

Index

Fane, Charles, 2nd Vt (1708–66), *262(1)*, *330*

Fangfosse cum Spittle, Yorks., inclosure, *17*

Farthingstone, Northants., inclosure, *367*

Faxton common, Northants., inclosure, *259*

Fazakerley, Nicholas MP (d. 1767), 161 n. 4

Felton common, Northumberland, inclosure, *409*

Fenchurch St, London, church, *212*

Ferrers, Mary, Countess, 76 n. 5, *501(3)*

Fetherstone(haugh), Sir Matthew, 1st Bt (d. 1774), *546*

Feversham, *see* Duras

Fitzgerald, John, 1st Earl Grandison (d. 1766), *34*

Fitzherbert, Thomas, of Swinerton, Staffs., *220*

Fitzroy, Mary Duchess of Northumberland (d. 1738), *295*, *452*

Flecknoe common, Warws., inclosure, *39*, *231*

Fleetwood, Henry, of Penwortham, Lancs. (d. 1746), 10, *306*

Fleetwood, William MP (d. 1594), 29 n. 6

Forester, William MP (1690–1758), 10, *100*

Fortescue, Hugh, 1st Earl Clinton (1696–1751), *423*

Foster, Sir Michael (1689–1763), 4 n. 2

Fownes, Thomas, of Iwerne Stepleton, Dorset, 123 n. 5, *153*, *243*

Fox, James, of East Horsley, Surrey, *308*

Francis, Rev. John, *60*

Francke, Evelyn Charles, of Preston, Lancs. (d. 1752), *469*

Freeman, *see* Cooke

Freeman, John, *539*

Gace, Joseph, of Panton, Lincs., *62*

Gage, Thomas, 1st Vt (d. 1754), *74*

Gape, Thomas, *221*

Gardner, John, solicitor, 14

Garnock, *see* Lindsay

Garrard, Thomas, of Lamborn, Berks. (d. 1746), 115, *293*

Gee, William, 10, *110*

George III, 61 n. 4

Georgia, trustees of, 14 n. 1, 64

Gibbs, Sir Vicary MP, attorney-general (1751–1820), 192

Gilbert, Alice, of Plymouth, Devon, *407*

Gilbert, John, name, *113*

Gilbert, Thomas MP (d. 1798), 74 n. 6, 177

Glanville, Sir John MP (1586–1661), 16 n. 4, 63 n. 3

Glenorchy, *see* Campbell

Gloucester: city, *356*; clothiers, *247(1)*

Glover, Richard MP (d. 1785), *471*

Goddard, Margaret, 113, *38(1)*

Godolphin, Ellen, 126

Godolphin, Francis, 2nd Earl of (1678–1766), *197*

Goldesborough, William jr, clerk HC, 23, 33

Goodflesh, Mark, divorce, *537*

Gore, William, of Barrows, Somerset, *170*

Gough, Richard (1735–1809), 3

Gould, Edward, *254*

Goulston, Francis, *20*

Goulston, Morris, of Mid. Temp., 14

Graham, Sir Reginald, 4th Bt (1704–55), *128*

Grandison, *see* Fitzgerald

Gratwood Heath, Staffs., inclosure, 137

Grenville, *see* Wyndham

Grenville, George MP (1712–70), 61 n. 4

Gresley, Sir Nigel, 6th Bt (d. 1787), *613(1)*

Greville, Francis, 1st Earl Brooke and Warwick (1719–73), *581(1)*

Grey, Harry, 3rd Earl of Stamford (1685–1739), *122(2)*; 4th Earl (1715–68), 123, *277*

Grey, Henry, Duke of Kent (d. 1740), 113, *3*, *11*

Grey, Lady Mary, 113, *33*

Griffin, Sir John Griffin MP (1719–97), *594*

Griffith, Joseph (d. 1721), 117–18

Grimston, William, 1st Vt (d. 1756), *265*

Grosvenor, Dame Mary (d. 1730), *19*

Grover, John, clerk HC (d. 1749), 43–5, 66 n. 2

Gunnerton, Northumberland, inclosure, *174*

Gwillym, Robert, *296*

235

Index

Manners, John, of Northumberland, *272*

Manners, John, 2nd Duke of Rutland (1676–1721), 9–10, 40, 106, 113 n., 124, *1*; 3rd Duke (1696–1779), 9–10, *96*

Mansfield, Paul, yeoman of Twickenham, Mddx, *337*

Marfleet, Yorks., inclosure, *582*

Market St Chapel, Cadington, Herts., *195*

Marlborough, *see* Churchill

Marshall, William (1745–1818), 148

Marsk, Yorks., inclosure, *454*

Martin, Samuel MP (1714–88), 68, 103

Mason, Thomas, gardener of Earls Croomb, Worcs. (d. 1749), *346*

Matfen, Northumberland, inclosure, *494*

Maty, Dr Matthew (1718–76), 2–3

Maty, Dr Paul Henry (1745–87), 3

May, Sir Thomas Erskine, 1st Bn Farnborough (1815–86), viii, 58 n. 3

Maynard, Sir John MP (1602–90), *123*

Meath, *see* Brabazon

Meijbohm, Johan, 79

Melbourne, *see* Lamb

Mercers Company, 175 n. 1

Merest, James, clerk HL (1700–52), 18 n. 2

Method of Proceedings, 27–8, 87, 90, 91, 94–5, 107, 108, 113–14, 190

Meynell, Littleton Pointz (d. 1751), *408*

Middlehurst, William, 158, 159

Middleton, *see* Willoughby

Middleton, —, receiver, 119

Middleton, Mrs, 125

Midleton, *see* Brodrick

Midleton, Alderman Sir Thomas, 118

Milbanke, Sir Ralph, 4th Bt (d. 1748), 7

Militia, 64, 70, 74–5

Mill, Barbara, *61*

Mitchell, William, *292*

Mitford, John Freeman, 1st Bn Redesdale, solicitor-general (1748–1830) 180 n. 3, 181

'Modus tenendi parliamentum', 4, 17, 30

Molineux, Crisp MP (1730–92), *497*

Molton, Devon, roads, *533*

Molyneux, Charles William, 8th Vt, Earl of Sefton (1748–95), *514, 524*

Molyneux, Richard, 5th Vt (1679–1738), *35, 138*

Montfort, *see* Bromley

Moore, Edward, 49 n. 2

Moore, Hubert Stuart, 5 n. 2

Moore, William MP (d. 1746), 12, *289*

Mordaunt, Charles, 3rd Earl of Peterborough (1658–1735), *97*

Moreau, David, divorce, *459*

Morgan, Richard, of Dublin, divorce, *459(1)*

Morice, Sir William, 3rd Bt MP (d. 1750), *438*

Morpeth, *see* Howard

Morse, John, goldsmith of London (d. 1739), *563*

Moyle, Thomas, *368*

Mundy, Wrightson, of Osbaston, Leics., *476*

Murray, Alexander (d. 1777), 27

Myddelton, Richard, *357(2)*

Myddleton, Sir William, 4th Bt (1694–1718), *251*

Myton, Yorks., *448*

Naish, Hugh, of Mid. Temp., *310*

Narborough, Leics, inclosure, *390*

Navy, *260, 316*

Naylor, John, clerk HC (d. 1761), 44

Nene, Northants., river, 147–8, *480*

Nevill, William, 16th Bn Abergavenny (1724–44), 77, *229*

Newcastle, *see* Pelham-Holles

Newdigate, Sir Roger, 5th Bt MP (1719–1806), 167 n. 2

Newland, William, of Gatton, Surrey (d. 1738), *360*

Newport, formerly Harrison, John (d. 1783): name, *122; 587*

Newport, Thomas, 4th Earl of Bradford (d. 1762), *341*

Newton, Yorks., inclosure, *512*

Noguier, Mary, 34 n. 1, 114, 115, *432*

Normanton, Lincs., inclosure, *419*

North, Frederick, 2nd Earl of Guilford (1732–92), 69

Northleigh, Stephen, *442*

Northumberland, *see* Fitzroy, Percy

Norton, Sir Fletcher, 1st Bn Grantley (1716–89), 98

Nugent, Robert MP (1709–88), 78 n. 9

Nunburnholme, Yorks., inclosure, *455*

Nuneaton, Warws., inclosure, *217*

Index

Nuneaton & Attleborough, Warws., inclosure, *48*

Oakeley, Richard, 123 n. 5, *287*
O'Brian, William 4th Earl of Inchiquin (d. 1777), *150*
'Observations' treatise, 20–2
Ombersley, Worcs., *389*
Onslow, Arthur MP (1691–1768), 4, 43 n. 2, 64; as speaker, 56, 59, 61, 62 n. 3, 131 n. 5
Onslow, Thomas, 2nd Bn (1679–1740), 114, *520*
Orme, Garton, 115, *276(1), 300, 353*
Osborne, John, yeoman of Sunbury, Mddx, *613(5)*
Osborne, Thomas, 4th Duke of Leeds (1713–89), *269*
Osmotherley moor, Yorks., inclosure, *456*
Ottringham, Yorks., inclosure, *510*
Ouse, river (Hunts. & Norfolk), 155 n. 6, *340(1)*
Overton Longville, Hunts., inclosure, 129 n. 4, 137, *31*
Owen, Humphrey, of Bodidda, Caerns., *262(2)*
Owen, William, publisher (d. 1793), 27 n. 1
Oxford canal, 167 n. 2

Packer, Robert, of Shillingford, Berks. (d. 1731), *142*
Pailton, Warws., inclosure, *154*
Palatine refugees, 64 n. 6, 78
Parker, Dr Samuel (1640–88), 23 n. 2
Parker, Sir Thomas, 1st Earl of Macclesfield (d. 1732), 124
Parkyns, Sir Thomas, 3rd Bt (1728–1806), *280*
Parliament, House of Commons
  bills, *see* that title
  chairman of ways and means, 31, 73, 102–3, 191
  clerks: of the house, 12, 31–2, 39, 43, 51, 66, 173, 190; assistant, 22 n. 3, 31, 38 n. 3, 44; of committees, 40–4, 48, 50, 74–5, 152; of elections, 44–5, 50; of ingrossment, 44–5; of journals, 39, 40, 57–50; *see also* Parliamentary agency
  committees: appointment of 96–7, 99, 181; attendance at, 14 n. 4, 99–

103, 148, 160 n. 4; on bills, 41, 42 n. 1, 53, 55, 57–8, 89, 96, 103, 154 n. 3; to draw bills, 58, 62; of enquiry, 37–8, 41, 68, 72 n. 5, 74, 78, 97 n. 3, 100–1, 123, 129, 135, 143–4, 148, 176, 180–4, 227–8; on expiring laws, 58, 72–3, 176, 181; of privileges, 45, 58, 97 n. 4; of whole house, 41, 53, 58, 75, 82
  fees: of clerks, 29–30, 33–9, 42–3, 128, 132, 147 n. 2; of serjeant, 29 n. 4; of speaker, 29–30, 32–3, 36, 64; *see also* Bills, cost of
  journals and records, 22–5, 43, 49–50, 106, 136, 187–8, 227
  speaker, powers of, 30–1, 54–5, 60, 98, 131 n. 5, 190
  standing orders, 15, 16, 86; development of, 38, 53, 61, 104, 106, 134–5, 141–2, 169, 173, 189; publication of, 17, 19, 25–7, 53; revisions of, in 1717, 41, 130, in 1761, 56, 61, in 1774–5, 134–5, in nineteenth century, 54, 58, 60, 99, 144–5, 150, 192–3
  time and order of business : order of bills, 30–1, 60–1; orders of the day, 58–61; time of meeting, 55–8, 62, 82; time for private business, 53–5, 61, 96
  treatises on procedure, 16–18, 20–2, 27–8
  Votes, 21 n. 4, 60, 134
Parliament, House of Lords
  amendments to Commons bills, 75, 130–2, 136–7 140–1; *see also* Bills, procedure on
  chairman of committees, 12, 91–5, 103, 124–5, 142, 189, 191
  chancellor, 29, 74–5, 105, 116, 189–90
  clerks: of the parliaments, 10, 190; assistant, 5, 10, 173, 181, 183; others, 37, 38 n. 3, 94, 147, 172, 175
  committee books, 94–5, 106, 137, 140, 226
  committees: attendance at, 89, 94–5, 107; on bills, notice of, 114, 130, 133–4, work of, 14, 76, 81, 116–17, 119, 125, 136–40, 162–3; of enquiry, 38 n. 3, 130, 147–8, 182–3, 226

Index

Portland, *see* Bentinck

Potter, Thomas MP (1718–59), 5

Powis, *see* Herbert

Powys, Edward, 123 n. 5, *235*

Powys, Richard, 130 n. 2

Poyntz, Newdigate, clerk HC (1715–72), 44, 75–6

Pratt, Sir Charles, 1st Earl Camden (1714–94), 43 n. 4

Pratt, Thomas, treasury clerk, 47, 69

Presbyterians, 45, 64 n. 3

Preston, John, merchant of Leeds, *386*

Price, Robert (1655–1733), 119

Privateers, *196*

Probyn, *see* Hopkins

Pryce, Sir John Powell, 6th Bt (d. 1776), *429*

Puleston, Thomas, *12*

Pulteney, Sir William, 1st Earl of Bath (1684–1764), 66

Puriton, Wilts., inclosure, *63*

Pusey, John Allen, of Pusey, Berks., 131, *394, 396*

Quakers, 64

Queeneborough, Leics., inclosure, 139–40, *53*

Radcliffe, James, 3rd Earl of Derwentwater (1689–1716), 74, *67*

Radway field, Warws., inclosure, *461*

Ram, Humfreys, of St Clement Danes, London, *578*

Rand, Thomas, of Anlaby, Yorks., *22*

Rash, Samuel, divorce, *326*

Rawstorn, William of Basseldon, Berks., *400*

Raymond, Hugh, of Langley, Kent (d. 1737), *548*

Read, John, clerk HC (d. 1760), 43 n. 7, 44

Read, William, of Sandhutton, Yorks., *507*

Regency bill, 1751, 43

Register of deeds, *166*

Relf, John, clerk HL (1660–1711), 19 n. 1

'Remembrances', of HL, 16–20

Rhodes, Gregory, of Ripon, Yorks., *266*; his daughter, Ann, 2

Ribble bridge, *165*

Rich, Edward, 8th Earl of Warwick (1695–1759), 81, 91, 92, 116

Rich, Thomas, *584*

Richardson, Samuel (1689–1761): printer, 25 n. 4, 43, 105; his will, 12, 40, 43, 46

Richardson, Sir Thomas MP, speaker (1569–1635), 63 n. 3

Richmond, *see* Lennox

Rigby, Richard MP (1722–88), 125, 127

Riley, *see* Wheelwright

Rip(p)on, Yorks., inclosure, 130 n. 4, *246, 266*

River navigations, *see* Bills

Rivers, *see* Pitt

Roberts, David, 125–7, *81*

Robinson, —, solicitor, 158

Robinson, George, of Bochym, Cornwall, 76

Robinson, William, of Gwersilt, Denbighsh. (d. 1739), *253*

Rochford, *see* Zuylestein

Rockingham, *see* Watson

Rogers, John, of Newcastle on Tyne, *324*

Rolle, Denys MP (d. 1797), *525*

Rolt, Edward Bayntun, 1st Bt MP (1710–1800), *210, 268*

Roper, Henry, 10th Bn Teynham (d. 1781), *328*

Roper, Trevor Charles, *465*

Rose, George MP, cler. Parl. (1744–1818), 70, 190

Rosier, John, clerk HC (d. 1796), 46–50, 68, 71, 167, 191

Ross, —, agent, 49 n. 2

Rotherham, Yorks., inclosure, *574*

Royal Society, 2–3, 187–8

Rugby school, *312*

Ruggles, Thomas, of Bocking, Essex, *580*

Russell, John, 4th Duke of Bedford (1710–71), 66, *137*

Russell, Lord John, 1st Earl Russell (1792–1878), 70

Rutland, *see* Manners

Rycroft, Rev. Richard, of St Andrew, Holborn, *613(4)*

Sacheverell, William (1638–91), 20 n. 2

St Andrew's university, *302*

St Aubyn, Sir John, 4th Bt (1726–72), *553, 609*

St John, Rev. Ellis, *440*

Index

Index

Wilbraham, *see* Bootle

Wilbraham, Randle MP (1695-1770), 161, 164

Wilbraham, Roger, of Nantwich, Chesh. (d. 1754), 163

Willes, Sir John MP (1685-1761), 112

Williams, Lady Frances Hanbury, name, *568*

Williams, Sir Hutchins, 1st Bt (d. 1758), *474*

Williams, Sir John Kt, of London (d. 1743), *331*

Williams, Orlo Cyprian, vii, viii; on clerks, 22 nn. 3 and 5, 23 n. 2, 29 n. 4, 39-45; on fees, 36-7, 145 n. 2, 146 n. 6; on parliamentary agency, 13-15, 41 n. 6, 47, 66 n. 2, 76 n. 1; on parliamentary counsel, 66, 68; on procedure, 85, 86, 131, 150-1

Williams, Richard, of Stoke, Suffolk, 116, *313*

Willis, Brown (1682-1760), *562*

Willoughby, Francis, 2nd Bn Middleton (1692-1758), *445*

Willoughby of Parham, Hugh, 5th Bn (d. 1765), 91, 92

Wilson, Ann, *595*

Windsor, Other Lewis, 4th Earl of Plimouth (1731-71), *237*, *270*

Wingerworth, Derbysh., inclosure, *489*

Winterton, *see* Turnour

Wisbech embanking, 155 n. 6

Wittewronge, Sir John 4th Bt (1695-1744) and family, 10, 118-20, *30*

Woide, Charles Godfrey (1725-90), 3

Wollesthorpe common, Lincs., inclosure, 12, *84*

Woodcock, —, agent, 49 n. 2

Woodhey, Hants., inclosure, *320*

Woods, John, merchant of Chilgrove, Sussex, 49, *565*

Woolwich church, *164*

Worth, John, 12, *159*

Wright, Henry, of Mobberley, Chesh. (d. 1744), 159, 163

Wright, Rev. Robert, of East Herling, Norfolk, *256*

Wyndham, William, 1st Bn Grenville (1759-1834), 52

Wyndham, Sir William, 3rd Bt MP (d. 1740), *566*

Wyndham, William, *383*

Wynn, Charles Watkins Williams MP (1775-1850), 56

Wytham, Lincs., inclosure, *393*

Yates, —, counsel, 166 n. 3

Yeates, Robert, clerk HC (d. 1769), 41, 45-7, 67, 166-7

York, archbishop of, *see* Blackburn, Dawes

York Buildings Company, *247(4)*

Yorke, Philip, 1st Earl of Hardwicke (1690-1764), 74-5, 76, 83, 132, 189; 2nd Earl (1720-90), *199*

Yorkshire cloth, 49, 73, *70*, *178(2)*, *613*

Young, Arthur (1741-1820), 149

Young, William, 1st Bt (d. 1788), *591*

Zuylestein, Frederick, 3rd Earl of Rochford (1628-1738), 116. 5

246